Fundamentals of Data Observability

Many people talk about data observability, yet only some fully understand it. This is where this book comes in, drawing from Andy's professional background and vast hands-on experience, it offers a simple-to-implement, smart, and applicable structure for considering and applying data observability.

—*Adi Polak, author of* Scaling Machine Learning with Spark

Data observability is a topic that hasn't received the extensive discussion it deserves. Andy Petrella does an excellent job conveying the what, why, and how of achieving successful observability within data products. This will help guide the future of data-driven decision making.

—*Matthew Weingarten, Data Engineer/Data Passionista*

Data observability is widely discussed and widely misunderstood. In this book, Andy provides an intelligent and practical framework for thinking about and implementing data observability.

—*Joe Reis, coauthor of* Fundamentals of Data Engineering *and "recovering data scientist"*

This book is a brilliant manifestation of Andy's extensive experience in data engineering and architecture in a career that has spanned in-the-trenches pipeline construction, software development, product design, and leadership. He guides the reader through data observability on all levels, bridging the gap between engineering technical mastery and organizational dynamics. This is the book we've been waiting for to move beyond the hype and make data observability a reality.

—*Matthew Housley, CTO and coauthor of* Fundamentals of Data Engineering

I've seen businesses of all sizes struggle with data platform reliability time and time again. Andy's book provides both a theoretical and practical foundation for addressing this challenge head-on. The text explores the principles of data observability and backs these up with technical implementations designed to address the common and repeated patterns that plague data teams. This book is a must-read for any technologist tired of struggling with data quality, unreliable platforms, and opaque data pipelines.

—*Emily Gorcenski, Principal Data Scientist, Thoughtworks*

Observability has gone mainstream in the past years, but one application area has been missing so far: data. With Fundamentals of Data Observability, you now have the missing piece at hand, explaining what observability means for your data pipelines and how to successfully implement it in your organization. An excellent hands-on guide that should be at the top of your reading list!

—*Michael Hausenblas, AWS*

This book paints a realistic and accurate view of data observability, shares the key tenants and mental models, and proves that observability is a critical requirement for any modern data organization and partitioner looking to remain competitive.

—*Scott Haines, Distinguished Software Engineer, Nike*

Fundamentals of Data Observability

Implement Trustworthy End-to-End Data Solutions

Andy Petrella

Beijing · Boston · Farnham · Sebastopol · Tokyo

Fundamentals of Data Observability

by Andy Petrella

Published by O'Reilly Media, Inc., 1005 Gravenstein Highway North, Sebastopol, CA 95472.

O'Reilly books may be purchased for educational, business, or sales promotional use. Online editions are also available for most titles (*http://oreilly.com*). For more information, contact our corporate/institutional sales department: 800-998-9938 or *corporate@oreilly.com*.

Acquisitions Editor: Aaron Black	**Indexer:** Ellen Troutman-Zaig
Development Editor: Gary O'Brien	**Interior Designer:** David Futato
Production Editor: Ashley Stussy	**Cover Designer:** Karen Montgomery
Copyeditor: Liz Wheeler	**Illustrator:** Kate Dullea
Proofreader: Piper Editorial Consulting, LLC	

August 2023:   First Edition

Revision History for the First Edition
2023-08-11:   First Release

See *http://oreilly.com/catalog/errata.csp?isbn=9781098133290* for release details.

978-1-098-13329-0

[LSI]

Table of Contents

Part II. Implementing Data Observability

Preface

Welcome to *Fundamentals of Data Observability*, a book designed to provide a robust introduction to a crucial, emerging field in data engineering and analytics.

As we venture into an era characterized by unprecedented data growth, the importance of understanding our data—its sources, destinations, usages, and behaviors—has never been more important. Observability, traditionally a term associated with software and systems engineering, has now made its way into the data space, becoming a cornerstone of trustworthy, efficient, and insightful data systems. This book aims to guide readers into the depth of this new and necessary discipline, exploring its principles, techniques, and evolving best practices.

Fundamentals of Data Observability is not just for data engineers or data scientists, but for anyone who interacts with data systems in their daily work life. Whether you're a chief data officer (CDO), a chief technology officer (CTO), a manager, a leader, a developer, a data analyst, or a business manager, understanding data observability concepts and principles will empower you to make better decisions, build more robust systems, and gain greater insight from your data resources.

This book begins by outlining the core concepts of data observability, drawing parallels to similar concepts in software engineering, and setting the stage for the more advanced material. It subsequently delves into the principles and techniques to achieve data observability, providing practical guidance on how to implement them. The final section discusses how to get started today with the system you are using or have inherited. The book concludes with thoughts about the future of data observability, exploring ongoing research and emerging trends that are set to shape the field in the coming years.

Every chapter in this book is packed with actionable advice to reinforce the topics covered. My aim is not merely to impart knowledge but to facilitate the practical application of data observability concepts in your real-world situations.

I hope that by the end of this book, you not only will understand the "what" and "why" of data observability but will also be armed with the "how"—practical knowledge that you can apply to improve the reliability, usability, and understandability of your data systems.

The field of data observability is still young, and there is much to explore and learn. As you embark on this exciting journey, remember that understanding our data and its usages is not just a technical goal—it's a foundation for making better decisions, fostering innovation, and driving the success of our enterprises.

Overview of the Book

Fundamentals of Data Observability is organized into three parts and eight chapters, each addressing specific areas of data observability:

Part I: The Foundations of Data Observability

Chapter 1 introduces the concept of data observability, explains why it has become an essential aspect of data management and sheds light on its role in facilitating accurate, reliable, and actionable insights from data.

Chapter 2 delves deeper into the components of data observability. It provides an understanding of its multifaceted nature and how to ensure its implementation aligns with both short-term and long-term organizational needs.

Chapter 3 describes the roles and responsibilities of a data observability platform within an organization. It covers its relationships with existing systems and practices, and explores the changes in workflow and management that it facilitates.

Part II: Implementing Data Observability

Chapter 4 outlines the APIs and practices required to make a data system observable. It includes a Python-based implementation example that can be adapted to suit any other programming language or system.

Chapter 5 focuses on automating the generation of data observations. It showcases a range of practices to lessen manual effort, thereby enabling data users to concentrate on more strategic tasks.

Chapter 6 covers how to implement expectations within data applications, supporting continuous validation, one of the crucial principles of data observability.

Part III: Get Started Today

Chapter 7 provides ready-to-use recipes for implementing data observability principles into various technologies used in data pipelines. The applications range from traditional data processing systems to machine learning applications and data visualization tools, broadening the scope of data observability.

Chapter 8 provides actionable intelligence to incorporate data observability into systems that are currently opaque or closed, or whose knowledge base has faded over time.

Through these three sections, *Fundamentals of Data Observability* offers a comprehensive guide to understanding, implementing, and leveraging data observability principles in various data systems, new or existing.

Who Should Read This Book

Fundamentals of Data Observability is a vital guide for anyone who plays a role in the world of data engineering, analytics, and governance. This book provides in-depth insight into the principles of data observability and its role in ensuring efficient and reliable data systems. Here's who should read this book, and why:

Data engineers and analyst engineers
> Whether you are just beginning your career or are an experienced professional, the book will empower you with the knowledge to architect and manage observable data systems. It delves deep into the tools, technologies, and practices that can improve the reliability, usability, and understandability of data systems. The book also provides practical advice and case studies to help you apply these concepts in real-world scenarios.

Lead data engineers and heads of data engineering
> This book is a resource for team leaders and managers responsible for designing, implementing, and managing data systems. The chapters guide you on creating a strategy for implementing data observability in your organization and offer advice on managing the change effectively. It provides the knowledge you need to mentor your team and facilitate their growth in this emerging field.

CDOs, CTOs, and heads of data
> For those in executive roles, the book offers an overview of the principles of data observability and its significance in the broader data architecture landscape. Understanding this will allow you to make informed decisions about resource allocation, risk management, and strategic direction. It provides a firm grounding in the language and concepts of data observability, enabling you to engage more productively with your technical teams.

Data governance and architecture professionals
> For those involved in data governance and architecture, this book provides insights into how data observability principles can contribute to robust, secure, and compliant data practices. It addresses how data observability intersects with other data systems in place, helping you build a more integrated and effective data strategy.

Software engineers
> If you are a software engineer working on building data systems, the book's second part will be especially relevant to you. It provides practical guidance on how to make these systems observable, thereby ensuring they can be effectively maintained and their data properly utilized by data users such as engineers and analysts.

In a world increasingly dominated by data, understanding the principles of data observability is crucial. This book will equip you with the knowledge and skills to make your data systems more reliable, understandable, and usable, driving better decision making and business success. Whether you are a hands-on engineer, a team leader, or a strategic decision maker, *Fundamentals of Data Observability* is an essential addition to your professional library.

Conventions Used in This Book

The following typographical conventions are used in this book:

Italic
> Indicates new terms, URLs, email addresses, filenames, and file extensions.

`Constant width`
> Used for program listings, as well as within paragraphs to refer to program elements such as variable or function names, databases, data types, environment variables, statements, and keywords.

This element signifies a tip or suggestion.

This element signifies a general note.

This element indicates a warning or caution.

Using Code Examples

Supplemental material (code examples, exercises, etc.) is available for download at *https://github.com/Fundamentals-of-Data-Observability/oreilly-fodo-source-code*.

If you have a technical question or a problem using the code examples, please send email to *support@oreilly.com*.

This book is here to help you get your job done. In general, if example code is offered with this book, you may use it in your programs and documentation. You do not need to contact us for permission unless you're reproducing a significant portion of the code. For example, writing a program that uses several chunks of code from this book does not require permission. Selling or distributing examples from O'Reilly books does require permission. Answering a question by citing this book and quoting example code does not require permission. Incorporating a significant amount of example code from this book into your product's documentation does require permission.

We appreciate, but generally do not require, attribution. An attribution usually includes the title, author, publisher, and ISBN. For example: "*Fundamentals of Data Observability* by Andy Petrella (O'Reilly). Copyright 2023 O'Reilly Media, 978-1-098-13329-0."

If you feel your use of code examples falls outside fair use or the permission given above, feel free to contact us at *permissions@oreilly.com*.

O'Reilly Online Learning

O'REILLY® For more than 40 years, *O'Reilly Media* has provided technology and business training, knowledge, and insight to help companies succeed.

Our unique network of experts and innovators share their knowledge and expertise through books, articles, and our online learning platform. O'Reilly's online learning platform gives you on-demand access to live training courses, in-depth learning paths, interactive coding environments, and a vast collection of text and video from O'Reilly and 200+ other publishers. For more information, visit *https://oreilly.com*.

How to Contact Us

Please address comments and questions concerning this book to the publisher:

O'Reilly Media, Inc.
1005 Gravenstein Highway North
Sebastopol, CA 95472
800-889-8969 (in the United States or Canada)
707-829-7019 (international or local)
707-829-0104 (fax)
support@oreilly.com
https://www.oreilly.com/about/contact.html

We have a web page for this book, where we list errata, examples, and any additional information. You can access this page at *https://oreil.ly/fundamentals-of-data-observability-1e*.

For news and information about our books and courses, visit *https://oreilly.com*.

Find us on LinkedIn: *https://linkedin.com/company/oreilly-media*

Follow us on Twitter: *https://twitter.com/oreillymedia*

Watch us on YouTube: *https://youtube.com/oreillymedia*

Acknowledgments

Firstly, I want to express my deepest gratitude to my wife Sandrine, and our sons Noah and Livio. Your unending patience and support throughout the writing of this book made it possible. I may have missed a few rare sunny Belgian weekends tucked away with this project, but your understanding and encouragement never wavered. To my parents, thank you for providing me with the opportunities to pursue my studies and follow my passions.

My heartfelt thanks to Jess Haberman for entrusting me with writing about this emerging and significant topic. Your assistance in shaping the outline and message of the book was invaluable in getting this project off the ground.

To Gary O'Brien, the keystone of this project, thank you for your unwavering enthusiasm and tireless effort. Your dedication to improving the quality and coherence of this book was a source of inspiration, and your nerdy jokes provided much-needed levity during our countless discussions.

I extend my deepest appreciation to Joe Reis and Matthew Housley. Your continuous thought-provoking comments and suggestions greatly improved the content presented in this book. Your perspectives were particularly insightful when they aligned with the themes of your own work.

Adi Pollack, thank you for being a beacon of positivity throughout this process. Your excitement and constructive feedback on my proposals kept me reassured that I was headed in the right direction. Your countless refinements ensured that the content remained crisp yet easily digestible for readers.

To Emily Gorcenski, Matthew Weingarten, Scott Haines, and Simon Späti, thank you for your expertise in enhancing the robustness of the technical statements, and for your efforts to increase the clarity of the material from the reader's perspective.

I am grateful to Ines Dehaybe, Emanuele Lucchini, and François Pietquin for your friendly support, often provided after hours, which greatly contributed to this book's success and helped me stay on schedule.

I want to express my gratitude to Eloy Sasot, Doug Laney, and Chris Tabb for your diligent reviews, which helped clarify and tailor chapters for business-oriented readers and stakeholders.

Also, my thanks go to Becky Lawlor and Jenifer Servais for your tremendous help in structuring my thoughts and polishing my English prose.

To everyone who contributed, your collective efforts have shaped this book into what it is today. My sincerest thanks to you all.

## PART I

Introducing Data Observability

## CHAPTER 1

Introducing Data Observability

Once upon a time, there was a young data analyst named Alex who had a deep passion for data. Alex loved the way data could help businesses make informed decisions, drive growth, and achieve success. However, Alex was also aware of the dangers of misinterpreting data or not having enough visibility into the data.

Alex was working on a critical project with a data engineer named Sarah. Sarah was responsible for preparing the data and making sure it was ready for analysis. As they delved deeper into the project, Alex and Sarah realized that there were many variables at play, and the data they were working with was not as straightforward as they had initially thought.

One day, while Alex was iterating on his analysis to generate insights, it appeared to him that the results presented on that day were looking odd and hard to relate to what he had seen to that point. He went to Sarah to discuss the case, but Sarah needed more context on his previous interpretation was or what his expectations were, and what he was asking her to check.

After four days of collaboration, pair review, and several brainstorming sessions, Sarah and Alex discovered that subtle changes in the distribution of half a dozen variables of the incoming data shifted the generated insights, several transformation steps later. Some variables had more missing values, hence they were dropped in the cleaning transformation, others had their average value increased greatly, and one of the datasets was refreshed with almost twice as much data as it had in the past thanks to better extraction from the operational sources.

Although Sarah and Alex originally thought the quality of the data may have dropped, it appeared that the data simply changed, and their assumptions about the data had to be aligned. They realized that they were lucky this had happened before deploying the project in production, and this kind of situation would probably happen many times in the future. If they didn't anticipate these changes, they would be in trouble.

That experience made them realize the importance of data observability. They needed to have visibility into the data, its transformations, and its usage so they would be able to react quickly to any changes. They started to embrace data observability principles and instrumented their data pipelines to add the needed capabilities that provide real-time insights into the data, its quality, and its usage.

From that day on, they have been backed with dashboard and notification systems that track the health of the data in the pipelines and alert them to any issues that need attention to ensure that the client always receives accurate and reliable data.

Through this experience, Alex and Sarah learned that data is a living and breathing entity that needs to be continuously monitored and observed. They realized that, without data observability, they never would be able to react quickly to changes, putting the project's success at risk.

If you're reading this book, it's likely because you, like Sarah and Alex, have experienced or anticipate experiencing similar situations in your own work with data. You understand the power of data, but also the potential for disastrous consequences when even subtle changes go unnoticed.

But you don't know what you need to do or how to get started. There's no need to worry anymore. In this book you'll learn what Alex and Sarah did to embrace data observability principles and ensure that their data pipelines are reliable and that their clients receive accurate and trustworthy data. By applying these principles to your own work, you can avoid the pitfalls of unreliable data and build a strong foundation for success in your data-driven projects.

Before I dig further into what data observability is and offers at scale, let's first look at how data teams are evolving and identify the challenges they face.

Scaling Data Teams

More roles, more responsibility, more engineering.

A data team is a group of data practitioners who work together to collect, process, analyze, and interpret data to generate insights and inform decision-making to drive better business outcomes and improve organizational performance.

Because data teams play a strategic role in organizations, their operational efficiency can become a bottleneck to incorporating high-demand data into critical business operations. To cope with this, data teams evolved similarly to IT teams in the 1950s—dedicated roles such as systems engineers, web engineers, or backend engineers were added to support specific operations instead of having generalist roles.[1]

As data teams have increased their operational complexity with additional roles, more interactions and interdependencies across members and teams have been created, increasing the need for greater visibility, transparency, and standardization.

In the remainder of this section, I will use search trends as an example that illustrates the creation and scaling of data teams along with the data engineer role. The impact and challenges coming with it are addressed in the following section, which also describes other roles, such as analytics engineers, for example.

Let's start with a Google Trends search (Figure 1-1) for the term "data team" from 2004 to 2020. We can see that while data teams have always been around, the interest in data teams began increasing in 2014 and accelerated significantly between 2014 and 2020.

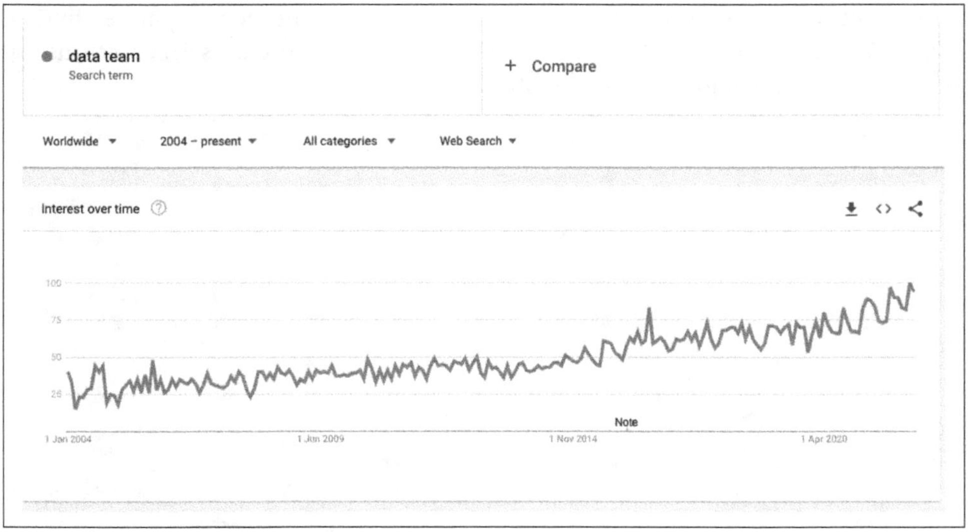

Figure 1-1. Google search trend for "data team"

---

1 Mary K. Pratt, "CIO (Chief Information Officer) (*https://oreil.ly/CRWyp*)," TechTarget, accessed April 11, 2022.

This is despite interest in "Big Data" decreasing (as shown in Figure 1-2).

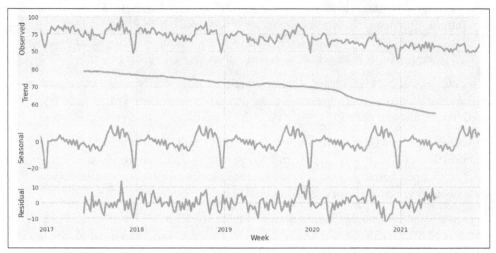

Figure 1-2. Analysis of "Big Data" search term on Google Trends[2]

Obviously, this doesn't mean that Big Data was not needed anymore, but, as Figure 1-3 shows, in 2014 the focus started to shift toward data science because its link with value generation was more intuitive.

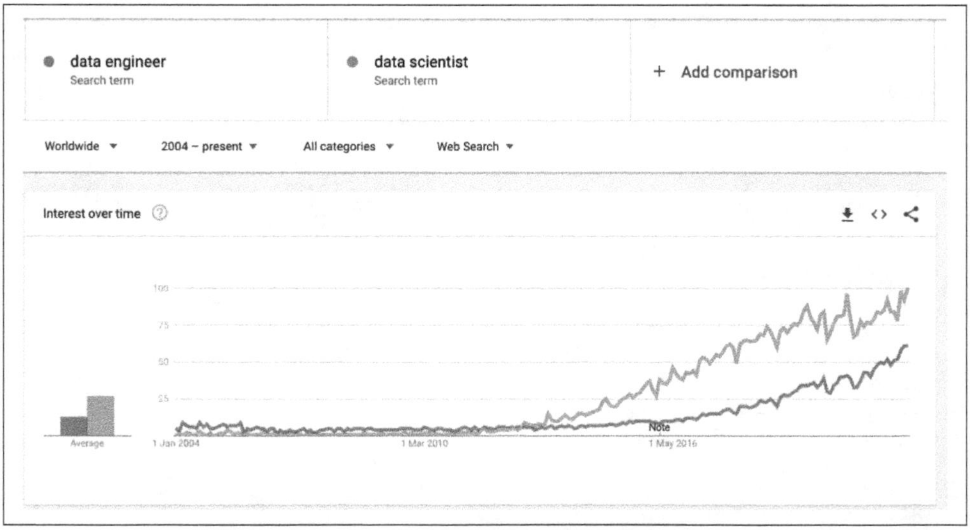

Figure 1-3. Google trends for search terms "data engineer" and "data scientist"

---

2 Cf. My O'Reilly report *What Is Data Observability?* (*https://oreil.ly/5TUbp*).

However, even as interest began to climb in data science, it was clear that data availability was a roadblock to many data science projects.

Data science teams have not replaced big data teams. Instead, data teams have embraced analytics, and thus added this relatively new role of data scientist.

As data and analytics became more central to companies' success, providing the right data to the right people has remained a constant challenge. Gartner noted that by 2018,[3] data engineers had become crucial in addressing data accessibility challenges and that data and analytic leaders must, therefore, "develop a data engineering discipline as part of their data management strategy."

Hence, it became evident that a role dedicated to producing data for downstream use cases was missing. This is why, since around 2020, as companies began to bring on engineers specifically to help build data pipelines and bring together data from different source systems, the search volume for data engineers has increased significantly. Today, as also shown in Figure 1-3, data engineering is trending toward catching up to data scientist in search popularity.

Data as a Metric

Data availability is one of the metrics driving data observability. There are important metrics and metadata relating to data availability, such as the time to live (TTL) and refresh rate (freshness) of a dataset. Still, there are also nuances we'll get into throughout the book such as sourcing data, privacy and security ramifications, etc. Meanwhile, though, separating roles allows the different skills time and space to be built and the resources to be focused on the different phases of data projects.

As previously introduced, scaling data teams this way with more people, roles, and responsibilities comes with its own challenges. Let's dig into that topic in the next section.

Challenges of Scaling Data Teams

As companies look to scale their data usage, they also must scale their data teams. I will cover the challenges and their consequences with the following examples:

- A description of the emergence of roles and responsibilities in a data team.
- An analysis of the operational complexity as the team grows.

---

3 Roxane Edjlali, Ehtisham Zaidi, and Nick Heudecker, "Data Engineering Is Critical to Driving Data and Analytics Success," Gartner Research, October 4, 2018, *https://oreil.ly/EPBEn*.

- An illustration of the challenges of (data) issuance management and their impact on the mood and efficiency of the data team.
- A note of caution to avoid failures on the ML/AI journey.

Consider a data team that starts with a single person tasked to do the data ingestion, data integration, and even the final report. For this person, a first project might consist of producing a view of recent customer acquisitions.

The data engineer would have to query and ingest the source data from the company's *customer relationship management* (CRM) system into the data lake, integrate it into the data warehouse, and create a report that gives the head of sales insight into the progress of the sales made over the past few weeks.

This first data team member is, in essence, a Swiss Army knife: covering both data engineering and data analysis responsibilities to deliver the project outcome (report).

In a larger data team, the skills required for this work are balanced between data engineering, data analysis, and business analysis. As a team of one, though, an individual must master the technologies required to build and run the pipeline, and reporting tools, and understand business key performance indicators (KPI)s. It is worth noting that each of these areas requires specific expertise.

So far, this person is happy, and the scope of work and responsibilities are as shown in Figure 1-4.

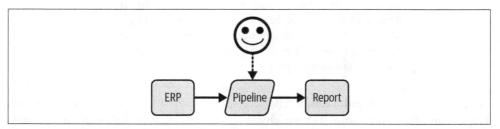

Figure 1-4. A happy single-person data team and its work

Of course, the process is not quite as simple. For example, an entire systems development life cycle (SDLC) should be followed to get the data into production and allow it to be available for analysis by the final user. At a very abstract level, however, this basic process outlined is what we mostly think of as "producing value" with a data project.

With only one team member and one data project, the whole data ecosystem is relatively under control.

The process is simple enough for one person, and the responsibility for the entire project is also attributed to that individual. Because there is just a single person on the team, they also have a close relationship with the business stakeholders—such as the head of sales—and have, therefore, built some domain knowledge around the use case and the business objective of the project. While this role is typically what a business analyst would perform, in this case, the data engineer takes on this role as well.

Thus, if the user raises any issues, it is clear who should work on troubleshooting. After all, they not only executed each step of the process but also know each area of the process.

However, as stakeholders become aware of the potential and value data can provide, more requests are made to this person for new reports, information, projects, etc. As a result, there is an increase in the complexity of the demands and ultimately, the individual reaches their limits of production capacity under the current setup. Consequently, it becomes urgent to grow the team and invest in specialized members to optimize productivity.

In the next section, we'll see how this team starts growing as specific roles are created, as presented in Table 1-1, which also highlights each role's responsibilities and dependencies.

Table 1-1. Data team (extended) roles, responsibilities, and dependencies.[a]

Title/role	Responsibilities	Dependencies
Software and Operation Engineer	Build and maintain the platform; manage security and compliance; oversee site reliability engineering (SRE)	Receive recommendations from other teams about what to monitor and what to consider an error
Data Engineer	Build the data pipelines and manage the data from deployment to production	Rely on IT to build the platform and set up the tools to monitor the pipeline and systems, including data observability tools
Analytics Engineer	Similar to data engineering with a stronger focus on data modeling and reusability	Rely on data engineering team to make the operational data sources available in the analytic platform
Analytic/data scientist	Build analytics and AI/ML models that can analyze and interpret data for the business team's use cases	Rely on the data and analytic engineering team to build the pipeline to generate the data they will be using in their report and machine learning models
Data Steward	Ensure data is under control and respect data governance policies; also facilitate data product or project scoping with their understanding of the data and its potential and quality	Rely on the metadata and other information available about the data provided by the upstream teams to create and maintain trust in the data used by the downstream users
Business/Domain Stakeholder	Sponsor use cases and use data analysis to make business decisions	Rely on all upstream teams (likely across other domains) to ensure data and analyses are accurate

[a] Note: I have not added data owners and data product owners/managers because their needs and dependencies are relatively covered by the stewards and stakeholder. Of course, I am not saying they are the same!

There is also a shortage in data engineering, data science, and data analyst skills on the market, hence growing a team is extremely challenging.[4]

This is especially true at the beginning when everything needs to be built in parallel, such as the culture, the maturity, the organizational structure, etc. Thus, it becomes even more essential to keep the talent you have, and this means ensuring that their roles and responsibilities align with their skill sets. So, in the next section, we will discover how these roles are added, what they will be expected to do, and what will happen to the team over time.

Segregated Roles and Responsibilities and Organizational Complexity

The single-person team has reached its maximum capacity to build new reports and has added another member to get back on track with the pace of the incoming requests. As stated earlier, it is important to specialize the team members to maximize their output, satisfaction, and, of course, quality of work. So we now have a data analyst delivering the reports defined with the stakeholders, upon the datasets built by a data engineer.

The impact of segregating the roles is that the data engineer is now farther from the stakeholders and loses direct contact with the business needs. In a way, the data engineer loses part of the visibility about the project's final purpose and part of the responsibility for the final outcome. Instead, the engineer will focus all efforts and energy on their deliverables—the ETL, SQL, or whatever framework or system was used to build the data.

The team and its deliveries are represented in Figure 1-5, where we see the distance and dependencies taking place.

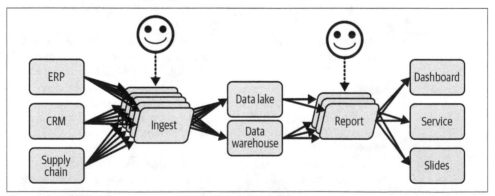

Figure 1-5. The team is growing, as is the complexity

---

4 Jen DuBois, "The Growing Demand for Data Engineers," Quanthub, April 26, 2023, *https://oreil.ly/0Yrqo*.

Figure 1-5 also shows the scope of produced work under the new management system by the data team after a few projects have been delivered. The data ecosystem begins to grow, and there is less end-to-end visibility, as it is scattered across both brains, and the responsibility across team members starts siloing.

Next, a data scientist is added to the team, as stakeholders are willing to explore setting up automated decision-making systems that don't require a human in the loop, or having someone on the team dedicated to overseeing the results and to scaling the value generated by the data.

As shown in Figure 1-6, this adds more scale, and those projects will require more data at a faster speed and more complex mechanisms, as the whole process needs to be automated to generate the expected results.

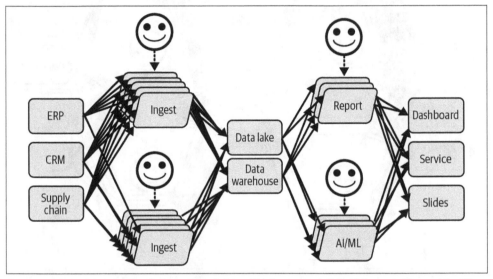

Figure 1-6. Data team evolving toward the use of automated decision making with AI

As time passes and the whole system scales, issues inevitably begin to occur. As noted in the Google paper, "Data Cascades in High-Stakes AI,"[5] there is a 92% prevalence for at least one data issue to happen in any project.

Because the system has evolved so much and so rapidly, these issues are hard to troubleshoot and resolve. What is happening? No one knows, in fact.

---

5 Nithya Sambasivan, Shivani Kapania, Hannah Highfill, Diana Akrong, Praveen Paritosh, and Lora M. Aroyo, "'Everyone wants to do the model work, not the data work': Data Cascades in High-Stakes AI," In proceedings of the 2021 CHI Conference on Human Factors in Computing Systems, pp. 1-15, 2021, *https://oreil.ly/ EbEAW*.

The lack of visibility within the system combined with its complexity makes it like a complete black box, even for those who built it (some time ago).

The organization's data ecosystem, as you can see in Figure 1-7, has become like a "legacy system" in IT—only it happened faster.

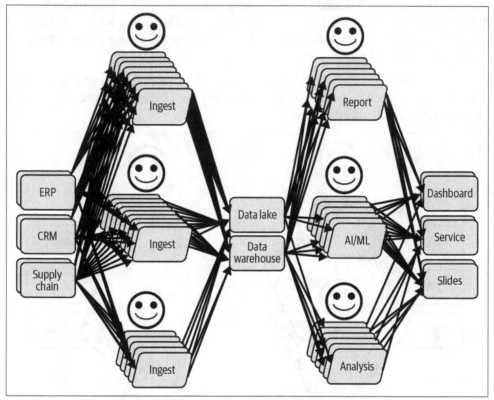

Figure 1-7. Efficient data team delivering projects in production after some time

In further sections, I will walk you through the journey of handling those issues and their consequences on the data teams' dynamics. However, before that, let's analyze the anatomy of such data issues.

Anatomy of Data Issues and Consequences

Data issues are a constant and common challenge for most organizations. In one survey by Dun & Bradstreet,[6] 42% of businesses said they have struggled with inaccurate data.

---

6 Dr. Anthony Scriffignano, "Data Management Study: The Past, Present, and Future of Data," Dun & Bradstreet, June 24, 2019, *https://oreil.ly/s1LVH*.

The most common reasons for data issues are:

Regulatory
Data privacy or other data regulations require changes in how data is collected, ingested, or stored, which can create unforeseen issues. For example, the passage to GDPR forced retail companies to change the data they collected and to limit it to only that needed to optimize their recommendation engine in full respect of the customers' integrity.

Business demands
Different business use cases require different configurations of data. For example, a business use case would rely on the shipping address and not the billing address. Therefore, the billing address can be discarded from the data. However, if the financial office uses the same data, they may need those billing addresses, but may have lost access to them, because this usage was not "known."

Human error
Often, data issues are caused by simple human error. For example, a data engineer accidentally publishes a transformation application that deletes all negative values for an amount column instead of setting them with the null value. Consequently, the data user gets less data than expected, which reduces the accuracy of their analyses.

Latent information error
This is a not a data error but an error of interpretation of the data. For example, because of a transporter strike, the sales of blue-colored sneakers dropped a lot, due to stock not being refilled. However, the sneakers' popularity was so good, buyers bought brown ones instead. The marketing team, unaware of the ground truth (e.g., a latent variable related to the transportation efficiency and availability of stock), estimated that brown was the new blue. So more brown sneakers were produced, and remained unsold when the strike stopped a week after.

Data drift error
More insidious, this error is also a misinterpretation of the data, likely due to a latent variable; however, the interpretation was initially accurate. Over time, the data genuinely changes so much that the assumptions no longer hold true; therefore, the insights are wrong. An example of such drifts can occur in fashion, when a product is appreciated by people aged, say, 28-31, but the ranges in the data are 25–30 and 30–35. In this case, the next year, it is likely that the interest in the 25–30 range (the 29-year-old people) drops dramatically, but moves to the 30–35 range (the 30–32-year-old people); hence the associated products to recommend must change to accommodate the most represented range.

One of the most challenging aspects of what causes a data issue is that the engineers involved in creating the change to the data or application often don't realize the implications of the changes they've made. And unfortunately, the issue isn't usually discovered until the end of the data value chain. All in all, the whole point of this book is to teach how everyone can take part in the responsibility to react fast to any such situations, while continuing to assess, communicate, and validate their understanding and assumptions about the data.

Usually, as we discussed in the scaling data team story, business users are working along like normal, running reports, etc., and realizing through a gut feeling and their own previous experience using the data that the numbers "don't look right."

But, at that point, it's already too late. Business decisions may have already been made based on faulty data before the inaccuracies were discovered.

With no time to fix data issues, data teams scramble to figure out who has the knowledge and skills to help resolve the issue. Yet, it's often unclear who is responsible, or what knowledge and skills you need to address the issue. Analysts? Engineers? IT?

And the responsibility can change from one moment to the next. Perhaps the analyst changed how some information is calculated that is now impacting sales reports, but perhaps even before that, the data engineering team adjusted one of the connections supporting the sales analytics tool the business users use to run the sales reports.

To try and resolve the issue, everyone relies on everyone else's knowledge about what was done, how things work, where the documentation is, if it is accurate, the understanding of the last changes in the (code) history, and the list goes on. After all, it boils down to manually trying to find and fix the issue collegially or the hard way (alone and in the dark). This is because no one is certain about what fields or tables will affect downstream data consumers.

The expense and time involved in resolving the issue and its negative impact on businesses' productivity, sales, overall revenue, and even reputation are significant.

The Dun & Bradstreet report also tells us that almost one in five businesses has lost customers due to incomplete or inaccurate data. Nearly a quarter of companies say poor quality data has led to inaccurate financial forecasts, and, of course, the remaining 75% have likely suffered from inaccurate data, but for other usages. Still, a 25% wrong financial forecast is impressive for such a crucial topic for the stability of a company.

Constant data issues can lead to a lack of confidence in making business decisions based on data insights. In a recent study of 1,300 executives, 70% of respondents said they aren't confident the data they use for analysis and forecasting is accurate.

Impact of Data Issues on Data Team Dynamics

First and foremost, the data issue is detected by the data user, who starts having doubts because either the data received seems odd compared to what was expected, or the results of the analyses are not what was anticipated. The direct side effect of those doubts is the sentiment of mistrust that gets installed in the user's mind against the team that produced the data, or the whole data platform.

Issues Could Also Be Data Changes in Disguise

This case can happen even when the data has no "issues," because data changes naturally, as it represents reality, which changes without notice. In such a case, the user simply might not yet be aware of the changes. However, for simplicity, I will assume that the issue is real for the remainder of this discussion.

Figure 1-8 depicts the current situation, where one of the consumers is starting to have concerns about the data, and who imagines that the issue just discovered may have other, yet-to-be-discovered, consequences in some or all applications that use it (also known as data cascade, issue propagation).

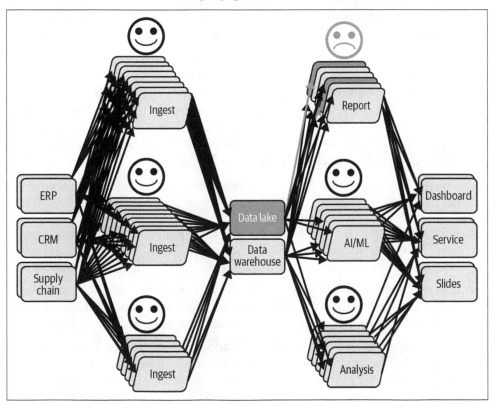

Figure 1-8. A user not cool about what has been discovered: a data issue

In this scenario, users always detect issues at the wrong moment for them. They need the data at that moment; otherwise, they wouldn't be accessing or checking the data.

So the user is stuck and of course, becomes grumpy. Indeed, instead of working on the planned tasks, the user has to find out how the data can be "fixed." Consequently, the final stakeholders will not have their data on time.

Moreover, finding how the data can be fixed is not straightforward, as the received data might have been corrupted by any of the applications that produced it. At this point, the process to follow depends on how the (data) operations are organized; an example could be, creating an "incident" (a ticket) with the comment "data is not right, please fix ASAP."

Eventually, in our example process, the faulty data has a data steward attributed to it. The data steward is responsible for unblocking the user (at the very least) and analyzing the potential for other consequences, which may result in more incidents.

To resolve such an incident, the data steward will have to involve the team or person responsible for producing that data. And now, the timeline depends on the availability of those who will need time to diagnose the symptoms and elaborate on a solution.

Well, this sounds easier than it really is. The incident needs to be reassigned to the producer, who is probably already busy with ongoing projects and unlikely to identify the issue instantly. That's assuming you can even identify the right producer! Instead, likely all producers will be contacted, probably summoned to a meeting, to understand the situation. They will challenge the "issue" (e.g., "are you sure this is an issue"?), and ask for more details, which loops back to the already angry user (who is most likely not going to be very cooperative).

Consequently, the applications that are touching this data and identified as potential culprits have to be thoroughly analyzed, which involves the following tasks:

- Access the production data to manually verify and understand the data issue by running a series of exploratory analyses (e.g., queries, aggregation computations in Spark). Given that, the permission to access the data might not be granted yet.

- Repeat this operation by time-traveling the data (when possible) to identify when the issue started to show up (e.g., a delta table can help to do the time-traveling, but the time when the problem appeared still needs to be found).

- Access the production logs of the applications (by SSHing on the machines or from the logging platform), to analyze their behavior and even review their history (version, etc.), in case the application's business logic has changed, which could impact the results. Given that, as for data access, the logs might require special permissions to be accessible.

- Analyze the business's logic to trace back to the original data consumed by the applications to identify potential data cascades (issue propagation).

- Repeat until the root cause is found, you know which data and applications need some repair, and finally, execute the back-filling (to reestablish the truth).

So, let's be honest—because time is critical (remember, the user is upset), it is likely that the root cause won't be tracked, but either one of these two temporary-definitive patches will be applied:

- Run an ad hoc script (aka data quality tool) to "fix" the data that is causing the process to become out of control (e.g., outside the lifecycle of the data, etc.).

- Update one of the applications to "clean" the received data. This involves fixing the problem locally, and is likely to have awkward side effects, such as removing or imputing null values that can change the distribution of the variables if the number goes up and have side effects downstream (e.g., bad decisions).

In fact, this process, called "troubleshooting," has puzzled many people, many of whom weren't even needed for this incident. It is worth noting that while the troubleshooting was happening the scope of the issue has grown significantly, as shown in Figure 1-9.

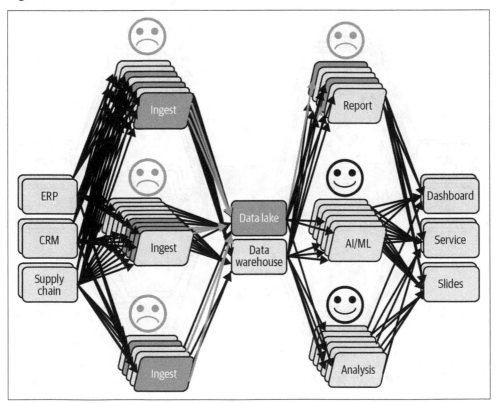

Figure 1-9. People involved in the incident analysis (troubleshooting)

Moreover, the issue detected on this data may have other consequences (remember, data cascades!) on other projects, users, and decisions, which has the effect of further expanding the scope of the issue to all usages of the data.

Another process, called impact analysis, is somewhat close to the troubleshooting we've just covered. However, its goal is slightly different, as it aims to prevent or communicate issues.

In fact, not only is the goal different, but an impact analysis is also much trickier and more sensitive, because it requires requesting time from all users to check their data, results, analyses, or decisions.

Even worse, some may discover that decisions were wrong for a longer period of time, potentially as long as the issue has appeared, with everything happened silently.

At this point, the scope of the data issue, considering both the troubleshooting and the impact analysis, is as big as Figure 1-10 shows. And the data steward has to resolve this as fast as possible.

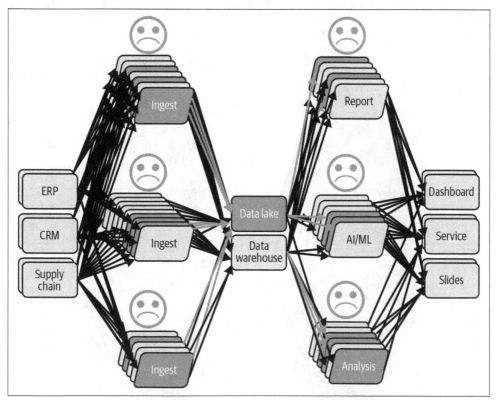

Figure 1-10. The scope to resolve a data issue

This is why we call data a "silent killer." In our example, it slowed everyone down, destroyed all trust, and generated stress, anger, and anxiety without raising any alerts or "exceptions" (as in software). In fact, data doesn't raise alerts, or exceptions—*yet*, anyway; however, there is a way to enable this capability, which we will see in the next chapter.

In this analysis, I have highlighted the challenges around the time and the people involved in the process, and the significant efforts wasted on ad hoc patching, which just creates more data debt. Despite the importance of those challenges, there is another inestimable resource that we lost instantly at the time when the issue was detected: trust in both the data and the data team.

This trust has taken months, if not years (e.g., for sensitive AI-based projects) to build, but because nothing had been anticipated to maintain it, it fell apart like a house of cards, within seconds. This kind of scenario and the resulting consequences for the general mood lead to discouragement and turnover of highly talented team members.

Hence, we can identify many questions raised throughout the incident management process that can be mood destroyers if they are raised at the wrong time:

- Who is responsible for this issue?
- Why am I the one who:
  — Discovered the problem?
  — Should be questioned about it?
- Why is the user telling me the data seems inaccurate?
- Is the data really inaccurate?
- What apps could be causing this?
- What upstream data could be the cause?
- What are the unknown consequences of this issue (i.e., what other projects is this data used in that could also be impacted)?

Understanding why these questions are raised allows us to identify the very source of the problem, and it goes beyond any data issues and their causes. The challenge to address is not the data itself; it is the lack of clarity about accountability and responsibility across the data team members and stakeholders, strengthened by the lack of visibility into the data processes in the wild (i.e. production, during its use).

Consequently, when these questions are raised by or posed to data teams, they can create and reinforce barriers to the creation of value from using data as they will incur the following costs:

- Take significant time to resolve, during which the data is still unusable by the consumer.

- Require significant energy and imply that there is a diminished capability to solve the problem at the source and that a local "patch" will be the likely default solution.

- Provoke anxiety and exacerbate the loss of confidence in deliverables, data, and suppliers.

This is where data observability plays a key role—helping to generate greater visibility into the health of the data and the data ecosystem, and better assigning (distribute, decentralize) of both accountability and responsibility.

Scaling AI Roadblocks

In the previous section, we covered the challenges many face when scaling up data teams. In this section, I will focus on one of the most critical achievements that any organization expects from their data teams, scaling their AI capabilities.

However, these same types of visibility challenges that limit value when issues arise also create significant challenges when implementing AI.

In an analysis performed by Gartner (see Figure 1-11) the most important roadblocks faced by companies in developing their data and AI programs included data volume and/or complexity, data scope or quality problems, and data accessibility challenges.

The good news is that data observability helps with these roadblocks, but before we get into how, let's look a bit deeper at the primary barriers and why they exist.

The survey results indicate that technology-related challenges account for 29% of issues and the complexity of existing infrastructure accounts for 11%. Interestingly, almost half (48%) of respondents indicated that they experience challenges relate to a lack of visibility due to the complexity of the system in place and a lack of clarity on who was responsible for remedying the issues.

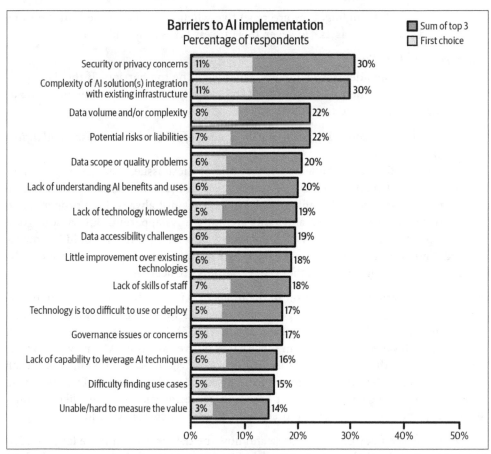

Figure 1-11. Gartner survey's results about AI roadblocks. Source: Gartner (March 2023)

Let's take a look at some of the common roadblocks:

Security/privacy concerns or potential risks or liability

Nearly one-fifth (18%) of respondents to Gartner's survey picked these issues as their biggest barrier to AI implementation. Risk management security is all about knowing who, why, and for what purpose the data will be used. There is also a potential risk or liability if the outcomes from the data are inaccurate because the data itself is wrong, which can lead to bad business decisions. Finally, there is concern that the outcome may not meet certain ethical constraints.

Data volume and complexity

This issue was the top barrier for 8% of respondents. The complexity and the size of the data require a lot of experimentation to understand and derive value from it. Because of a lack of visibility on experiments that were performed, such as profiling and wrangling, they are repetitive when being performed on the same big and complex datasets. However, this process takes time and effort.

Data scope and quality

For 6% of respondents, data quality issues were the top barriers. If the data quality is unknown, then it's very difficult to have any confidence in the outcome or final results produced from the data.

Governance issues or concerns, lack of understanding of AI benefits and uses, and difficulty finding use cases

A total of 16% of respondents felt that one of these issues was the biggest challenge in implementing AI. Data governance is a big issue because documentation is manual and time consuming, which means it's not always done properly, and therefore its overall impact and value are not always apparent. But without good data governance, the quality of the data fed into AI algorithms could be impacted, and without visibility on the data quality, stakeholders may worry about the security of the data and whether the AI outputs are accurate.

At the time of writing, a disruption in the usage of AI, namely its accessibility by the public, has emerged, with the usage of generative AI for text generation based on a type of model called a Large Language Model (LLM). The most popular tool built using this method is ChatGPT, from OpenAI, as it gives any non-AI-savvy person the ability to chat with an algorithm; meaning, have a structured discussion where each new answer considers the remainder of the discussion (the context). The discussion generally aims at generating content based on some instructions (yes, like coding), such as blog post, definition, structured point of view, pitches, and so forth.

However, the accuracy of the response and how the data is used in these large models was highlighted from the very first weeks of its general availability. For example, Italy forbade access to the service for some time as it was considered to potentially help spread misinformation and bias. Although it was reopened after its compliance with age policies had been verified, clarity about inaccurate or biased information hasn't been similarly provided.

For such tools, used by millions or even billions of persons around the globe, it is crucial to set the right expectation (e.g., accuracy, timeliness, etc.) to avoid inappropriate decisions or global movements relying on wrong "generated" information. This is nothing but taking what was discussed in this section to yet another level of magnitude, that is, not only to companies mature enough to leverage AI regularly for business decisions, which is likely to impact their ecosystems,[7] but also applying the logic to small businesses and individuals as well.

---

7 Of course, the ecosystem can be dramatic for large companies, but still…

So far, I have taken you on the journey of scaling data teams and AI, and we have identified several challenges, such as a lack of visibility (data pipelines, data usages,), and a lack of clarity about responsibility and accountability that results in distrust and chaos, leading to a loss of interest or confidence in data. This highlights the overall importance of data management. Therefore, the next section covers its challenges at scale, which will allow everything to come together, and introduces data observability as a glue, a solution for these challenges.

Challenges with Current Data Management Practices

As with any company transformation, data transformation and the associated creation of data teams poses the question of the teams' locations within the organization. Should there be one central data team? Should it be in IT? Or, maybe there should be one data team per business domain? Should they be under IT, or in each domain? But then, how do they collaborate, and how do they stay consistent, and efficient? Et cetera, et cetera.

Those questions are being addressed in many ways; Data Mesh (addressed in Chapter 3) is one of the few (not to say the only one) that has addressed them by rethinking data management at all levels, including at the architectural, cultural, and organizational levels.

However, independently of the position of data teams in the structure, let's analyze the impact that scaling them up has on data management.

Data management is a vast topic that is widely defined in the literature. For this analysis, I will concentrate on how data management is defined by DAMA[8] in their *Data Management Body of Knowledge v2* (DMBOK2)[9] book.

In DMBOK2, data management comprises many areas, such as data architecture, metadata, and data quality. All those areas are participating in leveraging the value of the data, alongside data governance, which is meant to dictate the policies that must be respected to ensure the data value is generated efficiently and according to the organization's core principles.

This is very well represented in the Data Management Wheel of the framework shown in Figure 1-12.

---

8 DAMA (*https://oreil.ly/IVx5U*) is a global data management community.

9 DAMA International, *Data Management Body of Knowledge (DMBOK)*, Second edition. (Technics Publications, 2017).

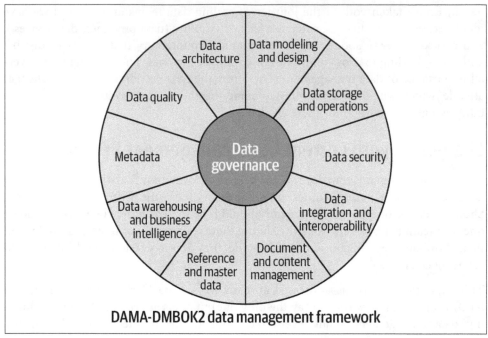

Figure 1-12. Data Management Wheel from DMBOK2 (Copyright © DAMA International)

With more businesses becoming data businesses, both data-savvy business teams and data teams are spreading throughout organizations. Therefore, data culture is no longer restricted to a well-defined center of expertise, but is a value that must be included in the whole organization's values.

Consequently, the areas delineated by the wheel have evolved to adapt to the different situations and needs. One of the most prominent areas that has seen an increase in global exposure since 2017 is data governance, which is covered in the next section. For example, we'll discuss how this exposure impacts other areas, such as data quality and metadata.

Effects of Data Governance at Scale

Many challenges result from the evolutions of data management practices and technologies, but I'll concentrate on one specific challenge: how to control, at scale, how that the data culture is sustained, by respecting not only data governance principles but also the definition and the implementation of the resulting policies. Data governance defines the policies, and each area is responsible for defining, planning, and executing the implementation.

However, along with the implementation, many dependencies across different areas are introduced, plus the fact that everything scales; without a harmonized, defined, and global control layer, any area that presents a default can break the machine.

This is why I am proposing not necessarily to change the structure of data management as presented in the DMBOK2, but to extend it with an extra area, surrounding the data governance area.

This new area is for data observability, which will extend the data management practices of organizations by giving them the ability to measure the health and usage of the data within their system, as well as health indicators of the overall system.[10] Nevertheless, a more detailed definition of data observability will be explained in the section "The Areas of Observability" on page 27

Having data observability at this position in the wheel makes it apparent that everyone is responsible for implementing it. Its principles and policies should be integrated throughout all areas.

The result is presented in Figure 1-13; however, it doesn't mean there is necessarily a need for a data observability role, team, or division. It states that at scale, the control must become explicit, as data observability becomes a challenge, when, at a smaller scale, it can be handled in a more ad hoc fashion.

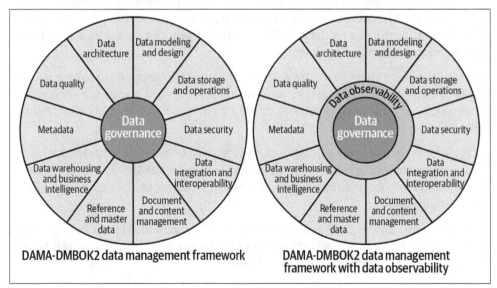

Figure 1-13. Data Management Wheel extended with data observability (Copyright © DAMA International)

---

10 Petrella, *What Is Data Observability?*

In the remainder of this book, we'll look at how observability extends from the IT DevOps landscape and how to apply it to data and data teams.

At this point, it should be clear that transversal challenges (data management) and local challenges (within a data team) have become bottlenecks to scaling up data strategies and enabling the maximum return on the investment in data in the last few years. Let's now talk about a solution to address those challenges across the board, that is, with data observability.

Data Observability to the Rescue

Up to this point, I've discussed the challenges faced by data teams as they grow and the roles that a lack of visibility and an absence of clarity about responsibilities play in making it difficult for organizations to scale their data and analytics strategies.

However, this is not the first time we've encountered such challenges; the closest example is when IT scaled rapidly, which led to the development of DevOps culture.

DevOps has evolved over the years, as more IT practices (e.g., the service mesh) have required more best practices and associated tooling to support them efficiently.

The most well-known example of such best practices is probably CI/CD (continuous integration and continuous deployment), but observability at the infrastructure or application level has also become part of any architecture meant to give more visibility and build confidence in their application and systems while also speeding up the time to market and reducing downtime.

Associated markets have therefore emerged and grown to support these observability requirements. A variety of companies have developed DevOps-related services and technologies at all levels of maturity of the IT environment (e.g., Datadog, Splunk, New Relic, Dynatrace, etc.).

In IT, "observability" is the capability of an IT system to generate behavioral information to allow external observers to reconstruct (modelize) its internal state. By extension, continuous observability allows an external observer to continuously modelize the internal state.

Fundamentally, an observer cannot interact with the system while it is functioning (e.g., we can't log onto the server); it can only observe information that can be perceived, which are therefore called "observations."

Now, let's discuss what those observations are.

The Areas of Observability

An IT system is complex by nature as it is composed of several categories that can drastically expand in number, such as infrastructure, cloud, distributed, machine learning, deep learning, etc.

In this book, however, I'll avoid getting too fine grained, but will aggregate the categories of an IT system that can be "observed" into several areas, and one of them is related to data, as represented by Figure 1-14.

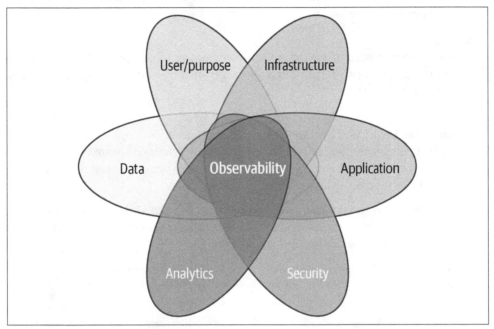

Figure 1-14. Areas of IT observability

These areas are not totally independent of each other, as they have a lot of interactions as they encode the system's complexities. This is why a Venn diagram seemed to be the best representation.

Before covering the "data" area and "data observability" in detail, let's briefly review the others:

Infrastructure
> Using infrastructure log metrics, you can infer the performance characteristics associated with internal infrastructure components. Proactive actionable alerts can be set when there is a failure or certain performance parameters aren't met.

Application

Observing application endpoints, versions, open threads, number of requests, exceptions, etc., can help determine how well the application is performing and identify if or why there are issues.

User/Purpose

It is useful to understand and "observe" who is using or implementing applications, what the purpose of a project is, and the goal of the project. This helps to understand the most frequent projects or goals, detect duplicate efforts, or compose centers of expertise.

Analytics

Observing analytics, from simple transformations to complex AI models, helps identify and learn from the ongoing usages of data and the insights generated from them.

Security

Observing security-related operations, such as modifications of who is granted access or assigned roles, or metrics on which roles are used more often than others, gives visibility on the efficiency of the security system in place, and possible areas of improvement.

Some of these areas have already been well-covered in the DevOps literature. However, we are focusing specifically on data observability. Therefore, we conclude that data observability can be defined as the following:

Data observability is the capability of a system that generates information on how the data influences its behavior and, conversely, how the system affects the data.

A system is data observable if it has the "data observability" capability.

A system is (fully) observable if it has the "observability" capabilities (infrastructure, application, user, analytics, security, and data).

It is worth noting that Gartner has defined data observability as the following, which aligns well with our definition:[11]

Data observability is the ability of an organization to have a broad visibility of its data landscape and multi-layer data dependencies (like data pipelines, data infrastructure, data applications) at all times with an objective to identify, control, prevent, escalate and remediate data outages rapidly within acceptable data SLAs.

Data observability uses continuous multi-layer signal collection, consolidation, and analysis over it to achieve its goals as well as inform and recommend a better design for superior performance and better governance to match business goals.

---

11 Gartner®, "Quick Answer: 'What is Data Observability,'" Ankush Jain, 8 June 2022.

The Gartner definition also discusses how data observability can be used (e.g., to prevent issues). However, I didn't include this as part of my definition because I want to focus on what it is, not what it does (also, I don't define an apple as a fruit that can satisfy my hunger).

That said, it is important to know the benefits of data observability. In the next section, we'll dive into data observability use cases in more detail.

Nevertheless, both Gartner and I agree that there is an important "multi-layer" or "multi-area" component that should be considered. I have, however, used the term "areas" because layers imply there is some independence, which, in reality, is not the case.

From this definition, we can look at the dimensions composing data observability as a result of its interactions with the other areas of observability.

I will start with the main dimension formed from observations intrinsic to the dataset. Those observations are essentially metadata such as the fields (e.g., columns, JSON attribute), the format (e.g., CSV), the encoding (e.g., UTF-8), and to some extent, the definitions of the information available.

They allow an observer to understand (mainly) the dataset's structure and how it changes over time.

If we were to stop here, we wouldn't be able to leverage data observability to its maximum capacity. For this, we must connect those core observations to the other areas we highlighted earlier to give the observer the following benefits:

Infrastructure
> Identify where the data resides physically (e.g., file path on a server, the server hosting a database—ideally its connection string), and whether it could impact the data itself or the following areas.

Application
> Be aware of which components of your organization's data system are storing or using the data (e.g., a transformation script, a web service); this could also include the code repository and the version.

User/purpose
> Contextualize and ease the knowledge handover with information about who was involved in the data production or consumption, its security settings, and in which projects (which have purposes) the data has shown itself to bring value.

Security/privacy
> Control how liable and appropriate are the data collections, accesses, and usages.

Analytics
> Understand how value is created with the data, through transformation (lineage), AI (machine learning training, predictions,), or even, simply, migration.

As for any new concepts, especially those that touch the organizational culture, ways of working, and technologies, it is crucial to understand their use cases. Therefore, I will cover the most common and valuable data observability use cases in the next section.

How Data Teams Can Leverage Data Observability Now

The main use cases of data observability are currently oriented toward data issue management. However, as data continues to proliferate and its uses expand, there will be many more use cases to come.

Low Latency Data Issues Detection

The more synchronized data observability is with the application (its usage context), the smaller the delay between the issues and their detection will be. In fact, data observability can be leveraged at the exact moment of data usage to avoid any lags between monitoring and usage. This will allow you to detect data issues as quickly as possible, helping you to avoid having data users find issues before you.

Leveraging data observability this way reduces the time to detect (TTD) issues, as data engineers are alerted in a timely manner because any data usage issues are observed in real time (aka synchronized observability).

Efficient Data Issues Troubleshooting

In most organizations, when data issues arise, data engineers spend a lot of time figuring out what the problem is, where it originated, and how to fix it. And every step of the process takes a lot of time. With data observability, the time to resolve (TTR) is much faster because there is visibility into the entire system, thanks to contextual observability, which provides information on the data and its usage context. This enables data engineers to fix issues before they impact downstream business users.

Preventing Data Issues

When implemented as part of the entire development lifecycle, including production, data observability provides continuous validation of the health of the data and the data ecosystem. Continuous validation can perceptibly improve the reliability of the applications and prevent data issues, lowering the total cost of ownership.

Decentralized Data Quality Management

Service level agreements (SLAs) can manage and ensure data quality, just as they are used in IT DevOps to ensure reliability and other key metrics. This new managing data quality requires data observability, which on the one hand, can provide synchronized (near-real-time) and continuous validation of the data, which further improves the efficiency of any service level agreements (SLOs) in place. But more importantly, on the other hand, data observability will allow SLAs and SLOs to be defined at the granularity of their usage, and within the context (the application, for example). This capability solves one of the most important roadblocks of data quality management programs, the definition of SLAs by owners, stewards, or subject matter experts (SMEs) who have a hard time defining a single set of constraints that will supposedly meet all usage expectations. Hence, they cannot come up with a single (central) set of SLAs, as each use case is likely to perceive the SLAs differently. The key difference with data SLAs is that they can take a very large number of forms that feels quickly infinite; for example, you could have SLAs for the min representation, number of nulls, number of categories, skewness, quantile 0.99, etc., for a single field from a random CSV file. Hence, leveraging data observability to decentralize the SLAs in a contextualized manner (the usage) is key to managing data quality and defining a culture of accountability and clear roles and responsibilities.

Complementing Existing Data Governance Capabilities

Remember the DAMA-DMBKO2 data governance framework from earlier? Because data observability is part of that architecture and surrounds all of the areas of data governance, it provides visibility into all of the different components that interact at the data level. This enables data teams to automatically create documentation using the same kind of data, data storage, and data modeling, and provides greater visibility into the different data models that exist, what data has been published to the data catalog, which analytics have been run on what data, and which master data was used.

The Future and Beyond

By better understanding the different use cases for data observability, you should now be able to understand how data observability can be used to help optimize your data systems as well as data teams.

In the coming chapters, I'll go even deeper, detailing how to set up these use cases and covering best practices to capture the information necessary for each use case in the most efficient and valuable manner.

Conclusion

Data observability is an essential capability for modern organizations that rely on data to achieve their objectives. As data teams continue to grow in size and complexity, it becomes increasingly important to establish practices that promote transparency, governance, and data validation. This book focuses on the technical aspect of data governance through the lens of data observability. By embracing simple yet powerful habits, organizations can ensure that their data efforts are visible, controllable, and manageable across the entire data lifecycle. The following chapters will explore the core principles of data observability and best practices and recipes for making a system data observable.

## CHAPTER 2

Components of Data Observability

As introduced in Chapter 1, data observability is an area of (IT) observability inter-secting with other areas, such as applications or analytics. In this chapter, we will cover how data observability and its interactions, shown in Figure 2-1, can be added to a system.

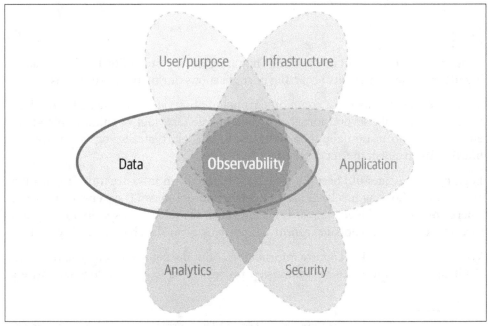

Figure 2-1. Areas of observability intersecting data observability area

As discussed in Chapter 1, data observability gives observers a broader spectrum of observations to interpret a system's internal state by combining all its areas. However, this combination can become a challenge itself if some precautions are not respected. This chapter will give you a deeper understanding of what observations are and what they should contain.

This chapter presents the three foundational components of data observability: the *channels* where observations are accessible, the *observation model* describing the structure of the observations, and finally, the *expectations* providing proactive capabilities to your data system.

Channels of Data Observability Information

The first component of data observability is the channels that convey observations to the observer. There are three channels: logs, traces, and metrics. These channels are common to all areas of observability and aren't strictly linked to data observability.

The following sections will define each of the three main channels of observability. You are likely already familiar with these channels, but if not, hundreds of books and blogs delve deeper into defining them. If you want to read more, I recommend the book *Distributed Systems Observability*,[1] which dedicates a full chapter to defining these channels. I also recommend part two of *Observability Engineering*,[2] as well as *Cloud Observability in Action*.[3]

Logs

Logs are very common in any system. They are generally lines of text in a file (called a log file) representing events occurring in applications during their executions.

Therefore, *logs* are the most common channel of observation produced by an IT system. They can take several forms (e.g., line of free text, JSON) and are intended to encapsulate information about an event. A *line* of a log (typically, logs are a stream of lines), is the result of the act of logging.

Logging is a decades-old best practice in IT, especially in infrastructure, applications, and security. Logging has been used to debug and optimize IT systems or processes. There are even developed standards for logs, such as Syslog, that specify the log structure and allow heterogeneous infrastructures to be controlled by a central system.

While logs are crucial to capture information about the behavior of a system, it is difficult to use logs to recreate a multistep process. This is because logs comprise all

---

1 Cindy Sridharan, "Chapter 4. The Three Pillars of Observability," *Distributed Systems Observability*, (*https://oreil.ly/XvdB8*) (O'Reilly, 2018).

2 Charity Majors, Liz Fong-Jones, and George Miranda, *Observability Engineering* (*https://oreil.ly/4TE4N*), (O'Reilly, 2022).

3 Michael Hausenblas, *Cloud Observability in Action* (Manning, 2023).

---

activities within the system, and the logs of a process are likely interleaved with other concurrent processes or scattered across multiple systems (e.g., distributed system, service mesh).

Traces

The excellent book *Observability Engineering*[4] introduces tracing as a "fundamental software debugging technique wherein various bits of information are logged throughout a program's execution to diagnose problems."

Traces can be thought of as a specific case of logs—the reconnection of the steps executed by a process. Because traces represent the links between all events of the same process, they allow the whole context to be derived efficiently from logs. This concept has been extended to address distributed systems needs, commonly called distributed tracing, where trace events (aka spans), such as calling a web service, accessing a file, or querying a database, are produced in the different systems but linked to each other as a global trace (generally an ID).

Traces, with their spans, are an efficient way to follow operations across services and servers, as information such as the server, the service, and the timestamp of the event are conveyed. So an observer can easily browse the logs of the service, on the server, at the given time to analyze the logs of the specific event for which they need to produce observations.

Data Lineage Is a Form of Trace

This element signifies a general note.

A different form of trace in the data and analytics context is the data lineage, which is covered in the next section. Although a data lineage is not strictly a trace (because it doesn't connect events), it connects data sources to encode the provenance or the generational model. However, in certain situations, data lineages can help with troubleshooting a process or discovering opportunities to optimize.

In practice, spans also convey logs that might be relevant for the observer to analyze on the spot, instead of only functioning to reconnecting the trace information.

Nevertheless, some systems may not yet support distributed tracing; thus, traces are not natively supported (made observable). Those systems may already be tagged as non-natively observable. In such a situation, a solution could be to leverage the

---

4 Majors, Fong-Jones, and Miranda, "Chapter 6: Stitching Events into Traces," *Observability Engineering* (O'Reilly, 2022).

existing logs to interpret their content to reconstruct traces based on information scattered across log lines (this possibility is addressed in Chapter 6).

The last channel of observations is metrics, which is closely connected to logs and traces, as both can contain metrics. However, because of their simplicity, metrics have a significant advantage over logs and traces.

Metrics

Every system state has some component that can be represented with numbers, and these numbers change as the state changes. Metrics provide a source of information that allows an observer not only to understand using factual information, but also leverage, relatively easily, mathematical methods to derive insight from even a large number of metrics (e.g., the CPU load, the number of open files, the average amount of rows, the minimum date).

Due to their numerical nature, they need to be recorded. This is why metrics were once part of logs as well as present in traces. Because their usefulness is so straightforward, we have seen standards to simplify the publishing or collection of metrics independently of regular logs and traces over the years.

In Figure 2-2, however, I present a case where all components are mixed up (which happens quite frequently); two applications are sending logs about events forming traces, and several metrics are available somewhere in the unstructured (logged) text. This can give you a better understanding why standards have emerged to simplify the collection and usage of traces and metrics.

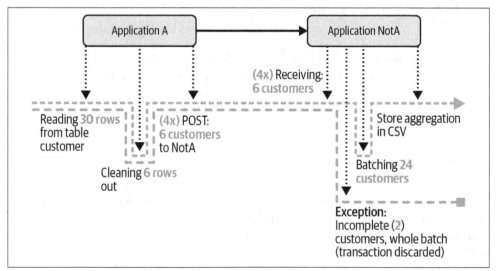

Figure 2-2. Two applications logging unstructured messages, exceptions, and metrics along two traces

Based on what I've described, it may sound odd to talk about logs, metrics, and traces as being produced by data (a number such as "3" cannot log, measure, or trace anything; it is a number). This is why it is vital to consider data observability as an area that intersects others, such as applications and analytics, implying that the information produced by logs, metrics, and traces from several areas must be connected. Let's tackle this in the next section.

Observations Model

To ensure comprehensive data observability, it's crucial to model observations that come from various channels and formats, and that relate to multiple areas. In the following sections, I present a model that encodes the dimensions of data observability and supports the solutions for the use cases I presented in Chapter 1.

I want to emphasize that the model I'm proposing is one I have seen work in many projects and use cases. Though the model may change over time to include more complexities or encode more relations, I intend to show you in detail how the observations from the different areas can work together easily as long as the connections between them are well enough anticipated to avoid reverse engineering or approximations.

This model will, at the very least, give you a viable starting point to generate information representing the state of the system you need to observe. However, you can consider it a core model that you could extend to address additional, potentially custom, needs. In Chapter 3, I will explain the different strategies you can use to generate most of the information of the model automatically, and, in Chapter 4, the associated ready-to-use recipes for several common data technologies (e.g., Python pandas, Apache Spark, SQL).

Emerging Standards for Data Observation

It is true that other areas of observability have not necessarily introduced such models yet, and this limits their ease of use. Having logs, metrics, and traces coming from many infrastructures or applications without a clear structure to recombine them (the intersections) makes generating insights about their internal state cumbersome. The information is therefore recombined in a best-effort manner, using a posteriori analysis, which also depends on human intervention.

At the time of writing, data observability is an emerging practice. Therefore, my intent is to avoid repeating the mistakes made in other areas by introducing a model to 1) accelerate its adoption 2) ensure its ease of use. With a clear model to follow for all disciplines that touch on observability of data, we will be able to communicate more effectively

In Figure 2-3, the model is designed as an entity graph, where each entity provides some bits of information about the state of the system and how they are linked to each other. The links clearly identify the intersections between data observability and other areas. For example, later in this chapter, you will learn that a data source (data observability) is linked to a server where it is accessible (infrastructure observability); hence, the link itself is part of the intersection of these two areas.

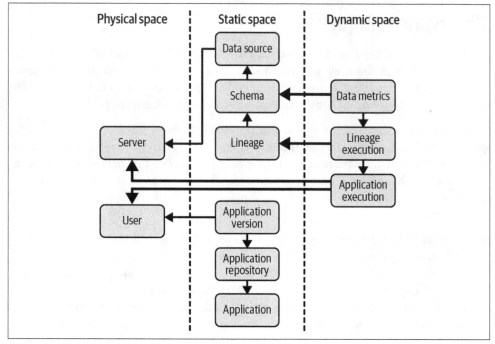

Figure 2-3. Data observability core model

The model presented in Figure 2-3 aims to structure data observations to maximize their overall interpretability for an external observer and to provide a common language that can be used independently of the people, time, and technologies involved in the observation.

To improve the readability of the model, it is split into the three spaces:

The physical space
(Left in Figure 2-3) links observations with tangible entities. Even though a server might be virtual or a user may be a system or applicative user, the physical space represents a space that can be physically checked.

The static space
> (Center in Figure 2-3) represents the entities changing relatively slowly in opposition to the dynamic space. It represents a state of the system that could be built manually.

The dynamic space
> (Right in Figure 2-3) is part of the system that is evolving or changing so fast that it cannot be consolidated, documented, or built manually. This is where automation is not even a question—but a necessity.

Within each space, entities are introduced to enable some observability. Let's go through each of these entities to understand their purpose and how their relation to other entities plays a role in data observability.

Physical Space

In this section, I will cover the information in the data observability area that can be considered tangible: the server and the user (or their virtual alternatives, such as containers and system users), as highlighted in Figure 2-4.

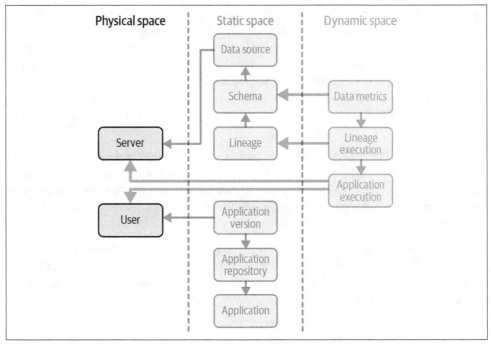

Figure 2-4. The physical space of the data observability core model

Let's start with the server first.

Server

The *server* is related to the machines running the IT system being observed. It is meant to provide information about physical appliances. However, in the era of cloud computing, it can also represent a container, a virtual machine, a pod, etc., that gives access to infrastructure observations. Because I am defining the core model, I kept the server component simple, without encoding containers, virtual machines, or clusters, for example—which can be extensions of the model.

However, the core information about the server must help the observer to tap into other systems (e.g., Datadog) to analyze the infrastructure status. To ensure this capability for the observer, the type of information the server must convey includes IP, container ID, machine name, or anything that can identify the underlying infrastructure appropriately.

In "Data source" on page 41, we'll see an example of how and when the server helps the observer.

User

In a data usage context, several types of users are involved, in as many different manners. The two most obvious ones are data users and data consumers. However, we can also consider data owners, data architects, and other roles defined in data governance, or more generally in data management organizations. The users we'll consider more specifically in data observability will be data producers and consumers, and this via their actions with the data or the system—the core model shows two examples that will be discussed in the sections "Application version" on page 48 and "Application execution" on page 49.

We are interested in observing the *user* because this is probably the easiest actionable information source that an observer can use to improve their understanding of a situation. We can simply ask the user about data issues or anything they can offer to help us understand the process; they generally hold some knowledge about the data and how the system is supposed to work.

Like the server, the user can be a virtual abstraction, such as an identifier that doesn't hold personal information (e.g., a GitHub account ID) or a so-called system or service account such as a *root* or *sparkuser*, that gives the observer a hint about the impact of the user on the behavior of the system (e.g., security) or on its liability (e.g., privacy).

In later sections related to the applications within a system, I'll discuss the advantages of having such information on hand.

While so far I have limited our considerations of physical space to users and servers, other elements such as geolocation (e.g., the geospatial coordinates of the server hosting a database) can also be part of the physical space. However, I recommend starting with a simple model to get the core visibility needed, then eventually growing it with additional use cases. That said, geolocation does fit nicely in the user and infrastructure observability areas.

Now let's address the static space, which includes most of the exclusive data observability entities.

Static Space

Physical space allows the observer to link events about data to "things" that can be accessed (even virtually). In this section, I introduce the static space (see Figure 2-5) that gives the observer the ability to analyze the status of the system at rest, or wherein the dimension of time has less influence than the physical space on its status (e.g., the existence of a server, the code change of a user). The entities are related to data and applications and their structural evolutions and act within the static space.

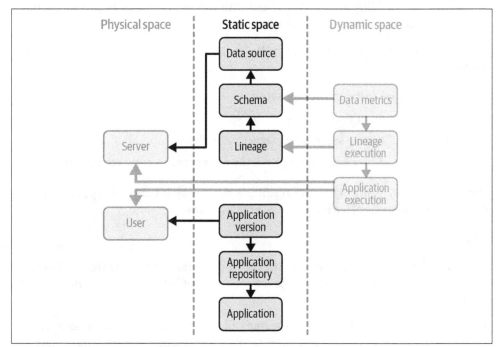

Figure 2-5. The static space of the data observability core model

Data source

The *data source* provides information about what data exists and how it is used— whether that's as a simple CSV file, Kafka topic, or database table. The local file path, the topic name, and the table name are the kinds of information that are typically part of the data source.

The data source is present in the static space because data sources do not change rapidly. Of course, files can be copied or moved to other locations, but the model would consider the copied or moved files as new data sources. Renaming a table in a database is also similar to moving it. It's important to note, though, that renaming and moving data sources can have big consequences. Applications can fail as they expect the data to be at a specific location, but the location may change in production because the data has been moved (e.g., mv). In such cases, there will be several data source entities, one for each data source location, as moving a data source from one location to another is copying then deleting it. This action of copy then delete is actually a transformation that will be represented by its own entity—this lineage will be introduced further in this chapter.

The data source is also an element of observation that resides in the main component of the data observability area and is linked with the server, which is part of the intersection with the infrastructure observability area.

Some use cases highlighting where you can gain observability of the data source include:

- Data migration to/from another server
- Data duplication or redundancy
- Data availability on a server (e.g., server migration or upgrade)
- Data access (i.e., if a machine is physically connected to access the data)

However, the data is not only a source, it is a repository for several types of information. In the next section, we'll explore what this means.

Schema

While the data source introduced in the previous section provides information about how data can be accessed, it doesn't cover what type of information the user may find in the data.

The schema entity provides visibility into the structure of the data source.[5] The schema is an essential component of *metadata* (others would be definition, tags, etc.) and conveys information about fields (or columns), including those that are potentially deep (embedded), available in the data source. Each field of the schema has

---

5 The name schema relates to concepts such as XML Schema, JSON Schema and the like.

at least a name and an associated type, which could be *native* (e.g., `string`, `int`, `address`) or conceptual[6] (e.g., `address`, `SKU_ID`), or both.

Even though the schema is in the static world, it is still a changing entity. It provides a dynamic example for a database data source, in the form of a table that can have columns added, removed, or renamed. However, the schema makes it relatively manageable to keep track of the changes.

The schema is linked to the data source because it allows the observer to identify the types of information available in a data source.

Because the schema of a data source is likely to change, the model can encode these changes by keeping all schema versions in two different but non-exclusive methods. Each method supports interesting use cases:

- Each modification of the data source's schema creates a new schema entity, along with the time of change or version. Here is an example of how the observer can leverage this information:
  — Instantly see what has changed between the new and old schemas.
  — Validate the new schema is matching new requirements.
  — Notice an unplanned change due to a mistake in a transformation.
- Each consumer of the data source creates a schema entity related to its own usage of the data source. This gives the observer the opportunity to:
  — Be aware their usage will fail due to missing information and issue a request for information.
  — Acknowledge new information that can be used to improve their results.
  — Change their usage appropriately to match renamed information.

Interestingly, depending on the semantics, the schema is an observation that is either part of the (a) main component of data observability or (b) an intersection between data and analytics observability.[7]

At this point in the model, we can recover decent visibility of the data. However, we still lack a fair amount of information about how the data plays out in the remainder of the system, especially in applications and analytics. The remainder of this section will focus on achieving data observability within these two areas.

---

6 As in ontology's concepts.

7 Which we could name "data usage observability." This is probably taking the idea a bit too far…

Lineage

The *lineage* entity, or more precisely the *technical data lineage*, is probably the most difficult information to uncover, and therefore the least represented observation available (at the time of writing)—consequently, it is also the least used observation, so we still have a lot to learn from it.[8] There is a lot of literature on how a lineage can be used (several examples will be listed at the end of this section), but there is little available about how to collect it, concretely.

Lineage, literally line + age, refers to the direct connections between data sources. A data source's lineage is its set of direct upstream data sources and their lineages. The technical data lineage can be at either the data source or the field level. We should consider that the schema level is a more complex level to work at than the data source level, as it provides information on how data sources' schemas are connected to each other. That results in a connected graph where each field of a data source has its own lineage that connects it to the fields of the upstream data sources, as shown in Figure 2-6.

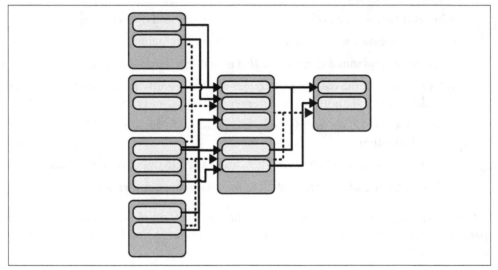

Figure 2-6. Example of technical data lineage (dark gray and dotted lines: data source level; light gray and plain lines: field level)

The connections between data sources are created using applications that execute *transformations* of inputs (sources) into outputs (results). These transformations can include events like the following:

---

8 And that's pretty cool!

- An SQL query issued by a Java web server transforming a table (input) into a JSON HTTP response (output).

- SQL generated by a reporting tool computing and presenting (output) a key performance indicator from a series table (inputs).

- A Spark job that creates a view in a data warehouse (output) from a number of Parquet files (inputs).

- A Kafka application using a streaming API that consumes a topic (source) and produces another topic (output).

- A machine learning script training a model (output) on a feature matrix created from a CSV file (input).

Even a human copying figures from a sheet of paper (input) into an Excel sheet (output) is a lineage.

The information contained in the lineage is essentially the mapping between input and output data sources and/or schemas.

To encode this mapping with the data source and schema, the model presented in Figure 2-3 shows that the lineage is linked to schema, enabling the following use cases:

- Instantly know the minimal subset of information needed to comply with the transformation, which helps for optimization.

- Allow further processing optimization by distributing a subset of the data by partitioning it along the columns dimension.

- Separate the transformation from the data source storage and location to ease change management (e.g., from code processing files in a data lake to distributed SQL on tables in a lakehouse).

- Generate semantic (usage) information from the dependencies between the information from inputs and their outputs.

Although conceptually simple, lineage is complex because of the following characteristics:

- Cumbersome to document: all data sources must be documented, and each operation applied to all fields.

- Likely to change: even a simple modification of an SQL query will change the data lineage.

- Numerous: so many transformations happen continuously on a company's data. Even a simple CRUD application is composed of many transformations.

Despite these complexities, I have left lineage information as part of the static space because a lineage relies on humans who transform data to create their desired output, and the static space provides us with the ability to observe those changes.

When considering lineage outside of the main component of data observability, we can see that it also fits well with:

Analytics observability
Lineage contains the analysis structure and how it is performed with data.

User/purpose observability
Lineage encodes what can be achieved with the data sources.

Application observability
Lineage is executed by an application, and a data application exists to execute lineage.

There's a lot to explore when speaking about the contribution of lineages to user/purpose observability and application observability, which is something we'll discuss further.

Application

The *application* gives access to another aspect of data observability because it is key to providing data visibility. In fact, applications are at the center of all information: they are the product of the user, the container of the analytics, the consumer and producer of data, and they run on infrastructure while also configuring or implementing their security.

Information about the application must be recorded so the observer can understand which system is at play and the associated logic.

I tend to consider the application as like a door to the other areas of observability, because the application is relatively central to everything. In fact, referring to an application can be as simple as:

- The `groupId: artifactId` of a Spark job.
- The path to a workbook in Tableau.
- The `organization/module name` of a Python script.
- The URN of a step in an orchestrator descriptor (e.g., GCP Workflow) scheduling an SQL.

Figure 2-3 shows that "Application" does not refer to anything, but because it still is in the most central position in the observability model, it must be executed. I will explain how this is done in "Application execution" on page 49.

One could argue that lineage should be directly connected to an application. For example, SQL joining two tables in Oracle and creating a view in Snowflake is coded in the application that will run it, hence creating a direct connection between both entities.

However, I believe that this view couples the "data" and "application" observability areas too strongly in the static space. In several cumbersome instances this direct connection is completely inappropriate:

Lineage modification
> When the lineage is modified and a new lineage is created, the initial lineage is no longer part of the application. In this case, the lineage should be connected with the application version (see "Application version" on page 48).

Lineage is generated at runtime
> When the lineage is generated at runtime, such as SQL created on the fly, all the SQL does not exist in the application until it runs and is used. In this case, the lineage would be connected to the runtime (execution) of the application (see "Application execution" on page 49).

Of course, the application is not disconnected from the lineage; it just won't link to it directly. Instead, it plays the role of a container by embedding most of the observation model via the two components, the application repository and application version.

Application repository

The *application repository* is often seen as the outlier in the model presented in Figure 2-3, because it gives information about where the source of the application resides (e.g., source code, report configuration).

At first glance, there seems to be little or no connection to the data. However, the information provided by the application repository is intended to encode the connection between data observability and application observability.

Because an application's source can move around, the application repository can represent its latest location (hopefully not several at the same time) and hint where it resided in the past. I have chosen to encode this notion of temporality in a different entity—in the application version.

One of the primary usages of the repository is to give the observer the direct location where they should be analyzing the system. For example, if there is an issue with generating a data source by an application, knowing the application repository location tells the observer exactly where to look. However, they will also need to know the application's version to analyze the situation appropriately—as it was when the issue happened—which is where an application version is useful.

Application version

An application version is the final entity—and one of the most critical, as it is the glue between the other entities—in the static space. The *application version* is the entry point in the observations model that refers to the exact version an application was running when an issue occurred with the data.

The version can be:

- The version number (e.g., v1.0)
- A git hash (e.g., d670460b4b4aece5915caf5c68d12f560a9fe3e4)
- A timestamp (e.g., 1652587507)

The version allows an observer to browse the history in the application repository for the running application under supervision. The version is also useful when conducting root cause analysis. If the version is too old, it may indicate that the application has not been updated (yet). If the version is unknown/newer, it may indicate that a bug in the logic has been introduced or an unknown transformation has occurred.

You'll see the version is not directly connected to the lineage or any entity closer to the core data observability entities (e.g., data source, schema). Thus, to create a bridge between the application and data observability, we must take into account what is executed, read, transformed, and produced. This is what the dynamic space is for.

Dynamic Space

The *dynamic space* (see Figure 2-7) allows the observer to leverage the behavior of the system that uses the data. Its main purpose is to create visibility on the *runtime* (i.e., data runtime context).

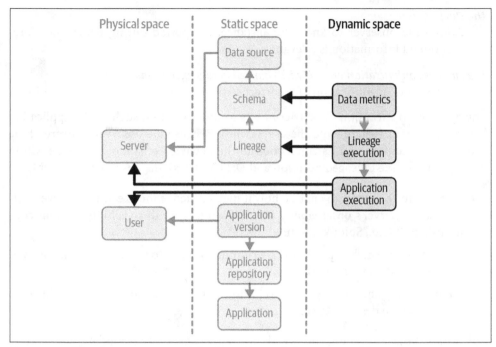

Figure 2-7. The dynamic space of the data observability core model

Also, the status of the environment is very sensitive to events that occur during runtime, such as the data changing due to real-world events, the application being killed due to a virtual machine reboot, etc. In other words, it is very dynamic and unpredictable (at least deterministically), which is why I call it the dynamic space. The composition of the dynamic space is described in the structure that follows, starting with the application execution.

Application execution

The *application execution* entity provides the observer with information about the application running and its use of data.

As previously noted, the application is the artifact that opens the door to greater visibility of other components within the observation model because its source describes the analytics (e.g., lineage) using the data. By capturing the real runtime and its execution, the application execution conveys information to the observer, such as:

An ID

Allows the observer to identify which application observability information is relevant to review (e.g., in an application logging system)

The starting date
> Allows the observer to know, for instance, the period during which the afore-mentioned information is relevant

The current configuration and how it's changed across executions
> Allows quick identification of incorrect settings

The application execution directly connects to other entities, such as the application (what), the server (where), and the users (who). Because the observer is aware of the application execution and its connection to the behavior of some data usage within the application (see Lineage Execution and Data Metrics), the observer will be able to:

- Connect to the server to analyze how it may influence the execution or, even better, use the server's observability information to gain this visibility without connecting to it (e.g., Splunk, Elastic).

- Know exactly which applications are running or used to run on a server, and analyze their performance or load.

- Identify easily and quickly who has performed the execution and thus is likely to be able to help describe the situation.

But what about the connection with the application? The model presented in Figure 2-3 doesn't connect application execution to the application because what is most important for an observer to know about the execution of an application is its version. Additionally, because the version refers to the source code, you can infer that it also refers to the application.

Having the information about which version is being executed is extremely powerful. This information provides instantaneous insights, such as whether the version deployed is not the latest or which changes may have caused an issue (e.g., `git diff`).

Also, consider that an application will likely be executed in different versions across different servers (e.g., environments), making the information described in this section even more valuable.

Lineage execution

The *lineage execution* entity is the less obvious, but also the most complex, to create because it will likely have a large number of instances.

A lineage execution simply gives information about the execution of a lineage. Therefore, it can represent many different things, such as the execution of an SQL job, a Python transformation, a copy command, machine learning training, etc. Lineage execution is meant to provide the observer with explicit information about how a lineage behaves, including how often and at what time connections to data sources occur.

I wouldn't say that a lineage execution conveys a lot of information intrinsically, but it is a keystone of the observation model. Without lineage execution, most of the use cases of data observability presented in Chapter 1 are fantasy or rely on best effort reconciliation, which inevitably leads to spurious correlations (mainly while reconciling the data and application observability areas).

A lineage execution is rich in information about its connections to other core entities, such as lineage and application execution. If the link to lineage is clear, then the observer can tell which lineage is observable and can analyze the link further.

A lineage can't be executed alone because it only represents the connections between data sources (schemas), not *how* these connections are implemented. This information is available in the code, which can be observed using the application version. For example, a data transformation could have been implemented in Spark RDD, then in Spark DataFrame, then in Spark SQL, then a materialized view in Snowflake, etc.

To understand how a lineage (a transformation) is executed, the observer has to use information about the application execution introduced in the previous section. It is like a lineage is executed as a subprogram (or a subapplication, a subprocess) started by the application itself, for example, an application creates an entry in a table when certain events are consumed from Kafka, then it executes the related lineage.

Moreover, an application is not limited to running a single lineage, or each lineage only once, or even always the same lineages. Because of this diversity, giving the observer visibility of this extreme (nondeterministic) situation is essential, as it is unthinkable that this complexity could be held in a person's brain.

Due to the centrality of lineage execution in the model, the observer gains holistic visibility (but is not limited to) on what is shown in Figure 2-8.

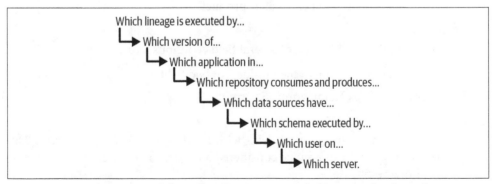

Figure 2-8. Using contextual data observations to gain holistic insight about data usage

In graph lingo, we call this a traversal (collecting information while walking a graph). I call this a *mind-blower*, as the observer can easily navigate deeply across the many layers of information, as shown in Figure 2-8, from a lineage to the user who changed one of the schemas it involves.

But we can extend this visibility further with data metrics. One of the exciting things about data metrics is that it has the potential to support data quality in a bottom-up, scalable, and real-time fashion.

Data metrics

Data metrics is the specification of metrics in observability. Data metrics are often the most common suspect when discussing observability, as they are easily leveraged in analysis to infer or predict (future or dependent) events—e.g., using their temporality dependencies with multivariate time series analytics, Markov chains, and the like.

In this context of data observability, I am focusing on the metrics that we can relate directly to data, such as descriptive statistics. However, the data metrics entity comes with a subtlety that can have a huge impact on its usefulness—the metrics are always attached to their analytical (e.g., transformations) usage.

The role of data metrics is to give information to the observer about what the values of the data look like under certain conditions during their consumption or production. At least three metrics types can be considered:

Univariable
  A metric related to one of the fields/columns of the observed data source. For example:

  - Descriptive statistics of a column (e.g., min, max, nulls, levels)
  - Distribution (e.g., density, skewness)
  - Formula (e.g., the sum of squares, product)

Multivariable
  The result of the combination of several fields/columns. For example:

  - Formula (e.g, the sum of the products of two fields)
  - Combined (e.g., Kolmogorov–Smirnov)

Extrinsic
  The result of the aggregation of fields with fields from other data sources. This metric is tricky, and can even be considered a borderline metric, as it is too close to a KPI or a result.

It is important to note that these metrics are not intended to replace the exploration analysis required during the analytical phase of a data project (e.g., data science, analytics report). Those metrics are meant to allow the data to be understood in the context of their usage, not before. In other words, the primary usage of the data metrics is not to provide potential users with the initial insights they may find.

Nevertheless, it is key for data metrics' potential users to gain trust in the likelihood of the data being reliable, because if the source is reliable for other uses, there is a good chance that their own data usage will also be dependable. Remember that trust (particularly related to data quality) requires time and is stronger when the reliability of the data is tied to real and understandable usages.

Data Reliability Is Not Universal

The likelihood in the preceding sentence is important because it is not fully granted that if a data source is reliable for the applications of user X, it will also be reliable for the applications of user Y. Users X and Y are likely to use the data differently. For example, imagine if user X computes the arithmetic mean of a field and user Y its geometric mean. In this case, how would a single unexpected zero impact each model?[9] And what if the data source is suddenly empty? How would that also change the impact on the different use cases?[10]

Hence, the data metrics must be linked to the data source exposing the *behavior* (the correct term should be *status*) to the observer. In Figure 2-3, I show that data metrics are linked to the schema. This is because the metrics are highly dependent on the fields present in the data source during its usage.

Finally, those metrics have to be linked to the data source usage, represented by the lineage execution, which indicates when the data sources' combination is executed. This link comes with a never-seen-before power in observation models—giving the observer the ability to understand the status of a data system. For example, it allows the observer to perform the following analyses:

- The percentage of the data transformed and how its fluctuation impacts the output
- The impact of the statistical variation of a subset (with a filter) of the data involved in an analysis
- The increase of the time period of data used in machine learning training and its impact on the performance (e.g., one year versus 18 months of data).

---

9 The user Y ends up with the value 0, while the value of X has probably not changed a lot (especially if there are many values).

10 Boom… division by 0. At least, Y would get an error this time.

Extensibility of the Core Model

The model presented in this section is meant to be a core model. Hence, it can be easily extended to introduce entities from other areas, such as the analytics area. For example, a machine learning algorithm is trained on some data sources serving as training and test sets. This is a case of lineage where some inputs play a specific role at a given time. Regarding the output, the trained model can be saved (e.g., a linear model in Python saved as a *pickle* file). This turns the model into a data source, with associated metrics related to the performance of the training phase (e.g., R2), and its content (e.g., number of weights, number of zero weights).

Therefore, the reasoning used to create the core model described in the previous section can be reused to structurally increase the coverage of observations in the model to define a global observability model, which is beyond the scope of this book and left as homework.[11]

So far I have introduced you to the observations a system needs to produce to be considered data observable. Now, I will extend this capability to their usage by the system itself, or its creators or users.

Expectations

So far we have covered the types of information and the entities that give an observer the ability to understand how data behaves in a system.

In this section, I am going to address the third component of data observability, which pertains to creating visibility when the data continuously satisfies assumptions about its content (e.g., the *age* is available, there are at least *10,000 rows*) or its behavior (e.g., subtracting *income* from the *outcome* is positive). These assumptions generally come from business rules, data explorations, or simply data definitions, and they guide which transformations must be applied. Therefore, when the applications executing these transformations are deployed, these assumptions can become expectations, as they seem to have been validated enough during development to move on to production.

As you'll see, the expectations can come from different parts of the data ecosystem (e.g., users, applications, etc.). If expectations are visible to an observer, it gives the observer key insights into how the observed status of the data compares to how it is expected to behave.

---

11 This is a reminiscence of my past as a pure mathematics student when the demonstrations of "trivial" theorems were left as "homework"—each taking days, and often more, to accomplish.

By setting specific expectations, just as tests do in software development, the observer can better understand the behavior of the data that aligns with expectations. Moreover, if some expectations are not met, the observer instantly knows what requires their attention, just as test reports indicate to software developers where they need to focus their attention.

So they give visibility about what the observer expects to happen, representing either a positive or a negative event. For example, knowing that an expectation, such as "an address always starts with a number," is true for 99% of the entries, ensures that the data that can't be used is only 1%. There are no incidents. It just provides the observer two pieces of information: the expectation itself and if it is true or false. On the other hand, if a transformation is known to fail if a secondary is incomplete, in this case, when it becomes false, an incident can be created, triggered, and an associated decision can be made (e.g., not executing the transformation at all).

When setting expectations, you will want to both set rules for how the data should behave and detect anomalies. The next section will look at both of these areas of expectations and how an application can become its own observer and make decisions regarding the status of the data's behavior.

Rules

A rule is a common tool used in development and monitoring; it is basically a function that evaluates a *signal* (e.g., number of rows, list of fields) extracted from the data against a series of *checks* (e.g., "> 10,000"), which encode and validate that the expectations are met. If the current signal passes the rule, it will return a "true" response; if it doesn't, it will return a "false." The function's logic is often quite simple, so interpreting the result is easily relatable to the inputs. For example, rules using a machine learning model to return the result are more like anomaly detectors than rules.

Anomaly Detection Is Not a Rule

Oxford's definition of "rule" is "One of a set of explicit or understood regulations or principles governing conduct or procedure within a particular area of activity." I don't consider a trained machine learning model to be explicit, even if a fully explainable one would be borderline.

Therefore, rules for data observability would be created using information conveyed by schema, data metrics, lineage, etc. For example, if a data metric reports the number of null values for the field *age*, a rule could be the *number of null values for age must be below 10*, or *less than 5%*, or even *can't increase by more than 0.01% between two executions of the same lineage*. Another example, of using the schema information, would be *the age field must be present and of X type of integer*.

In fact, there are two categories of rules:

Single-state based

These rules act on the information about the state of the system only at a given time, such as in the example, where null ages must be below 10. The state information could also be combined to create intrinsic checks, such as comparing the number of null values to the total count (e.g., no more than 10%).

Multi-state based

These rules require more than one state, such as the states of one or several periods of time, continuous states, or sampling. Multi-state-based rules could even include a list of states randomly drawn from the available states.

And each category can be categorized into a single variable and multivariable, when a rule uses one or more observations from the same state. Figure 2-9 illustrates the four variations.

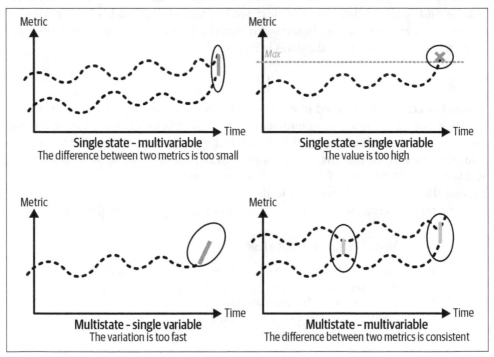

Figure 2-9. The four variations of rules

While the entities of the observation model are computed or extracted from available information, the rules are less factual and require more insight to create. The insights needed can come from several sources such as:

- Human knowledge and experience

- The history of the system
- Similarities with other systems

Let's look at two ways to make rules.

Explicit rules

Explicit rules are created by users as a representation of assumptions that they are building, and which they expect to hold true when their applications will run and be used in production.

Those assumptions come mainly from the following channels:

Experience
> A person's experience with the data or the addressed use case is a great way to generate rules because it is based on past experience or applied knowledge. For example, business rules are experienced in different ways: as constraints on how the business should be conducted, as a way to assert a business structure, or as a way to control or influence the behavior of the business.[12] I am also referring to intuition or gut feelings resulting from years of experience forming assumptions based on use cases or practical experience (e.g., networking, etc). However, it doesn't mean that those assumptions are always reliable. A person may be biased or misunderstand the full situation. Nevertheless, it is still worth considering these "instinctual" assumptions as they are far better than nothing, and, more importantly, they express the user's expectations. Then, if those rules are not met, thanks to the system's observability, the team can perform an analysis to determine the rules' validity and potentially discard or adjust them.

Exploration
> While working with data to create the pipeline, report, features, and other types of data transformations, a person will be learning, or at least better understanding, the data at hand.[13] Therefore, assumptions will be formed and integrated into the application based on these learnings. For example, if the data has no duplicates or a turnover is always above zero, you might come to assume that those conditions are true. Then, you will likely not make their roles explicit, or may not specify them in the business logic to be implemented, although those assumptions are a great source for rules. One way to help this process of developing rules would be to create data profiles (using profilers). Profiling data generates a series of static rules inferred from the data provided. However, these rules need to be used with caution and reviewed thoroughly, leveraging the team's experience to

---

12 Business Rules Group, "Defining Business Rules ~ What Are They Really?" July 2000.

13 Data at hand refers to the data available during the development phase.

select the most appropriate ones while avoiding introducing rules too close to the data at hand and therefore likely to fail rapidly in production.[14] The usage of data profilers will be detailed further in Chapter 6. They will be referred to as scanners.

Discovery

When applications and data are in use, new cases can be discovered, such as unknown-unknown (unexpected cases) or corner cases (not considered in the business logic). When discovered, they are generally considered incidents that need to be analyzed, and most likely fixed. As discussed in Chapter 1, several processes must be conducted, such as root cause analysis, troubleshooting, and impact analysis, to determine and fix the issue. Each of these analyses presents opportunities to introduce new rules that can be discovered (learned from history) along the pipeline—including discovering interactions or causality (strong, consistent, and invariable correlation) between events at different stages of the pipeline.

It is also important to note that rules can be outdated as the world constantly changes (e.g., products are boycotted, laws are adapted, and platforms are upgraded). Consequently, the maintenance of these rules must be considered. I often encourage teams to quickly review the rules, especially for experience-based ones, with every new version of the application using or producing the data, at the very least. Validating rules properly requires a simple feedback flow; however, there are alternatives, such as using assisted rules.

Assisted rules

In the previous section, I introduced rules created entirely as the result of human analysis. Here, I will introduce an alternative method, which allows rules to be discovered.

Although rules cannot be based on non-explicit behavior, they can still be discovered using simple analysis (e.g., heuristics) or even learned (e.g., association rule mining). Such rules are created with the assistance of the observations. In this way, they are "data-driven."

The power of assisted rules is not only the capability to create new rules, but also to update existing ones, even the explicit ones. Done efficiently, assisted rules lessen the burden required to maintain rules in the long run.

The way to introduce assisted rules in a data observability system is by keeping humans in the loop. Because rules are structurally comprehensive, they can be

---

14 It is similar to overfitting in machine learning.

reviewed by people with the knowledge to tune, accept, or reject them. Validating rules in this manner is important to increase the level of trust in the rules, and, ultimately, the accuracy of the issues the rules detect. For example, an assistant system can be estimated (e.g., based on self-correlation) that the *amount* seems to take its value around 19,945.62 with a standard deviation around 783.09, and therefore propose a few rules such as following some distributions—which could also either estimated from observations or be an observation itself like the Kullback–Leibler divergence with a few distributions a priori. The possibilities are limitless as long as we have enough observations at hand. That said, assisted rules should, over time, also leverage knowledge accumulated during the discovery processes, that is, the rules created after the fact, which provide information on how to anticipate *unknown-unknowns*.

The opportunity to recommend and update rules is an advantage over automated anomaly detection, which I will discuss in further detail. However, such anomaly detection, by definition, does not involve humans much; the lack of control they provide, and their randomness, are not generating a level of certainty about what is under control. To increase and strengthen this feeling, which is the goal of data observability, I will first tackle the relationship between rules and service level agreements.

Connections with SLAs/SLOs

Service level agreements (SLAs) and service level objectives (SLOs) have been around for quite some time to establish contracts and are a way to avoid subjective disputes about the expected quality of the service. They help build and maintain the trust between producers and their users, which is necessary to give confidence to both parties that they are engaged in a valuable and sustainable relationship.

These relationships also exist in the data world. Data teams are, in a fashion, a service; data teams produce data for dedicated use cases or to be made available for future consumption.

Thus, both data teams and data consumers/users have expectations, even if they are unspoken, undocumented, and not intuitively shared when it comes to data. This has created the issues I covered in the first chapter. SLAs and SLOs are good solutions to eliminating many of these issues.

SLAs for data are contracts between the parties involved consisting of expectations that can be met, and if not, a fine or other penalty to be applied. The fine/penalty is potentially as important as the length of time that elapses during which the expectations are not met. Hence, operational metrics such as "time to detection" and "time to resolve" are key for sustainable success.

To establish an SLA in data, it is a prerequisite to have the input of the users to ensure the service quality will be high enough for them to actually use the data. The more users are taken into account in the SLA, the greater the service, the higher the service levels, and the better the relationship is—as long as the associated cost to ensure the expectations is acceptable.

Several complex facts need to be considered when establishing the SLA for data:

How to define the constraints
> The user may have a hard time defining the important constraints due to the number of possible constraints. Consider that each field in a data source can have 10+ associated metrics (e.g., for age there can be min, max, mean, std but also the quantiles, the estimated distribution, the null values, the negative ones, etc).

Data usage will vary
> Each user will have a different use case for the data, resulting in a different set of expectations and, thus, constraints.

High number of users
> With self-serve data and analytics, the number of users is exploding, thus creating more data use cases and more constraints.

This is where data observability is essential. Data observations can be used as service level indicators (SLIs) by providing enough information about both the data and user behavior based on which rules can be identified, assisted, and maintained.

Because both producer and consumer generate these observations, it becomes easier to find a consensus on which KPIs from the SLIs should be used to determine which SLAs are possible for the data team to meet. This will set the bar for the SLOs across all SLAs while keeping the door open for other SLIs to be used later during the discovery of SLAs. In the meantime, both consumers and producers can use them as SLOs (or simply as a source of information, through a notification system, for example).

Without data observability, the scope is too vast if you consider the number of metrics that can be computed on, say, 100+ columns multiplied by the number of different checks. It is so huge that it feels daunting or even impossible for both parties to commit to a subset of expectations without sound evidence of their effectiveness and a way to improve them over time, efficiently.

Automatic Anomaly Detection

Rules are a powerful way to ensure data matches expectations in the context of where the data is used. However, rules depend on people to create and validate them (at least, this is what I strongly recommend). This dependency on people's time and availability is undoubtedly a bottleneck to scale exponentially with data validation. Companies reaching this stage need to have already reached a high maturity level.

Furthermore, assisted rules have a constraint on their structure, as they must be explicit and fully explainable, which may be a weakness over other more opaque solutions, such as learning-based rules.

Considering that rules are meant to intercept expectations that are not met, another method we haven't discussed yet is automatic anomaly detection using the data observability information available.

An anomaly is a state of the system that is different from the expected states. This is the connection between expectations explicitly encoded as rules and those implicitly discovered when unmet.

In our case, we have the system states corresponding to the history of the data observability information based on the core observation model. Hence, those states can also be seen as a stochastic process with many random but connected (non independent) variables (each instance of the entities could be considered a variable).

Automatic anomaly detection, therefore, is the process of leveraging some of the learning-based methods to infer or predict when a state should be considered an anomaly.

The methods that can be used are numerous and include machine learning:

Supervised learning
> This requires labeling data observability information (or the state itself) to work properly. Hence, it requires time to collect enough data to train the algorithm as well as time for the team to label (with high accuracy) the anomalies.

(Semi-)Unsupervised learning or statistical analysis
> Unsupervised learning approaches can help identify anomalies based on their statistical properties. For instance, statistical learning methods can automatically identify outliers and, with the assumption that anomalies are likely to show outlier behaviors, detect potential quality issues without requiring extensive foreknowledge of how anomalies appear.
>
> The risk here is that not everything that is an outlier is an anomaly, and perhaps not every anomaly is an outlier. A human review process is still necessary to validate the algorithm's outputs. Humans can bring both semantic context and subject matter knowledge to analyze the results to accept or reject the classifications. One downside is that this often requires input from subject matter experts whose time and availability are limited.

Reinforcement learning and active learning
> This method is quite advanced, and still requires some time from the team. Not only would agents need a lot of simulations to be validated, but the active learning is also essentially based on the human in the loop.

My intent is not to dig into each method, because it would require at least another book, and there are already enough papers and books on each topic. However, let me emphasize that although these methods are capable of scaling in theory, they still come with downsides:

The cold start problem
> For anomaly detection to be efficient, data and people are needed to ensure the learning phases are reliable.

The black box worry
> The methods introduced so far generate anomalies automatically but with little information about the reasons. Consequently, the team must reconstruct the context and understand the reasons.

The performance challenge
> Anomaly detection can't be 100% accurate. Therefore, the team's performance needs to be under control to avoid *alert fatigue*, where they start to ignore the detected anomalies.

Coming back to the black box worry, it is important to note that a lot of effort is put into making machine learning models explainable (which is, in my humble opinion, a component of analytics observability). This challenge is not fully solved, especially for methods such as deep learning. However, keeping an eye on the evolution of this capability is a must to reduce the effect of the black box worry.

I'll wrap up this section on anomaly detection by mentioning another method rarely considered to address the black box worry, and that provides an interesting mix of rules and anomaly detection—the learning of finite state machines. This method could be promising when data observability information is growing in volume, especially if the triggered rules are also labeled as true or false positives.

Prevent Garbage In, Garbage Out

One cause for which the data community should be fighting is the ban on the "garbage in, garbage out" (GIGO) excuse.

GIGO is an excuse, not an explanation. It is used when someone is pissed and asks about why they received irrelevant information, and the only answer they are provided is that it is irrelevant because the initial data was itself irrelevant. First, it doesn't explain anything, it is perceived as a waiver of the issue's importance, and it doesn't create trust, as the producer doesn't feel responsible for trying their best to avoid such a situation. Let's be honest; we've all been in that situation, and on both sides.

In other words, it is a "dodge" that creates more harm than good. An opposing view is that if an application can be aware that garbage comes in, it should be forbidden to generate garbage out. To do this, the application needs to be able to do these things:

- Assess whether provided data is garbage
- Qualify the classified data as garbage

But why such behavior is so common is an interesting question to ask ourselves. The answer must be related to the lack of visibility for the behavior in production and knowledge about what must be considered an issue. Also, the situation is extremely time sensitive, and generally involves some power imbalance (manager–contributor, buyer–seller, user–provider, etc.) which makes it awfully uncomfortable. Also, there is a natural tendency for the people addressed by this criticism to take it as if they must be able to solve all situations and avoid all problems. Let's make this clear once and for all: this is not what is expected. What is expected is to be able to analyze the problem and, ideally, to be able to anticipate, recover, and maintain trust. Not to avoid everything!

This is especially important to understand when the data is provided by external sources, and we have little (or no) influence on the data, in which case, it feels impossible to avoid everything and at the same time not be able to blame the producers (I mean, point fingers).

The good news is that the third component of data observability, the expectations, addresses these exact requirements.

With data observability implemented, here are the possible scenarios:

- Incoming data is classified as garbage before the application generates its results. The application can then either:
  — Not proceed and avoid the garbage out
  — Make best efforts to clean the data, ensure the cleaning process is observable, and then proceed
- Incoming data is classified as garbage based on the qualification of the results. The application can then either:
  — Roll back the data and log it
  — Log why the data is garbage, due to a posteriori discovery of garbage in
  — Like in the first case, try to clean the incoming data or its output, still ensuring those processes are observable

This logic could be implemented using two, non-mutually-exclusive procedures. The first is the use of conditions.

Pre- and post-conditions

Conditional statements are commonly used in programming, such as when implementing an HTTP endpoint. For example, if the endpoint's business logic is expecting a JSON payload encoded in UTF-8 that contains a non-null integer `age` field under the `customer` top-level field, and these conditions are not met, the application can decide to return an error to the client, or be lenient for certain cases, such as encoding by re-encoding before proceeding. Also, if the HTTP endpoint's side effect is to update a table and then get the current state of the data, but it gets several rows instead of one, it can take actions such as rollback, delete, or simply return an error, letting the client know about the potential garbage data it sent.

What I just described is something very natural for any programmer: it is even more than a best practice; it is intuitively used. Therefore, the idea would be to simply use this pattern when creating data applications, pipelines, and so forth.

The interesting advantage of implementing pre- and post-conditions directly within the data application is that it is well-guarded without depending on other external components to ensure its viability. Of course, the system used to build data needs to allow such practices, which have not systematically been addressed in some systems, especially the low-code no-code (e.g., ETL, reporting tools).

Ease of Access versus Accountability

In recent years, not only because of the influence of DataOps, which is a set of methods and tools to go to production faster, the data system has reduced the entry level required by people to use the data. Therefore, the practice of setting pre/post conditions is not necessarily well known or can seem like an additional unnecessary burden—as unit tests used to be considered in the early 2000s.

On the other side, the whole world is putting a significant focus on the culture of accountability and respect for data.

In my opinion, accelerating time to production, lowering the skill requirements, and increasing accountability are not playing well together unless the data systems allow the people also to mature and take some responsibility. Some technologies have partially included this concept, such as *dbt*, which includes data tests, but with the current limitation that tests are not executed in production. This is addressed further in this book (see Chapter 5).

In the next section, I describe the circuit breakers, which conceptually are not so different from the conditions described here, but structurally give an alternative when the system does not (yet) have first-class support for the conditions.

Circuit breaker

The circuit breaker originates from electrical circuits. In electrical systems, a circuit breaker is a safety device designed to protect an electrical circuit from damage.[15] This device closes the circuit to allow the electric current to flow until certain conditions are met that could break the circuit. In such an instance, the device breaks the circuit (opens it), forbidding the current to circulate until the underlying issues are fixed and an action is taken to close the circuit again.

This idea has been reused in software architecture by Michael Nygard[16] and supported by Martin Fowler,[17] where an additional component wraps a function to prevent its execution under certain conditions. The prevention could be as simple as returning an error directly when the wrapper is called and the *circuit is open*.

In a data pipeline, this may be more an alternative to pre/post-conditions, especially in the case where the user has no capabilities to introduce conditions into the system used to create the pipeline, such as in low-code no-code systems or restricted interfaces (whether graphic or API). Therefore, the system has extra components in the pipeline (circuit) to break it in case conditions are not met. In fact, implemented as such, circuit breakers are similar to pre- and post-conditions external to the applications.

The nice thing with circuit breakers is that they are easier to add after the fact (especially good for legacy systems). However, they do come with downsides. For example, suppose the conditions depend on the steps before and after (e.g., case-specific SLA/Os, custom checks). In that case, the circuit breaker is yet another application to maintain and align with the steps' logic.[18] Hence, circuit breakers are likely to be present before and after each step, which makes the pipeline three times as long as it would have been if the conditions had been added to the applications directly.

---

15 Wikipedia has a good description of a circuit breaker (*https://oreil.ly/EXHzB*).

16 Michael T. Nygard, *Release It!* (O'Reilly, 2007) (*https://oreil.ly/HAd64*).

17 Read Martin Fowler's take on his blog (*https://oreil.ly/9QbAr*).

18 This is likely to result in troubles…

Conclusion

Data observability is not a one-time project but rather a cultural shift that requires a set of practices to be embraced by all data practitioners. Data observability becomes natural and ingrained in the data culture through the development of habits and the standardization of observations across the organization. By adopting a standardized model of observations, organizations can increase communication and collaboration across teams and projects. Moreover, data observability introduces a framework for using observations to assess assumptions and validate expectations. In the next chapter, we will dive into the influences of data observability in an organization, exploring its impact on architecture and communication across actors and areas.

## CHAPTER 3

Roles of Data Observability in a Data Organization

In the previous chapter, you learned the definition of data observability and how data technologies and teams can embrace it. In this chapter, I will systematically look at data observability to analyze how it fits into the data organization, such as its data architecture and culture. Because the culture of data is a complex system itself, I will address it in two parts:

- Through the lens of data engineering roles in a data organization.
- The role of data in the evolution of our economy (and, thus, organizations).

Data Architecture

Data architecture is a critical component of a data organization. It sets the foundation of how data will deliver value for each department individually and collaboratively. The intent of this section is not to define the ideal data architecture, if there is such a thing, but to review where data observability must be introduced to support the sustainable management of data usage in the organization.

Not all organizations are equal regarding data architecture; some already have an established architecture expected to evolve or be replaced partially or entirely, and others are simply starting from a white page. Therefore, I will explain why you must consider data observability from the start when building a new architecture and how, despite its central role, it can be introduced as an add-on to existing data architecture.

Where Does Data Observability Fit in a Data Architecture?

To address where data observability fits into a data architecture, I have to split data observability into two pieces: the data-observable system and the data observability platform. This is to respect a fundamental principle of architecture: the separation of concerns.

The data-observable system

The data-observable system relates to the involvement of data observability as an element of data applications. As we recall from the first chapters, data observability is a capability that can be introduced from within data applications, which can generate the whole data observability core model.

Therefore, data observability is included at first in the application layer of the data architecture, as presented in Figure 3-1.

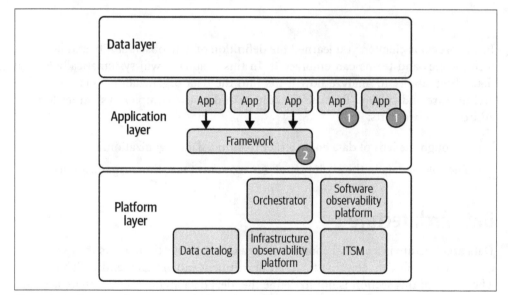

Figure 3-1. Data architecture including data-observable applications

Two different cases must be considered in this layer: when data tools, frameworks, and libraries are partially or not (yet) data observable and when they are natively data observable.

When the components supporting the creation of data applications are not fully data observable, an additional component must be added in one or two places depending on the tools and architecture. These places are represented by the labels 1 and 2 in Figure 3-1. Label 1 on the *App* represents the introduction of the data observability capability I will discuss in Chapter 4. Label 2 is where tools are extended with additional artifacts (e.g., agents) to generate data observations by default for all data applications built with them, as I'll discuss in Chapter 5.

In the future, however, all tools and libraries will be data observable by design or natively, which means all data applications will be data observable by default, so it will be taken for granted. Therefore, I'm not representing what is trivial to avoid bloating the architecture diagram and to accelerate the definition of new architectures.

In the meantime, however, I have to consider the tools that are either legacy or too closed (black box) to give us a chance to apply the practices presented in Chapter 4 and Chapter 5. For those, I reserve a place in the data-observable system, which has one foot in the data layer and another in the data observability platform. Chapter 6 covers this specific, yet temporary, case in detail.

The data observability platform

As Figure 3-1 shows, all applications are made data observable either natively or with appropriate extensions, which will be covered in the next chapters. A *data observability platform* is a system to aggregate and observe data observations generated by interconnected data applications.

The data observations generated by each application have the potential to tackle the challenges highlighted in Chapter 1. These challenges involve the need for a system that can detect data issues in a scaling environment, streamline the process of identifying and resolving root causes, and proactively anticipate their recurrence. By harnessing the power of data observations, we can develop solutions that effectively address these challenges, ensuring a more robust and resilient data ecosystem. Moreover, each application is most likely strongly (e.g., orchestration) or weakly (e.g., using the same data sources) dependent on others, such that there is huge potential value in the interplay of global data observations. For example, by respecting the data observability core model, it is possible to leverage the information about these dependencies (e.g., lineage) to automate the detection and resolution of data issues.

You also need to consider the value that exists in past data observations, because the current status of data in its usage context can be determined more efficiently based on past statuses. A simple example is a data ingestion application. The amount of data ingested most likely follows underlying patterns (e.g., time series) that can be learned to determine if the amount of current data ingested is an anomaly or not; see "Expectations" on page 54.

Consequently, data architectures must be extended with an additional central component, the data observability platform. At the very minimum, this component is responsible for ingesting all data observations, aggregating them, and ideally learning from them to offer those capabilities. Figure 3-2 updates Figure 3-1 with this platform next to other central components.

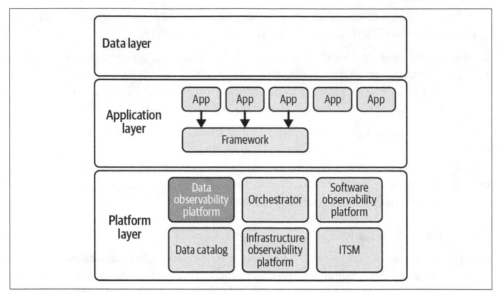

Figure 3-2. Data architecture including the data observability platform

The data observability platform does not operate in isolation but should collaborate with other platforms like the orchestrator or application observability platform. This collaboration is recommended because, as outlined in Chapter 1, data observability is a dimension of an observable system. Data observability serves as a buffer that provides control and visibility between data governance and all other data management domains.

Data observability also plays an important role in the efficiency of a data (engineering) team, which I'll discuss in a later section. First, let's look at when a data architecture must ensure the system will be data observable and how to introduce the data observability platform.

Data Architecture with Data Observability

In an ideal world, you would introduce data observability from the beginning. In the real world, however, delivering the platform and the first value always comes first. Monitoring and reducing the total cost of ownership (TCO) may become the next priority if time and capacity allow you to "not work on direct business value generation."

I have seen a lot of companies willing to drive a "Proof of Concept" on data observability, but, in fact, do we really have to prove that the concept of generating data observations to increase the information about a system is good? Okay, I understand that the data observability platform, the tool I mean, needs to be "tested" to validate that its capabilities match the expectations and needs. However, making the system data observable shouldn't even be questioned. It must be embraced by both the data architecture and the organization's entire data community. So, I recommend starting "yesterday" with the data-observable system and looking for the right data observability platform that will adapt well to your specific environment.

How can you do that? Let me cover two broad categories: the new and the existing architectures. Not all cases will fit those categories perfectly; some cases land somewhere in between. Thus, understanding both categories provides a good sense of which mix may work best for you.

The introduction of data observability in an architecture depends on the specific design and implementation of the system. In the case of a new architecture, selecting data technologies that are either already data observable or that can easily be made observable is advisable. I also recommended introducing the data observability platform in the foundational layer of the architecture, where other solutions, such as the orchestrator, are already available.

On the other hand, for established architectures, introducing the data observability platform in the foundational layer should not be hindered, as it can work independently. However, this does not automatically make the system built on the architecture data observable. To achieve data observability, it is essential to convert existing data technologies into observable ones, unless they are already observable. For inherited technologies, Chapter 6 may provide assistance.

When adding additional technologies to the architecture, choosing those designed to be natively data observable is important. This will enable the system to maintain a consistent level of data observability throughout its development and operation. It is crucial to prioritize data observability in the design and implementation of any architecture to ensure that data can be effectively monitored, managed, and utilized.

How Data Observability Helps with Data Engineering Undercurrents

Now that the data architecture has been extended to introduce the data observability capabilities, in this section, I will focus on the data engineering undercurrents introduced by Joe Reis and Matt Housley in *Fundamentals of Data Engineering* (O'Reilly) which I will discuss in depth in Chapter 5. The undercurrents are often viewed as complex and inconvenient, but they are much simpler to deploy on a foundation of data observability.

Let's start with security.

Security

Security must be embedded in the organization's culture, which means it cannot be complex or hard to do. Although it is challenging to automate all security tasks, systems are evolving to handle many of them. In software development, for example, a package with security issues can be detected, and a dedicated platform can create pull requests automatically.

The hard part for the engineers is that they must consider as many disastrous scenarios as possible, anticipate all the occurrences they'll want to observe, and automate prevention (e.g., filtering) and propagation (e.g., circuit breakers).

However, by combining the data-observable system with the data observability platform, we can make things easier by automating the tedious and time-consuming tasks and leaving only the knowledge-based ones (e.g., computing the percentage of masked data) to the engineers. These tasks are directly linked to the value they generate and maintain.

Hence, the standard information, such as the observations related to data access, is provided by design by data-observable systems in place. The data observability platform does the rest to match those observations with the platform's security observability and automation components, as depicted in Figure 3-3.

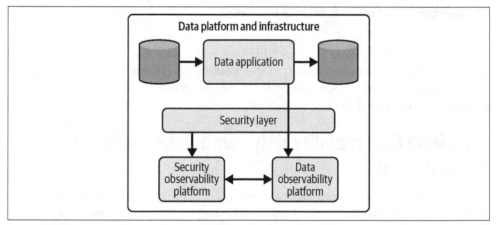

Figure 3-3. Data and security observability platforms work hand in hand.

Other observations will also support engineers taking care of security, such as from the user and application observability areas that deliver observations. To illustrate this, let me walk you through some examples.

The first use case is to detect new usages or changes in the usage as a data application suddenly fetches 50% more data than in the past, although the size of the data itself has not changed. Also, it is possible to prevent data from being exposed outside because the encryption step is not applied in the pipeline, as shown in Figure 3-4.

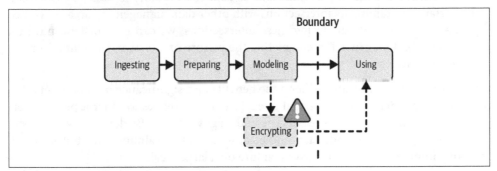

Figure 3-4. Detecting lack of encryption

Engineers can be notified when their custom metric about the percentage of masked data goes down, which may indicate data has leaked.

Another example is to alert that data flagged as important is not backed up, as there is no "backing-up" application running on it that's reading and writing it elsewhere, as represented in Figure 3-5.

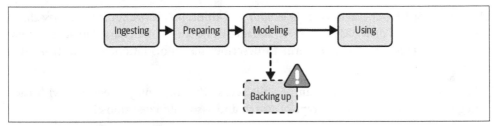

Figure 3-5. Oops, forgot to back up

Now that we can support the engineers to achieve a satisfactory level of security without dramatically increasing the intrusiveness in their daily work, let's tackle an important and broad undercurrent—data management.

Data Management

In Chapter 1, I proposed that the DMBOK2 data management framework can introduce data observability as a new area surrounding data governance as a control layer across all others (Figure 1-13). In this section, I will reinforce this message, mainly through the lens of data governance as it is proposed in *Fundamentals of Data Engineering*.

Data governance

To fully understand the impact and value of data observability in data governance, it is important to examine its intersections with other data management areas governed by data governance. By analyzing these intersections, we can gain insight into how data observability is crucial in completing the picture of effective data culture implementation at scale.

In other words, to fully comprehend the benefits and significance of data observability in data governance, it is essential to explore how it relates to other aspects of data management that fall under the purview of data governance. By doing so, we can gain a more comprehensive understanding of how data observability contributes to successfully implementing a data-driven culture on a larger scale.

Discoverability.   Data has to be reused across projects and domains. For this, it needs to be discovered during the analysis phase of a new project scoping, for example. This means that the characteristics of the data are exposed to an engine that will allow a human or another system to match it according to their needs. If this is not the case, all data needs to be analyzed systematically to find the most appropriate use, which would eventually require ever-growing time and resources. In short, it would very quickly become unsustainable.

Another word for *characteristics* is *metadata*. I think it is more intuitive to say that a user searches for data based on its characteristics than its metadata. However, metadata is the generally accepted term to describe this information, so I will use that term.

The metadata to be exposed can be split across the following categories, with each category addressing a specific type of search and associated decisions:

Business metadata
> Project, usage, (data) definition

Tech metadata
- Descriptive metadata: location, lineage, schema, pipeline
- Content metadata: volumes, missing data, density

Ops metadata
> Runtime identifier, dependencies (orchestration)

Reference metadata
> Lookup data, codes, etc.

These metadata are similar to most observation entities presented in Chapter 2 or can be derived from them.

Therefore, a data-observable system can also be described as a discoverable system, as the observations about the involved data will be automatically generated and consolidated in the data observability platform.

This is the role then of the data observability platform—to cooperate with the data catalog, the data management component generally used for data discovery. This cooperation will enable the data catalog to always return to its users the most appropriate data based on their searches, or eventually push the information to users who had shown interest in being notified when data about certain characteristics became available.

Accountability. Because engineers use or generate the entirety or a portion of the data, they hold a certain accountability for these specific operations. For example, suppose some incoming data used in the process is not satisfying engineers' assumptions. In that case, the engineers will be considered responsible for either not noticing it or, worse, having generated inappropriate data (e.g., GIGO).

So, to be confident in this new responsibility, engineers must build practices to introduce defensive approaches (introduced in Chapter 2 and described in later chapters) to increase their chances of success without impacting their capacity to deliver. They have to make the data systems they build and use data observable. Then, they have to couple the generated observations with the following two processes:

- Assumptions checking (±SLO)
- Expectations handling (±SLA)

The last option, which is a fallback—a safety net if you like—is to rely on the data observability platform to create visibility about latent constraints that might be interesting for the engineers to monitor continuously.

Data quality. The role of a data engineer is often challenging when it comes to ensuring data quality. This is because the engineer is providing a service in response to a business request for new or adapted data, typically from a subject matter expert (SME). The request is often triggered by a range of factors, such as an exploration of reports, analysis of the market, specific knowledge about the domain, or awareness of peculiar events that may impact the business.

However, it can be challenging for the SME to explain these factors to the engineer, who may not have the same level of domain-specific knowledge. As a result, validating the final result can be difficult for both the engineer and the SME, as the amount of results could exceed their individual areas of knowledge.

Moreover, even if the SME is able to express how the final result can be validated by outlining the constraints or expectations they have, it is not always possible to ensure exhaustiveness. Additionally, the validation process of the results may not hold up in the long run or in a changing context, which is another important consideration. Then comes the fact that the produced data is often reused by the original requester or other users, potentially from other domains, who find the data valuable for their own use cases.

On paper, it would be possible for engineers and stakeholders to define a set of constraints to validate the data quality. In practice, this results in an uncomfortable series of discussions where none of the parties can really make firm decisions and, thus, assume full responsibility. For the stakeholders, it is complex and risky to be assigned the responsibility to provide the "a priori" definition of what is "good data" now and in the future. Engineers often experience anxiety when deploying a project in production without being certain that all the transformations they have applied are producing valid data.

In reality, a continuous improvement process is essential to achieving agreement between all parties involved. Each party should have a well-defined role in this process. It is important to acknowledge that data issues are inevitable and that a limitless number of potential issues could arise. By recognizing this and implementing a continuous improvement process, everyone can work together to ensure that data issues are identified and resolved in a collaborative and constructive manner.

Therefore, the time and resources involved in anticipation of data issues must be well balanced to provide a sufficient (or "good enough") agreement of what will be validated and the iteration necessary to upgrade this validation process.

We can now revisit the roles and responsibilities to achieve an efficient collaboration between engineers and stakeholders:

- Engineers validate known constraints.
- Stakeholders describe known constraints.
- Engineers generate observations to the data observability platform.
- Stakeholders use the data observations to maintain or create constraints—however, the platform should be smart enough to automate this.
- Engineers and stakeholders should work hand in hand when new types of issues are discovered and need to be anticipated in the future.

This separation of concerns allows for an iterative, less time-consuming process, setting the right level of expectations and risks on both sides. In other words, this is the only way to be in a win-win situation.

Master data management and data modeling. It takes time and resources to define the entities related to an organization's business or internal processes. Those efforts aim to formulate standards of formats, structures, and characteristics that must be respected across data teams and projects.

Data observability helps identify the cases where those definitions are not followed appropriately. To provide an example, let's say that a data pipeline is responsible for writing date information to a data source. The format of the date information must be consistent across all entries. To ensure this consistency, a data observability metric can be implemented to track the number of entries that do not match the required date format.

This metric can be checked by a rule (expectation), and the pipeline is considered to be in failure if the count of unmatched entries is not zero. By monitoring this data observability metric, data engineers can proactively identify and resolve any issues related to inconsistent date formats, ensuring high data quality and minimizing the risk of downstream issues.

Again, data observability acts as an important control layer to ensure that practices and conventions are respected, sustained, encouraged, and rewarded in the organization.

Data Integration and Interoperability.   With the explosion of specialized SaaS applications, each having its specificities and associated personas, it is not uncommon for organizations to have several tools with a relatively significant overlap. Plus, there is an established awareness that combining data across domains is expected to yield surprising results, such as unknown niches or underused opportunities.

Consequently, most tools offer capabilities to share their data, integrate external data, or both. This can be more easily achieved using either programming interfaces (e.g., Python, ETL) or higher-level tools (e.g., a low-code no-code ELT such as Matillion).

Hence, the number of connections between the tools themselves or via the data platform is increasing as fast as the complexity of setting them up is decreasing. This is where data observability brings value—to controlling the network of interconnections and ensuring the prevention of issue propagation.

Data lifecycle management.   This is a vast topic. I'm limiting myself to only the deletion and archiving of data, for example, to cope with security or privacy requirements. In those cases, data observability provides an embedded capability to expose whether or not delete operations are executed, and their effects (how much data is deleted) or the archives created (how much, often, and when).

The other way around is also a valid usage of data observability, as it provides the opportunity to expose data (or a subset) that is rarely used that can be deleted or archived.

Ethics and privacy.   With the growing awareness of what data can achieve (good or bad), an organization also needs to have a defensive approach against inappropriate usage or sharing of data. This is something that must be implemented as part of the organization's data culture, because most problems are unintended and happen by mistake. Data observability provides, first and foremost, visibility, which in the case of ethics and privacy is key, as the organization must be as transparent as possible.

Data observability provides great support for ethics and privacy, as new usages and shares of data are logged, including with whom the data was shared. Note that data observability is not a complete security mechanism. In fact, if the associated checks can be executed by the application responsible for sharing the data (e.g., using computational sharing policies), then sharing can be avoided. However, it is not data observability but genuine applied security. Nevertheless, data observability allows inappropriate usages of data to be exposed, so preventive actions can be taken to avoid the same situation in the future.

Another case to consider is when there is an automated decision process that may be biased because the data used to define the process was biased. This happens for different reasons, the most common being that the data was *skewed*, which means that some categories were overrepresented compared to others. This situation can also be supported by data observability, for example, by controlling the variations of the *skewness* metric or simply showing the histogram of a categorical field.

DataOps

DataOps has not necessarily been a well-defined perimeter. However, in *Fundamentals of Software Engineering*, Joe and Matt did a good job describing the areas that will likely be constant across definitions or understanding: automation, observability, and incident response.

I am connecting these areas with a set of practices and tools designed to achieve multiple goals for data engineers. These include:

- Ensuring fast and efficient deployment to production while maintaining the reliability and accuracy of the outcome.
- Facilitating ease of debugging in case of issues or errors.
- Providing a spectrum of automated issue detection to catch and resolve problems as quickly as possible.

By implementing these practices and tools, data engineers can work with greater efficiency, confidence, and peace of mind. Let's see where data observability fits in this picture, starting with automation.

Automation.   Scaling is all about scaling data ambitions. And, to scale smoothly and sustainably, the following conditions must be met:

- Complexity must decrease—to find more talent.
- Frictions must be reduced—to go faster in production.
- Repetitive tasks must be automated—to gain time.

Therefore, all activities related to creating and maintaining trust in this highly automated system must be automated. Otherwise, they become the bottleneck and will simply be skipped when teams are under time pressure. That is why data applications must be made data observable by design, or extend that way, as proposed in Chapter 5.

Observability.   This section pretty much closes the loop, as data observability is an area of observability. Nevertheless, observability must be a best practice that can be automated as much as possible, ideally by design, across all steps and tools of the data transformation process.

Observability also brings value to issue management, as discussed in the next section, and is responsible for generating the information needed to optimize the whole process. As introduced in Chapter 2, data observations are the data that bring visibility about the data usage. Therefore, as introduced in some optimization theories (e.g., operational research), they can be used to optimize in relevant dimensions, such as time, resources, or outcomes.

Without data observations that would be assimilated into monitoring, a system cannot be self-improving or have a deterministic improvement process. I have addressed this topic in another book, *What Is Data Governance?*, in which I cover the aspects of *maturity*. In the third section, I highlight the 5th level of maturity as:[1]

> Optimizing (Level 5)
>
> The data governance program focuses on continuous improvement, monitoring the quality and performance of processes and their role in meeting business objectives. The organization efficiently and consistently improves and adapts its practices to strategic changes.

Incident response.   The last part of DataOps is related to issue management, mainly the processes related to providing a response to reported incidents. In fact, if it is clear to everyone in a data organization that incident response is a "big thing," meaning it is extremely expensive, it is also the one that is the least tracked and measured.

---

1 Andy Petrella, "Chapter 3. Maturing Your Data Governance Program," *What Is Data Governance? Understanding the Business Impact* (O'Reilly, 2020).

After seeing this in hundreds of scenarios and hearing ten times that many reports, my explanation is that when something goes wrong with data, without data observability and the associated practices described in this book, everything is done in a rush in a vain effort to recover trust as fast as possible. So nothing is apparent, but the people who have been involved on either side of this situation feel the ineffectiveness of the whole process.

Rephrasing my introduction line: it *feels* like issue management is inefficient, and lots of money is wasted.

Hence, the role of data observability is to provide visibility about issue management, from issue detection to resolution, and through post-mortem, and to help determine what constitutes the appropriate process for incident response.

Based on the data observations, which include user involved and code changes, organizational improvement or prevention mechanisms can be drawn from their correlation with the number of tickets resolved, their frequency, the data involved, the system involved, the duration of the resolution process, etc. Consequently, you can associate cost estimation to TTD or TTR and so estimate and even predict (for budgetization) the total cost of ownership (TCO) of the system that takes into account all costs associated with acquiring, implementing, and maintaining the system.

Orchestration

It is often crucial to determine the order of execution of applications in a pipeline, as they have to follow the underlying dependencies at the data level. For example, a batch application reading a CSV must start before the CSV has been updated with the latest data, especially if freshness is important.

Managing those weak dependencies is doable when the pipeline is simple, with a limited number of contributors (ideally one), and only one orchestration tool. But if any of those parameters change, then any application producing data can change its behavior without knowing if another application relies on it, because of factors like these:

- It is not clear whether the next application in the orchestrated pipeline is using the data.
- It is not known if there is another application from a pipeline orchestrated in another tool.
- It is not clear what the requirements are for the data from the next application (e.g., the schema changed).

ETLs Are Not Orchestrations

An orchestration solution is creating a DAG (directed acyclic graph) of applications. It is not an ETL, so some of those examples don't apply (in the case where there is only one orchestrator).

It turns out that with data-observable pipelines, a solution comes by default to those cases, as described in Figure 3-6. This is because data-observable pipelines generate, by design, the data observations necessary to detect issues individually (rules checked in the applications) or by the data observability platform (see *expectation validator* in Figure 3-6).

Then, the pipelines automatically break themselves (see circuit breaking) as some of their steps are self-declared as failed, having taken this decision based on the detected issues returned, for example, by a health status service (Figure 3-6).

With this flexibility enabled by data observability, the interconnections existing across pipelines—potentially orchestrated by several different orchestrators—can be managed externally, without the orchestrations themselves necessarily requiring strong coordination or even adding an extra burden on the data engineers or Data-Ops to create additional "data quality" scripts or applications surrounding all the steps along all pipelines. For example, we could look at adding such a checking script before and after three applications running in two different orchestrators (or DAGs), involving five data sources—we'd be talking about twenty additional scripts (or queries) to be added to the whole pipeline, which is now 4 to 10 times bigger than it should be.[2]

---

2 That's unreal, isn't it?

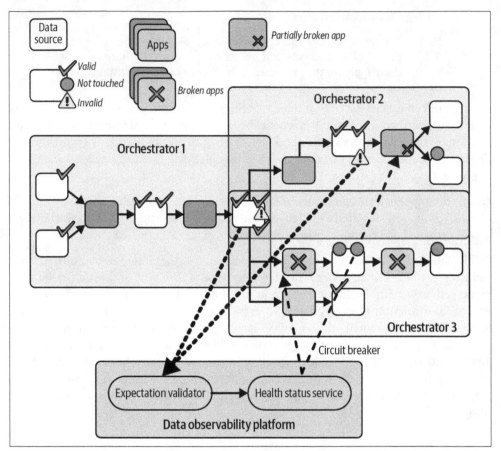

Figure 3-6. Weakly connected data-observable pipelines orchestrated by potentially different orchestrators and the data observability platform

Software engineering

There's an important undercurrent in the data engineering milieu, although it's obviously not limited to that role. The value of the panel of practices that have been built and improved over the last few decades, especially since computer science has become more mainstream, is often underestimated.

It is true that *data* is not directly mappable with *software*, or more precisely, *softwares*, as there are many subcategories to be considered with their own peculiarities that segregate the applicability of this or that practice—embedded softwares, web applications, or, simply, websites, for example, have lots of dedicated best practices.

Consequently, it is not completely absurd to consider *data* as part of *softwares*, as data can't really exist without processing.[3] Hence many *software* practices apply to data engineering. You'll find several covered in *Fundamentals of Data Engineering. I* would add data observability, especially *making applications data observable*, as an additional practice that must be encoded in all data practitioners' DNA, like it is for software engineers to log, test, and check the validity of a received message (e.g., encoding, formatting, etc.) in their production code, for example.

Now that we have covered architectural and practical concepts, it makes sense to cover organizational concepts where data observability plays a strong role. For this, I will use a paradigm I strongly believe in—data mesh.

Support for Data Mesh's Data as Products

I'll start this last section with a disclaimer: my intent here is not to explain what data mesh is—I'll leave this to its creator, Zhamak Dehghani, or other experts investing a large stake of their time thinking about it. My goal is to give you some advice on why data observability is undoubtedly part of the practices and technological components of data mesh, at least of its implementation in an organization. If you want or need an explanation about data mesh, there are two things I suggest you to do, now, which are:

- Read the genesis (*https://oreil.ly/ZdhgI*) on Martin Fowler's blog.
- Read Zhamak's book *Data Mesh* (*https://oreil.ly/bQIQW*) (O'Reilly).

Of the many concepts supporting data mesh, I will focus on *data as a product*, which consists of the delivery of what could be considered an asset for the organization (e.g., it can be monetized).

In *Data Mesh*, data as a product is a principle supporting the implementation of a data product, artifacts that can be combined via input and output APIs, plus an additional API for its exposure outside of the pure data flow, the control API. The book represents this as a hexagon, shown in "Observations Model" on page 37. You can see that the APIs are annotated with *standardized and domain agnostic*, for mostly the same reasons I introduced in Chapter 2.

---

3 Unless we consider our brains as such, as we extend our cognitive power to computers.

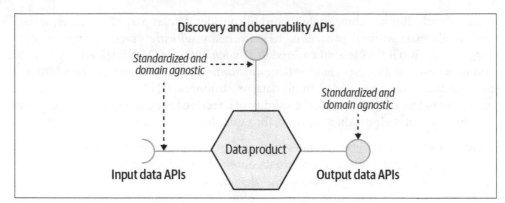

Figure 3-7. A data product with its input, output, and control APIs

Putting aside the important concept of domains in data mesh, we can picture, as in Figure 3-8, data as products connecting their input and output APIs to form a graph (a mesh).

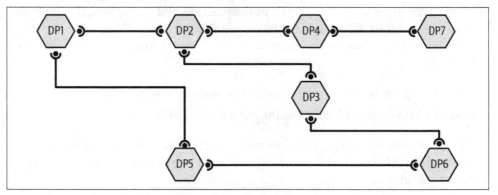

Figure 3-8. Data as products in a mesh

You can see the mesh is connected with APIs. In fact, the line with connectors in Figure 3-8 represents data in flight, as data is exchanged via input and output APIs and controlled by the control API. However, to explain data observability in such a mesh, I use a dual graph.[4] The dual graph, in this case, is when we consider the input and output APIs connections as the nodes, and the links represent the control APIs alone.[5] As this can be tricky to represent, Figure 3-9 shows the dual graph for the mesh in Figure 3-8.

---

4 See this explanation of a dual graph (*https://oreil.ly/i1DZD*).

5 Hence we'll not consider the "data" itself anymore, as it is abstracted out anyway.

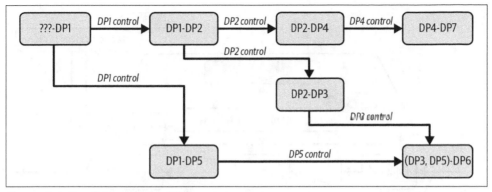

Figure 3-9. Dual data mesh of Figure 3-8

In fact, this dual graph could be called the "Data Usage Mesh." We can see that data products DP1 and DP2 are present twice. This doesn't mean those product are duplicated, but that controlled information of a data product is highly dependent on its usage (the way the output API is used).

If a node is not fulfilling expectations, then the next edge can be disconnected to avoid propagation, which is the circuit breaker in place creating a (potentially isolated) subgraph linked to the found issue. In these examples, let DP2 be wrong only in the context of DP4; this would propagate the issue in the data mesh graph and flag all downstream data products impacted—DP3, DP4, DP6, and DP7, instead of DP4 alone. By adding the data usage mesh into the decision-making process, only DP2, DP4, and DP7 are impacted, and thus DP3 and DP6 are kept safe.

This shows the importance of contextual management of expectations and highlights what is nice about data mesh—it's structured around APIs. This benefit is clearly exhibited, versus the general-purpose quality of data sources (e.g., file, table, etc.) that access randomly without controlled APIs (e.g., JDBC, filesystem access, etc.).

That said, I still have not covered how data observability supports creating and managing data as products in a data mesh. For that, I have to open a data product and look where data observability can be added (see Figure 3-10).

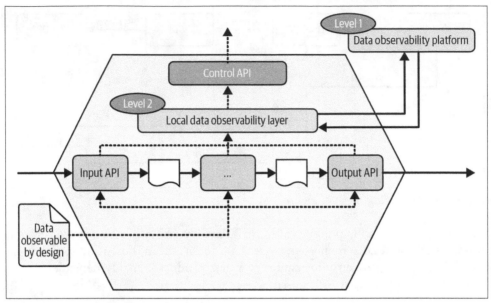

Figure 3-10. Data as a product and data observability

It turns out that there are two levels of data observability, in a way, involved here.

The first level is external to the data product and involves exposing, via the control API, the visibility and trustworthiness for the other data products built on it. However, it is likely coarse-grained because the intent at this level is not to explain all the nitty gritty details of how the data product works—which is likely to change over time anyway, without necessarily impacting the consumers—but to validate the data coming out of the output API.

At this level, the visibility of the connection (upstream data lineages) with the input API is important to demonstrate and analyze, within the boundaries of the data product (its internals), if a detected issue at the output API has been either propagated from the input API, or is the result of a misuse of the data (within the pipeline).

However, a data product is atomic in a data mesh, meaning its internals can be extremely complex and not exposed.

Therefore, when an issue is due to the behavior of the data product, the second level of data observability, which is local to the data product level, is needed, as it brings the visibility to address it.

This fine-grained data observability provides the necessary mechanisms to operate at the data product level efficiently and can be, in fact, the source of the aggregated view delivered at the higher level—the data product level.

Because the first level of data observability is a somewhat coarse-grained (an aggregation) of the finer-grained information available in the second level, I have connected the data observability platform only to the latter to maximize the amount of visibility without redundancy.

Mixing both levels allows the definition of the SLOs at the data product level, which are first linked to the SLAs associated with what is exposed to the control API (bottom up). And secondly, the SLOs can be adapted by leveraging the continuous validations happening in the data observability platform at the input API of the dependent data products, which could also be exposed in the control API, to provide this information to the upstream data products.

Conclusion

This chapter has introduced data observability as a crucial element in building a robust data ecosystem. By implementing it at the foundation layer of their data platforms, organizations can foster a strong data culture and efficiently manage their data. Data observability also aligns with the DataOps vision and supports all its pillars.

Additionally, it bridges the gap in data organization to ensure the implementation of data strategies at scale, and it is integrated with related paradigms like data mesh. However, it is essential to note that the data observability platform cannot function independently and requires data products and pipelines to be data observable. The upcoming chapters will explore how to achieve this goal.

## PART II

Implementing Data Observability

## CHAPTER 4

Generate Data Observations

As explained in Chapter 3, data observability combines technology and people to gather information about the state of a system from the data perspective, and the expectations of that state. It then uses the information to make the system more adaptable or resilient.

This chapter explains how to apply the data observability practice. I will start with "data observability at the source," a method to introduce collection strategies in your day-to-day data work, and I'll show you how to minimize its impact on efficiency. Then, the chapter elaborates on implementing expectations that will subscribe to the software delivery lifecycle, such as continuous integration and continuous deployment (CI/CD).

As with any emerging practice and technology, to increase data observability adoption, you need to lower the barrier to entry; that way, people have less reason to argue against the change. However, people are also part of the solution, as their involvement in the process is crucial to identify their expectations and codify the rules. To this end, you'll learn several ways to reduce the effort required to generate observations and understand how to introduce them at the right moment of the development lifecycle.

At the Source

Chapter 2 explained the sources and types of information that help the observer. But how do you generate and collect the information from these sources?

It starts with *data observability at the source*. The term "source" refers to the applications responsible for reading, transforming, and writing data. These applications can either be the root cause of issues or the means to solve them, as explained in

Chapter 3. Additionally, applications are within our control as engineers and organizations, unlike the data itself.

Hence, the method of data observability at the source turns on the ability for applications to generate data observations following the model covered in Chapter 2; in other words, the applications are made data observable.

Pure data and analytics observations—such as data sources, schemas, lineages, and metrics—correlate to reading, transforming, and writing activities. The strategies described in this section address these activities by explaining what to consider when running them.

Generating Data Observations at the Source

Producing data observations at the source begins by generating additional information capturing the behavior of specific activities with data: reading, transforming, and writing. For example, developers can add lines of logs that contain the information needed to generate visibility about what their application does. The instructions use the channels—that is, the logs, metrics, and traces or lineages—covered in Chapter 2 to convey the observations that can be centralized in a logging system.

In the next section, you learn how to create data observations in JSON format that can be collected (published) to local files, a local service, a distant (web) service, or similar destinations. For example, following the data observability core model in Chapter 2, the data source and schema entity of a Postgres table would look like Example 4-1.

Example 4-1. Example of data observations encoded as JSON

```
{
  "id": "f1813697-339f-5576-a7ce-6eff6eb63249",
  "name": "gold.crm.customer",
  "location": "main-pg:5432/gold/crm/table",
  "format": "postgres"
}
{
  "id": "f1813697-339f-5576-a7ce-6eff6eb63249",
  "data_source_ref": {"by_id": "e21ce0a8-a01e-5225-8a30-5dd809c0952e"},
  "fields": [
  { "name": "lastname", "type": "string", "nullable": true },
  { "name": "id", "type": "int", "nullable": false }
  ]
}
```

This ability to collect data observations in the same model on a centralized platform is key to generating the value of data observability at scale, such as across applications, teams, and departments. That's why using the data observability core model is important to aggregating data observations with ease, especially along lineages.

Let's see how to generate data observations in Python using a low-level API, which will be used to introduce higher-level abstractions (covered in the next chapters).

Low-Level API in Python

This strategy of using a low-level API requires a lot of your time and involvement because you are responsible for creating every observation explicitly. However, this strategy also gives you the greatest flexibility, because it doesn't involve any higher-level abstractions.

On the flip side, the support of data observability at this level, especially during exploration and maintenance, requires the developer to be consistent and always think about what they may want to observe in production (for example, any senior developer should be producing as many lines for logs and checks as for business logic).[1] During development, developers must then create visibility about the modifications brought to the logic or behavior of the application with the generation of the associated observations. Examples of such observations include a connection to a new table, the creation of a new file, or the alteration of a structure with a new field.

In the following sections, you will go through a complete example of data applications written in Python that generate data observations alongside their data usage by doing the following:

- Understanding applications without data observability capability
- Adding instructions to generate data observations and their purpose
- Gaining insights into the pros and cons of using this strategy

Description of the Data Pipeline

Throughout the remainder of the chapter, I will use a data pipeline written in Python that we will make data observable. The code of the pipeline (*https://oreil.ly/6X5ge*) on GitHub allows you to run the examples in this chapter. It uses the pandas library to manipulate CSV files and is composed of two applications, *ingestion* and *reporting*, as presented in Figure 4-1.

---

1 This is what led me to start thinking about the data-observability-driven development method.

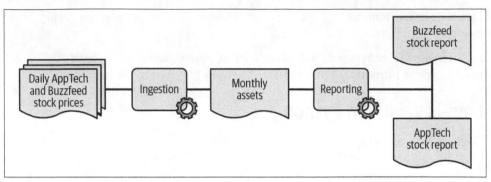

Figure 4-1. Structure of the example pipeline

Both applications (`ingestion` and `reporting`) use Python and pandas and share data from the "Daily Stock Prices" data source to create two downstream reports (Buzz-Feed stock and AppTech).

The `ingestion` application reads the CSV files for the daily stock prices that the stock market team provides each month. The team partitioned the files by year and month, then merged the prices into monthly views stored as a separate file, as shown in `ingestion` in Example 4-2.

Example 4-2. Data ingestion application

```
import pandas as pd

AppTech = pd.read_csv(      ❶
    "data/AppTech.csv",
    parse_dates=["Date"],   ❷
    dtype={"Symbol": "category"},   ❸
)
Buzzfeed = pd.read_csv(
    "data/Buzzfeed.csv",
    parse_dates=["Date"],
    dtype={"Symbol": "category"},
)

monthly_assets = pd.concat([AppTech, Buzzfeed]) \   ❹
    .astype({"Symbol": "category"})
monthly_assets.to_csv(
    "data/monthly_assets.csv", index=False
)
```

❶ The `ingestion` application processes two CSV files for the following stocks:

- BuzzFeed
- AppTech

The application reads the files from the *"../data"* folder, for reference; a row in these files looks like this:

```
1  Date         Symbol  Open    High    Low     Close  AdjClose  Volume
2  2022-01-03   APCX    14.725  15.200  14.25   14.25  14.25     1600
```

During exploration, our data engineer determined that the files have two fields that need to be preprocessed. **❷** The `Date` field must be parsed as a date, **❸** and the `Symbol` field must be treated as a category.

The application reads and processes the daily stocks before making them available in memory. Then, the application merges them into a single variable, which in this case is a new pandas DataFrame, containing all categories in *Symbol*.

❹ The script writes the result into the same folder as a new file named *monthly_assets.csv*. This way, other analysts or data engineers can start there if they need all daily stock prices for further analysis.

After this first script runs and the file is available, the remaining pipeline scripts can run to generate the BuzzFeed and AppTech stock reports. This example has only one script, the reporting Python file, shown in Example 4-3.

Example 4-3. Data reporting application

```
import pandas as pd

all_assets = pd.read_csv("data/monthly_assets.csv", parse_dates=['Date'])  ❶

apptech = all_assets[all_assets['Symbol'] == 'APCX']  ❷
buzzfeed = all_assets[all_assets['Symbol'] == 'BZFD']

buzzfeed['Intraday_Delta'] = buzzfeed['Adj Close'] - buzzfeed['Open']  ❸
apptech['Intraday_Delta'] = apptech['Adj Close'] - apptech['Open']

kept_values = ['Open', 'Adj Close', 'Intraday_Delta']

buzzfeed[kept_values].to_csv("data/report_buzzfeed.csv", index=False)  ❹
apptech[kept_values].to_csv("data/report_appTech.csv", index=False)
```

This application performs the following actions:

❶ Reads the data source created by the previous application

❷ Filters out the data for the two reports it creates: BuzzFeed and AppTech.

❸ Computes the `Intraday_Delta` scores, which are the daily stock evolutions to report.

❹ Reports the `Open, Adj Close`, and the computed score `Intraday_Delta` values in the dedicated files for each stock.

Simple Yet Complex, Depending on the Context

The pipeline presented here is quite simple, on purpose. However, analyzing their behavior can still be tricky as the source codes are available from code repositories, such as the GitHub repository mentioned. However, both applications may be developed by different individuals or teams, and thus, their lifecycles are independent of each other but dependent at the data level.

To execute the pipeline appropriately, it is important to respect the dependencies between the reporting and ingestion applications. That is, you must run the `ingestion` application successfully before you run the `reporting` application. Otherwise, the pipeline will fail. A solution to achieve this is to use an orchestrator that runs `ingestion` before `reporting`, such as Dagster and Airflow. In fact, the orchestrator is another application to configure by explicitly hardcoding the dependencies between applications at the data level. However, the applications themselves are still ignorant of their downstream dependencies.

The flip side of hardcoding the dependencies in an orchestrator is that it is a new asset to maintain (e.g., the accuracy of the explicit dependencies). Also, additional constraints are imposed when creating a pipeline because teams must stay independent and therefore can't simply update an existing pipeline to meet their own needs. Thus, an extension must be created at a higher level by adding a new, separated DAG, which could disconnect the explicit dependencies.

Returning to our pipeline, let's discuss the functional dependencies between the applications; that is, `ingestion` must run successfully before `reporting` can be run. But what does *successfully* mean?

Definition of the Status of the Data Pipeline

To determine whether an execution of a data pipeline is successful, I will analyze the opposite question: What kind of failures can occur in the `ingestion`?

Explicit failure

> This causes the application to crash. This type of failure is easy for the orchestrator to handle if you use one, because it's a flag not to trigger the next application: the `reporting` application, in our example.

Silent failure

> In this case, the application finishes, without, for example, an error code or log. Because it doesn't run as expected, you must consider the notion of expectations introduced in Chapter 2.

An observer of the `ingestion` application would face explicit failures like these:

File not found errors

> Occur when any of the data files, such as *Buzzfeed.csv*, aren't available in the folder because it was renamed or changed to lowercase, or the file wasn't created before running the `ingestion` application.

Type errors (`TypeError`)

> Occur if some values aren't coercible to match the types provided to the `read_csv` function, such as when the symbol should be a category.

Hardcoded name errors

> Occur when any of the fields explicitly used in the code to access the values, such as the column name `Date` in Example 4-3 ❶ and `Symbol` in this case, aren't present or the name has changed.

Filesystem errors

> Happen when the files aren't readable or the folder isn't writable for the user who runs the application.

Memory errors

> Happen when the files increase in size to the point that the memory allocated to the application is no longer sufficient.

System errors

> Triggered if the disk doesn't have any more space to write the aggregated result.

But from the perspective of the engineer who observes it, the following examples indicate silent failures:

- The `Date` column isn't parsable as a date because it's malformed, the pattern changed, or the time zone isn't consistent. In this case, the column isn't a `date time` anymore but an `object`.

- The `Date` column contains values but not for the current month. All values are past or future dates.

- The `Date` column contains values in the future because the generator might have run later and generated information about the future to compare to the month in which it's processing. This situation can generate duplicates later, or inconsistent values for the same dates, and can likely fail some aggregations.

- The `Symbol` category changes for various reasons, such as because of a typo or a capitalization change, length, or reference. This category is used across the files and is written in the output file as a category.

Also, the `reporting` application might regard the `ingestion` as failed because it provoked the following failures in `reporting`:

- The monthly aggregated file wasn't written when the reporting started, making it unavailable when the reporting tool is scheduled to run at a given interval.

- Any of the fields used to filter in the arithmetic aren't available or their name changed.

- The same errors occur with read/write access, size, and space.

Also, `reporting` can fail silently due to the silent failures of the `ingestion`, plus:

- The `APCX` and `ENFA` symbols aren't available in the provided file.

- `Adj Close` or `Open` are missing values, which generates garbage in the `Intra day_Delta` output. This problem can also be an explicit failure, in which case the values become pandas' `NA`.

- The aggregated file doesn't contain information about the current month, but the dates are in the past.

Because any of these failures can occur, you must have visibility when they happen and—even better—anticipate them earlier to prevent their propagation (see "Fail Fast and Fail Safe" on page 151) from the `ingestion` application.

The explicit failures should already have been made visible, as a development practice, to catch those errors explicitly (`try…except` in Python). However, for an observer to identify and discover silent failures, they need the application to produce the appropriate observations.

Data Observations for the Data Pipeline

In this section, I will provide an overview of the data observations the data pipeline must generate. For this, let's have a quick glance at Figure 4-2, which shows how a low-level API implements the model presented in Chapter 2. It is interesting to note that they share a similar structure and even some entities (labeled); in the next paragraphs, I will detail each portion individually to highlight these facts.

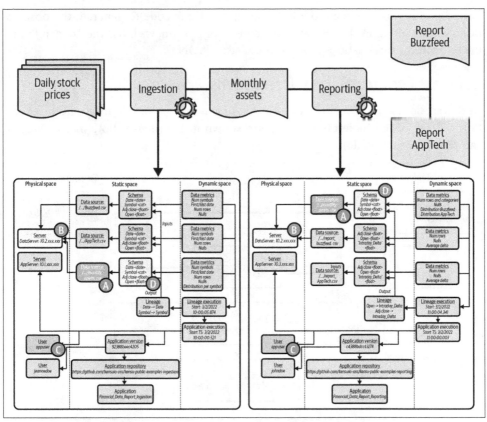

Figure 4-2. The observations for ingestion and reporting and their similarities (a larger version of this figure is available at https://oreil.ly/TaQGV)

In this diagram, you'll notice labeled entities as uppercase letters A, B, C, and D in circles. The "A" data sources highlight the observations generated by the `ingestion` application about the data it generates, and by the `reporting` as it is reading it, hence making explicit the implicit dependency.

In fact, both applications generate several similar observations, which represent all dependencies that tie them together. In Figure 4-2, the following similar observations are also highlighted:

- The "B" entities observe the server the data was retrieved from.
- The "C" entities observe the user executing commands.
- The "D" entities observe the schema of the data generated by the ingestion, as read by the reporting.

Let's dig into what we need to add to the application's code to generate the observations shown in Figure 4-2. Because the code is in Python, we'll use the logging module to print the observations that are encoded in JSON.

Generate Contextual Data Observations

In this section, I will cover the code needed to generate observations about the execution context of the ingestion application shown in Figure 4-3 (note that reporting can reuse the same code).

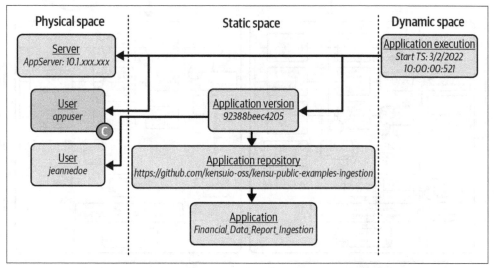

Figure 4-3. Data observations about the execution context of the ingestion application

Insert the code in Example 4-4 at the beginning of the file to generate the observations for the ingestion application.

Example 4-4. Generate data observations about the ingestion application

```
app_user = getpass.getuser() ❶
repo = git.Repo(os.getcwd(), search_parent_directories=True) ❷
code_repo = repo.remote().url
commit = repo.head.commit
code_version = commit.hexsha
code_author = commit.author.name
application_name = os.path.basename(os.path.realpath(__file__)) ❸
application_start_time = datetime.datetime.now().isoformat()
```

❶ Retrieve user name information.

❷ Retrieve git information.

❸ Retrieve information about the application execution.

The extra instructions in Example 4-5 create variables for the observations, but nothing is done yet with them. To log the information as mentioned previously, we use a JSON representation of the information model, encoded as in Example 4-5.

Example 4-5. Modeling data observations about the ingestion runtime

```
application_observations = {
    "name": application_name,
    "code": {
        "repo": code_repo,
        "version": code_version,
        "author": code_author
    },
    "execution": {
        "start": application_start_time,
        "user": app_user
    }
}
```

This code creates the JSON that's formed with all the observations created so far. However, this section is about using a low-level API for data observability. As we move on, we will encounter a similar pattern, giving us the opportunity to create functions to simplify the code and share it across the `ingestion` and `reporting` applications, or any other Python applications in the future.

To create an API, we create a model that mimics the observation core model in JSON, turns each entity into a *class*, and converts relations into references (see Example 4-6).

Example 4-6. Modeling the application data observations using dedicated classes

```
class Application:  ❶
    name: str

    def __init__(self, name: str, repository: ApplicationRepository) -> None:
        self.name = name
        self.repository = repository

    def to_json(self):
        return {"name": self.name, "repository": self.repository.to_json()}

class ApplicationRepository:  ❷
    location: str
```

```
        def __init__(self, location: str) -> None:
            self.location = location

        def to_json(self):
            return {"location": self.location}

    app_repo = ApplicationRepository(code_repo)
    app = Application(application_name, app_repo)
```

That means the application entity has to have an `Application` ❶ class with a property *name* that can hold the name of the file as an `application_name` variable, and a reference to an `ApplicationRepository` instance. This `ApplicationRepository` entity will be encoded as an `ApplicationRepository` ❷ class that has a property `location` set as the git remote location. This structure will help build the model and generate a JSON representation more easily that will be reusable and able to lead to standardization.

An additional benefit of encoding concepts into API classes is that it gives them the responsibility to propose helpers to extract associated observations, as in Example 4-7 ❶.

Example 4-7. Leverage classes to define helpers related to modeled entities

```
class ApplicationRepository:
    location: str

    # [...]

    @staticmethod
    def fetch_git_location():  ❶
        import git
        code_repo = git.Repo(os.getcwd(), search_parent_directories=True).remote().url
        return code_repo


class Application:
    name: str

    # [...]
    @staticmethod
    def fetch_file_name():  ❶
        import os
        application_name = os.path.basename(os.path.realpath(__file__))
        return application_name


app_repo = ApplicationRepository(ApplicationRepository.fetch_git_location())
app = Application(Application.fetch_file_name(), app_repo)
```

This strategy might be a straightforward way to implement the model. However, we prefer another approach that weakens the links between entities. In Example 4-8, all information will be logged in one JSON with entities spread into the tree of information with `Application` at its root. This encoding forces us to create all observations before logging the root one, which is the `Application` instance. The `Application` constructor would become something like Example 4-8.

Example 4-8. Bloated constructor for Application without separation of concerns

```python
class Application:
    name: str
    def __init__(self, name: str, version: ApplicationVersion,
                 repo: ApplicationRepository, execution: ApplicationExecution,
                 server: Server, author: User) -> None:
        pass
```

To avoid this complexity and constraint, a better way is to reverse the dependencies between the entities. Instead of having the `Application` contain its `ApplicationVersion` or `ApplicationRepository`, we'll create the `Application` alone and then add a weak reference to it from within the `ApplicationVersion` and `ApplicationRepository`. Example 4-9 shows how this model would look.

Example 4-9. Reversing the dependencies between entities and introducing `id`

```python
class ApplicationRepository:
    location: str
    application: Application
    id: str

    def __init__(self, location: str, application: Application) -> None:
        self.location = location
        self.application = application
        id_content = ",".join([self.location, self.application.id])
        self.id = md5(content.encode("utf-8")).hexdigest() ❶

    def to_json(self):
        return { "id": self.id,
                 "location": self.location,
                 "application": self.application.id }

    @staticmethod
    def fetch_git_location():
        import git
        code_repo = git.Repo(os.getcwd(),
                             search_parent_directories=True).remote().url
        return code_repo
```

With this model, we can log the observations individually—the two calls to `logging.info`—reducing the amount of information to retain. Because we need to recompose the entity relationships, we introduce the `id` variable to reduce the amount of information to log and observations to link. Using the logs, `id` can reconstruct the links in the model, like the dependency between the `ApplicationReposi tory` and the `Application`, by their `id`s, because they have already been logged.

In this example, the application generated `id` locally, resulting in a poor design that will make it inconsistent across several executions. To circumvent this problem, we must define a functional `id` that can identify the entities across executions, deployments, and applications. This notion is known as the *primary key* in modeling. You can use a primary key as an input in a hashing algorithm, for example, that will generate the `id` in a deterministic fashion, in this case using `hashlib`.

Example 4-9 illustrates how to use the primary key to generate the `id` consistently, for example, by using `md5` ❶. We'll use this strategy throughout this chapter to generate entities.

Generate Data-Related Observations

Let's now cover the observations of the main data observability components: data source, schema, and data metrics. Figure 4-4 shows the observations we must log.

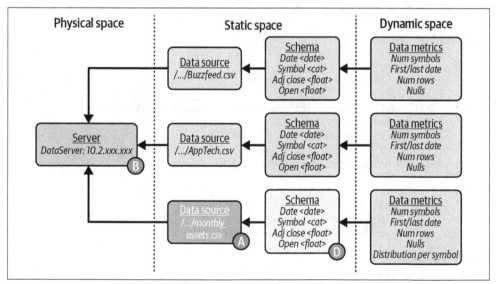

Figure 4-4. Entities data source, schema, and data metrics of ingestion.

The observations to generate are related to the data source that's read and written. Then, the transformation (lineage) is addressed. In the ingestion code, many sources are read using the pandas read_csv function.

The observation for the data source will be mainly the file path provided as an argument to the read_csv function. Another observation would be the data source format provided by the fact that read_csv is used without any specific parser attributes, such as *sep*, and thus the data is a "real" CSV.

Also, read_csv isn't given any information about the header. Therefore, the first non-blank line is expected to be the column names, which will help create an observation about the data the ingestion application accesses.

The type of columns is another piece of information that can be observable. pandas infers most of the numeric types. However, strings, categories, and dates are kept as *objects*. The read_csv function provides two hints: the Date is date information, and the Symbol is categorical data, or a string in this case.

Describe Function

You have likely used the describe function many times when exploring and developing your application. This function is essential for knowing what you must do with the data to achieve your goal. This exploration, which is based on a set of assumptions about data, leads to understanding the data. Therefore, logging the result of the describe function gives you the information to understand the data later if the assumptions about it hold true in the future.

For example, in Example 4-1, computing and logging as JSON, the BuzzFeed's *describe* could be logging.info(json.dumps(Buzzfeed.describe().to_dict())), which logs the following JSON line:

```
{"Open": {"count": 20.0, "mean": 4.4985, "std": 0.503014857999663,
"min": 3.72, "25%": 4.077500000000001, "50%": 4.43, "75%": 4.9525,
"max": 5.28}, "High": {"count": 20.0, "mean": 4.6921,
"std": 0.5150902731305302, "min": 3.98, "25%": 4.30675, "50%": 4.66,
"75%": 5.0425, "max": 5.57}, "Low": {"count": 20.0, "mean": 4.31515,
"std": 0.5218698441283289, "min": 3.622, "25%": 3.96, "50%": 4.27,
"75%": 4.595, "max": 5.24}, "Close": {"count": 20.0, "mean": 4.4345,
"std": 0.506894310586796, "min": 3.73, "25%": 4.0275, "50%": 4.39,
"75%": 4.71, "max": 5.29}, "Adj Close": {"count": 20.0, "mean": 4.4345,
"std": 0.506894310586796, "min": 3.73, "25%": 4.0275, "50%": 4.39,
"75%": 4.71, "max": 5.29}, "Volume": {"count": 20.0, "mean": 193095.0,
"std": 104746.62901245884, "min": 79300.0, "25%": 104350.0,
"50%": 168350.0, "75%": 234975.0, "max": 386500.0}}
```

With the values, pandas creates a DataFrame, a sort of table we can use to catch the information listed so far. Moreover, the DataFrame also allows us to compute additional intrinsic information about the values themselves, such as descriptive statistics. We use the describe function to compute these basic statistics on numerical values and other types like categorical or date values using the argument: include='all'.

Finally, the ingestion application writes the monthly assets CSV file by using the to_csv function on the DataFrame that holds in memory the values to be written. This function gives almost the same level of information as the read_csv function. So, we can derive the file path, columns, and types.

Let's see how we can model these observations in a reusable API. The first class is DataSource, which is relatively straightforward to modelize, as shown in Example 4-10. We mainly want to know the format and where the data source the application is reading or writing is located ❶. Therefore, it will model the path to the file.

Example 4-10. DataSource entity class

```
class DataSource:
    location: str
    format: str
    id: str

    def __init__(self, location: str, format: str = None) -> None: ❶
        self.location = location
        self.format = format
        id_content = ",".join([self.location, self.application.id])
        self.id = md5(content.encode("utf-8")).hexdigest() ❷

    def to_json(self):
        return {"id": self.id, "location": self.location, "format": self.format}
```

Also, id is generated based on the provided path, which is relative (starts with ./), and should be expanded to use the absolute path. ❷ Further, if we use a database table, such as a method other than read_csv, we'd need to add other helpers to handle connection strings.

Next, Example 4-11 can modelize the schema that the application manipulates in the data source.

Example 4-11. Schema entity class

```
class Schema:
    fields: list[tuple[str, str]]
    data_source: DataSource
    id: str

    def __init__(self, fields: list[tuple[str, str]], data_source: DataSource) -> None:
        self.fields = fields
        self.data_source = data_source
        linearized_fields = ",".join(list(map(lambda x: x[0] + "-" + x[1],
                                     sorted(self.fields))))
        id_content = ",".join([linearized_fields, self.data_source.id])
        self.id = hashlib.md5(id_content.encode("utf-8")).hexdigest()

    def to_json(self):
        from functools import reduce
        jfields = reduce(lambda x, y: dict(**x, **y),
                         map(lambda f: {f[0]: f[1]},
                         self.fields))
        return {"id": self.id, "fields": jfields, "data_source": self.data_source.id}

    @staticmethod
    def extract_fields_from_dataframe(df: pd.DataFrame):  ❶
        fs = list(zip(df.columns.values.tolist(), map(lambda x: str(x),
            df.dtypes.values.tolist())))
        return fs
```

The Schema class has the fields property, which models the columns of the CSV file. Here, we can extract it from the metadata of the pandas DataFrame: columns and dtypes. We chose it to represent the fields as a list of pairs *(field name, field type)* ❶.

The last class for this part is DataMetrics, which will model the metrics of the files that the ingestion application reads and writes. However, it's an incomplete version of the class because it encodes only the relationship with Schema. It must be extended to ensure it provides visibility into the data metrics for a specific usage. This purpose requires a lineage that comes later (see Example 4-15).

The current class looks like Example 4-12.

Example 4-12. DataMetrics entity class

```python
class DataMetrics:
    schema: Schema
    metrics: list[tuple[str, float]]
    id: str

    def __init__(self, metrics: list[tuple[str, float]], schema: Schema) -> None:
        self.metrics = metrics
        self.schema = schema
        self.id = hashlib.md5(",".join([self.schema.id]).encode("utf-8")).hexdigest()

    def to_json(self):
        from functools import reduce
        jfields = reduce(lambda x, y: dict(**x, **y),
                         map(lambda f: {f[0]: f[1]},
                             self.metrics))
        return {"id": self.id, "metrics": jfields, "schema": self.schema.id}

    @staticmethod
    def extract_metrics_from_dataframe(df: pd.DataFrame):  ❶
        d = df.describe(include='all', datetime_is_numeric=True)  ❷
        import math
        import numbers
        metrics = {}
        filterf = lambda x: isinstance(x[1], numbers.Number) and not math.isnan(x[1])
        mapperf = lambda x: (field + "." + x[0], x[1])
        for field in d.columns[1:]:
            msd = dict(filter(filterf, map(mapperf, d[field].to_dict().items())))
            metrics.update(msd)
        # metrics looks like:
        # {"Symbol.count": 20, "Symbol.unique": 1, "Symbol.freq": 20,
        #   "Open.count": 20.0, "Open.mean": 3.315075, "Open.min": 1.68,
        #   "Open.25%": 1.88425"Open.75%": 2.37, "Open.max": 14.725,
        #   "Open.std": 3.7648500643766463, ...}
        return list(metrics.items())
```

The metrics were chosen in this simplified form to represent only the numerical descriptive statistics as a list of pairs *(metric name, numerical value)*. ❶ These observations will convert directly from the result of the describe function called on the DataFrame that holds the data values. ❷

Now that we have defined all entities as classes, we can update our code (see Example 4-13) to ensure it generates the observations appropriately.

Example 4-13. Ingestion application including data observations entities

```python
app = Application(Application.fetch_file_name())
app_repo = ApplicationRepository(ApplicationRepository.fetch_git_location(), app)

AppTech = pd.read_csv(
    "data/AppTech.csv",
    parse_dates=["Date"],
    dtype={"Symbol": "category"},
)
AppTech_DS = DataSource("data/AppTech", "csv")
AppTech_SC = Schema(Schema.extract_fields_from_dataframe(AppTech), AppTech_DS)
AppTech_M = DataMetrics(DataMetrics.extract_metrics_from_dataframe(AppTech),
             AppTech_SC)

Buzzfeed = pd.read_csv(
    "data/Buzzfeed.csv",
    parse_dates=["Date"],
    dtype={"Symbol": "category"},
)
Buzzfeed_DS = DataSource("data/Buzzfeed", "csv")
Buzzfeed_SC = Schema(Schema.extract_fields_from_dataframe(Buzzfeed), Buzzfeed_DS)
Buzzfeed_M = DataMetrics(DataMetrics.extract_metrics_from_dataframe(Buzzfeed),
                         Buzzfeed_SC)

monthly_assets = pd.concat([AppTech, Buzzfeed]) \
    .astype({"Symbol": "category"})
monthly_assets.to_csv(
    "data/monthly_assets.csv", index=False
)
monthly_assets_DS = DataSource("data/monthly_assets", "csv")
monthly_assets_SC = Schema(Schema.extract_fields_from_dataframe(monthly_assets),
                           monthly_assets_DS)
monthly_assets_M = DataMetrics(
              DataMetrics.extract_metrics_from_dataframe(monthly_assets),
                    monthly_assets_SC)
```

Code Evolution

This version of the code requires tremendous changes and an extra layer of instructions. Reviewing this code to understand what it does helps us understand what we need to observe and how. Examples 4-14 and 4-21 show simplified versions with a function removing duplicate instructions.

Also, the next sections introduce many strategies to reduce the number of changes and work to the point where data observation generation is almost automated and invisible.

We now have code that generates the observations we need to observe the data behavior when running the `ingestion` application. However, plenty of code is almost identical. This function ❶ in Example 4-14 can be used to remove most of the noise.

Example 4-14. Wrapping duplicated code in higher level function

```python
def observations_for_df(df_name: str, df_format: str, df: pd.DataFrame) -> None:
    ds = DataSource(df_name, df_format)
    sc = Schema(Schema.extract_fields_from_dataframe(df), ds)
    ms = DataMetrics(DataMetrics.extract_metrics_from_dataframe(df), sc)
```

In this section, we work with files, but what if you have to deal with tables instead, using SQL to read, transform, and write the data? If SQL is used directly to perform these operations, it contains the same operations as a Python code would have. That is, it reads tables, transforms them, and eventually writes them; for example, an *insert* of a sub-*select*. However, SQL doesn't provide many capabilities to generate information *in-the-middle*, such as metadata extraction or metrics. Another application, which the database server should be responsible for, runs the SQL.

Remember SQL holds a lot of information that your application can leverage. It contains the names of the tables, columns, types, and transformations performed; hence, parsing the queries gives similar observations, as presented in Example 4-14. Actually, I recommend this extraction strategy for SQL queries because an SQL query is likely the result of several iterations and experiments until it does exactly what it is meant to do (like any code, in fact). Therefore, the SQL query implements all assumptions made in each iteration—for example, including the following:

- `IS NOT NULL` represents the assumption that columns can be null and it is fine to filter them out (assuming that their number is not impacting the final logic).

- `cast("Amount" as "INT64")` represents the assumption that the `Amount` is always castable as an integer.

An SQL Query Is a Program

SQL is procedural logic. Like Python logic, it is encoded in a domain specific language (DSL) and, like pandas, as a character string sent and processed by the database server. In fact, it is very similar to a Python code, being a character string sent and processed by the Python executable.

After adding the `ingestion` capability to generate data and application observations, we can work on another area that will provide even more information—observations about the analytical part—when the application is deployed.

Generate Lineage-Related Data Observations

To generate observations about the interaction at the data level between the applications in the pipeline, down to the column level, I will cover in this section how to generate the lineage entity as shown in Figure 4-5.

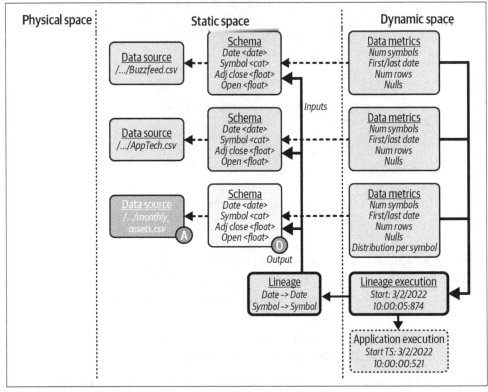

Figure 4-5. Entities representing the lineage executing by the `ingestion` application

As discussed in Chapter 2, the part of the model that connects the lineage—the data flow and transformations, in this case—glues the observations from the main component of the data observability area to the application component. It's in the analytics observability area, at the intersection of all three areas.

To encode this part, we must generate observations about which data sources (inputs) are used to produce other data sources (outputs). For the `ingestion`, the stock CSV files help generate the *monthly_assets* CSV file. Going one level deeper, `ingestion` concatenates all values from all columns and then writes the result in a file. The lineage at the field level is *direct*, meaning the input and output column names are identical and an output takes its value only from this column for each input data source.

Example 4-15 shows how to include the generation of the lineage—OutputDataLineage ❶—in the reporting application with a dedicated class defining the dependencies of an output with its inputs.

Example 4-15. Class to model lineage observations

```python
class OutputDataLineage:  ❶
    schema: Schema
    input_schemas: list[tuple[Schema, dict]]
    id: str

    def __init__(self, schema: Schema,
                 input_schemas_mapping: list[tuple[Schema, dict]]) -> None:
        self.schema = schema
        self.input_schemas_mapping = input_schemas_mapping
        self.id = hashlib.md5(",".join([self.schema.id]).encode("utf-8") \
                  + self.linearize().encode("utf-8")).hexdigest()

    def to_json(self):
        return {"id": self.id, "schema": self.schema.id,
                "input_schemas_mapping": self.input_schemas_mapping}
```

Example 4-16 presents a static function part of the OutputDataLineage that will map each input with the output at the field level, connecting them in this way: out put_field -> list of input fields for each input ❶. The generate_direct_map ping helper binds the data sources using an overly simple heuristic that maps output data sources when field names match.

This strategy fails in most real-life use cases, especially with aggregations, which require more conscientious tracking to manage all connections.

You can avoid this situation by using one of the strategies discussed in the next chapter.

Example 4-16. Helper method to generate a lineage easily

```python
@staticmethod
def generate_direct_mapping(output_schema: Schema, input_schemas: list[Schema]):  ❶
    input_schemas_mapping = []
    output_schema_field_names = [f[0] for f in output_schema.fields]
    for schema in input_schemas:
        mapping = {}
        for field in schema.fields:
            if field[0] in output_schema_field_names:
                mapping[field[0]] = [field[0]]
        if len(mapping):
            input_schemas_mapping.append((schema, mapping))
    return input_schemas_mapping
```

```
define linearize(self):
    [...]
    return linearized
```

Then, I define in Example 4-17 the lineage execution, ApplicationExecution, ❶ which makes the connection with the contextual (application-related) observations.

Example 4-17. Class to model the execution of a lineage

```
class DataLineageExecution:
    lineage: OutputDataLineage
    application_execution: ApplicationExecution ❶
    start_time: str
    id: str

    def __init__(self, lineage: OutputDataLineage,
                 application_execution: ApplicationExecution) -> None:
        self.lineage = lineage
        self.application_execution = application_execution
        self.start_time = datetime.datetime.now().isoformat()
        self.id = hashlib.md5(
            ",".join([self.lineage.id, self.application_execution.id,
                    self.start_time]).encode("utf-8")).hexdigest()

    def to_json(self):
        return {"id": self.id, "lineage": self.lineage.id,
                "application_execution": self.application_execution.id,
                "start_time": self.start_time}
```

Also, the data observability core model introduced in Chapter 2 linked the data metrics entity to the execution of the lineage to give visibility about the data when it's used or modified. Therefore, we adapt the DataMetrics model to represent that link by adding the lineage_execution property ❶, as shown in Example 4-18.

Example 4-18. Adding the lineage execution to the metric for context

```
class DataMetrics:
    schema: Schema
    lineage_execution: DataLineageExecution ❶
    metrics: list[tuple[str, float]]
    id: str

    def __init__(self, metrics: list[tuple[str, float]], schema: Schema,
                 lineage_execution: DataLineageExecution) -> None:
        self.metrics = metrics
        self.schema = schema
        self.lineage_execution = lineage_execution
        id_content = ",".join([self.schema.id, self.lineage_execution.id]
        self.id = hashlib.md5(id_content).encode("utf-8")).hexdigest()
```

```
def to_json(self):
    from functools import reduce
    jfields = reduce(lambda x, y: dict(**x, **y),
                     map(lambda f: {f[0]: f[1]}, self.metrics))
    return {"id": self.id, "metrics": jfields, "schema": self.schema.id,
            "lineage_execution": self.lineage_execution.id}

@staticmethod
def extract_metrics_from_df(df: pd.DataFrame):
    d = df.describe(include='all', datetime_is_numeric=True)
    import math
    import numbers
    metrics = {}
    filterf = lambda x: isinstance(x[1], numbers.Number) and not math.isnan(x[1])
    mapperf = lambda x: (field + "." + x[0], x[1])
    for field in d.columns[1:]:
        msd = dict(filter(filterf, map(mapperf, d[field].to_dict().items())))
        metrics.update(msd)
    return list(metrics.items())
```

Now all the pieces are ready to generate the observations shown in Figure 4-5. The final ingestion script can be seen in the GitHub repository (*https://oreil.ly/icKQy*).

Wrap-Up: The Data-Observable Data Pipeline

Before moving on with the analyses of how the observations help with the explicit and silent failures introduced at the beginning of this section, we reuse what we've done so far for the ingestion application to make the reporting application data observable. See Example 4-19.

Example 4-19. Reporting application with verbose data observations generated from code

```
import ApplicationRepository.fetch_git_location
import ApplicationVersion.fetch_git_version
app = Application(Application.fetch_file_name())
app_repo = ApplicationRepository(fetch_git_location(), app)
git_user = User(ApplicationVersion.fetch_git_author())
app_version = ApplicationVersion(fetch_git_version(), git_user, app_repo)
current_user = User("Emanuele Lucchini")
app_exe = ApplicationExecution(app_version, current_user)

all_assets = pd.read_csv("data/monthly_assets.csv", parse_dates=['Date'])

apptech = all_assets[all_assets['Symbol'] == 'APCX']
buzzfeed = all_assets[all_assets['Symbol'] == 'BZFD']

buzzfeed['Intraday_Delta'] = buzzfeed['Adj Close'] - buzzfeed['Open']
apptech['Intraday_Delta'] = apptech['Adj Close'] - apptech['Open']
```

```
kept_values = ['Open', 'Adj Close', 'Intraday_Delta']

buzzfeed[kept_values].to_csv("data/report_buzzfeed.csv", index=False)
apptech[kept_values].to_csv("data/report_appTech.csv", index=False)

all_assets_ds = DataSource("data/monthly_assets.csv", "csv")
all_assets_sc = Schema(Schema.extract_fields_from_dataframe(all_assets),
                all_assets_ds)
buzzfeed_ds = DataSource("data/report_buzzfeed.csv", "csv")
buzzfeed_sc = Schema(Schema.extract_fields_from_dataframe(buzzfeed), buzzfeed_ds)
apptech_ds = DataSource("data/report_appTech.csv", "csv")
apptech_sc = Schema(Schema.extract_fields_from_dataframe(apptech), apptech_ds)
# First lineage
lineage_buzzfeed = OutputDataLineage(buzzfeed_sc,
                            OutputDataLineage.generate_direct_mapping
                            (buzzfeed_sc, [all_assets_sc]))
lineage_buzzfeed_exe = DataLineageExecution(lineage_buzzfeed, app_exe)
all_assets_ms_1 = DataMetrics(DataMetrics.extract_metrics_from_df(all_assets),
            ❶ all_assets_sc, lineage_buzzfeed_exe)
buzzfeed_ms = DataMetrics(DataMetrics.extract_metrics_from_df(buzzfeed), buzzfeed_sc,
                lineage_buzzfeed_exe)
# Second lineage
lineage_apptech = OutputDataLineage(apptech_sc,
                            OutputDataLineage.generate_direct_mapping
                            (apptech_sc, [all_assets_sc]))
lineage_apptech_exe = DataLineageExecution(lineage_apptech, app_exe)
all_assets_ms_2 = DataMetrics(DataMetrics.extract_metrics_from_df(all_assets),
                ❶ all_assets_sc, lineage_apptech_exe)
apptech_ms = DataMetrics(DataMetrics.extract_metrics_from_df(apptech), apptech_sc,
                lineage_apptech_exe)
```

By adding the observations this way, we keep the modifications similar to what we did in the `ingestion` application. This approach enables us to build habits and abstractions, such as a framework, that will reduce the number of changes needed—almost an implicit law in development.

In Example 4-19, notice that the observations generated for the inputs shifted to the end ❶. We made this implementation choice for the simplicity of the example. An upside is the additional computations are done at the end without impacting the business flow. A downside is that, if something fails in between, no observations about the data sources and their schema are sent. Of course, it is possible to avoid this situation with some adaptations to the code. Also, for this introduction to a low-level API, we have to add some boilerplate to generate the right information, which may sound like noise, proportionally to the business code. However, keep in mind that the script initially had no logs. In general, logs are added sporadically to generate some information about the script's own behavior, which is what we've done, but for the data.

Also, keep these points in mind:

1. We reused the `OutputDataLineage.generate_direct_mapping` helper as is to create lineage mapping between the outputs and input. However, it won't work, because we aggregated `Adj Close` and `Open` from the *monthly_assets.csv* file into the new `Intraday_Delta` column. Because the fields don't have the same name, the "direct" heuristic won't pick up this dependency.

2. A warning message is displayed about reporting the same observations a second time for the *monthly_assets*. We did this because we encoded lineage per output. We now have two lineages, each producing output for the *report_buzzfeed.csv* and *report_AppTech.csv* files. Because the output reuses the same data as the input (filtered), we must report what the input looks like for each output to avoid them appearing as duplicates. As an alternative, we could reuse the observations or adapt the model to address this duplication. You might consider the following options instead:

   - If we change our strategy to read every time the data is accessed instead of loading it in memory, then if the data changes between the two writing operations, the observations will no longer be identical. If one output has issues, we prefer to synchronize the observations of the input with this lineage. The probability of this situation increases when you consider each writing operation can take hours, not seconds.

   - The `reporting` application generates all outputs at every run, but refactoring later can change this and make it parameterable. For example, only one output might be created, such as BuzzFeed. Therefore, each `reporting` dataset is generated by independent runs. In this case, the observations already represent this appropriately, so we don't need to adjust the logic. In other words, sending the observations of a given input as often as it is used to create an output represents reality, rather than trying to optimize to reduce data that might look like duplicates.

Let's address the first point and ensure that the lineage can represent the real connections between the data sources. To do this in a simplified manner, we will update the helper function introduced in Example 4-19 with extra information. Example 4-20 ❶ shows the new version of this helper which now includes an argument to provide nondirect mapping for each input. Later sections present strategies to handle this common use case in a much easier, efficient, maintainable, and accurate way, such as by using monkey patching.

Example 4-20. Generated field level lineage based on matching field names

```
@staticmethod
def generate_direct_mapping(output_schema: Schema,
                            input_schemas: list[tuple[Schema, dict]]):
    input_schemas_mapping = []
    output_schema_field_names = [f[0] for f in output_schema.fields]
    for (schema, extra_mapping) in input_schemas:
        mapping = {}
        for field in schema.fields:
            if field[0] in output_schema_field_names:
                mapping[field[0]] = [field[0]]
        mapping.update(extra_mapping)  ❶
        if len(mapping):
            input_schemas_mapping.append((schema, mapping))
    return input_schemas_mapping
```

Example 4-21 shows the final observations part of the reporting application.

Example 4-21. Reporting application made data observable with clean code

```
# First lineage
intraday_delta_mapping = {"Intraday_Delta": ['Adj Close', 'Open']}
a = (all_assets_sc, intraday_delta_mapping)
lineage_buzzfeed = OutputDataLineage(buzzfeed_sc,
                                     OutputDataLineage.generate_direct_mapping(
                                     buzzfeed_sc, [(all_assets_sc,
                                     intraday_delta_mapping)]))
lineage_buzzfeed_exe = DataLineageExecution(lineage_buzzfeed, app_exe)
all_assets_ms_1 = DataMetrics(DataMetrics.extract_metrics_from_df(all_assets),
                   all_assets_sc, lineage_buzzfeed_exe)
buzzfeed_ms = DataMetrics(DataMetrics.extract_metrics_from_df(buzzfeed),
                 buzzfeed_sc, lineage_buzzfeed_exe)
# Second lineage
lineage_apptech = OutputDataLineage(apptech_sc,
                                    OutputDataLineage.generate_direct_mapping(
                                    apptech_sc, [(all_assets_sc,
                                               intraday_delta_mapping)]))
lineage_apptech_exe = DataLineageExecution(lineage_apptech, app_exe)
all_assets_ms_2 = DataMetrics(DataMetrics.extract_metrics_from_df(all_assets),
                   all_assets_sc, lineage_apptech_exe)
apptech_ms = DataMetrics(DataMetrics.extract_metrics_from_df(apptech), apptech_sc,
                lineage_apptech_exe)
```

Using Data Observations to Address Failures of the Data Pipeline

Now, we can deploy, run, and monitor our pipeline by using the observations they generate each time they're run. The low-level API required quite a bit of extra effort and conviction to achieve. Nevertheless, we are satisfied with the results. Every minute spent on those tasks will give us 100 times the benefit in the form of avoidance of revenue loss—following the total quality cost rule, 1-10-100—when issues happen in production.

Let's look at the issues that can arise that were mentioned in this section, starting with the `ingestion` application failures:

Input files not found
> The `DataSource` observations are sent every run. After they've been read, the failing runs are, therefore, not sending any of them. Even for someone without any knowledge about the application logic, it's clear the files used until now are missing.

Type errors at read
> The `Schema` observations are sent and contain the field names associated with their type. Therefore, the expected type is clear for the observer without going to the application or the files for the previous months.

Errors due to missing fields
> The same observations as for "Type errors at read" help the observer quickly identify which fields were present in the previous runs that are missing in the current one.

Filesystem errors
> The exception thrown by the pandas library normally provides the path that resulted in an error. The remaining information available for the observer to identify the issue is which server this path used. The *IP* provided in the server observations associated with the `DataSource` gives instant visibility about which server was related to that path.

Memory error
> This issue happens mostly when the data increases suddenly. Many cases can be considered, but they are mostly handled intuitively by the observer using `Data Metrics` observations that contain the number of rows, the schema with the number of fields, or the number of `DataSources`. Regardless, it might require the observations to be sent earlier than at the end of the script, such as in the following two cases:
>
> - *One of the input files has a larger size than before.* The file is detected easily because no `DataMetrics` are available for it.
> - *The output has grown a lot because all files have grown.* The size difference is detected because the `DataMetrics` for the outputs are missing. Also, the `Data Metrics` for the inputs show an increase in the number of rows.

Filesystem space errors

These errors most likely happen when writing the output, considering that we're addressing data observability cases here. Therefore, the same information as for "Memory error" gives the observer instant visibility about why the available space is no longer sufficient and which files couldn't be written.

The Date is not parsable as a date

- In this case, the schema has the type observation for the date field change from date to something else, such as str or object.

Date column doesn't contain values for the current year/month

- The DataMetrics observations include the minimum and maximum time stamp, which gives instant visibility into the difference between the execution time and the available data. For example, let's consider the maximum time stamp is two days in the past to the time when the data source is read, then the data can be considered too old if the acceptable period is only one day.

Date column contains values in the future

- This one is easy, as the same kind of observations as for the previous failure due to missing values for the current month will give you this visibility.

Symbol categories changed

- If we consider only numeric DataMetrics, we can quickly identify this case by using the number of categories that would grow in the output file. One or some of the files wouldn't be consistent anymore, as they would refer to different categories.

Then, we must consider under what circumstances the reporting application might regard the ingestion application as failed, and where applicable, what the reporting application an observer could use. These situations include the following:

The monthly aggregated file is not available

- The DataSource observation or DataMetrics hasn't been sent by the ingestion application.

Aggregation uses missing fields, such as Close

- The schema of the monthly data sent by the ingestion application is missing those fields too.

Errors with read/write access, size, and space

- The same solutions apply to the `reporting` observer as the `ingestion` observer. There is no bias of information across teams or team members.

APCX and ENFA symbols

- The number of categories reported by the `ingestion` observer has changed, giving hints of what is happening, in some cases. However, we can extend `DataMetrics` to also report non-numerical observations and report the categories.

Missing values in `Adj Close` or `Open` leading to abnormal numbers

- The `DataMetrics` "number of nulls" covers this case because when the number of nulls is greater than zero, the computation of the `Intraday_Delta` will return NAs.

Wrong date in the monthly assets

- The same solutions used by the `ingestion` observer related to date failures apply here. For example, the application could use the minimum and maximum value for the `Date` column compared to the currently reported month.

We're now ready to handle various situations wherein the data is the source of a problem. Without this knowledge, these situations would require long, high-stress meetings to understand them and exhausting hours or days spent debugging that could turn into months, because we can't access the data in production.

The issues discussed so far are ones we know can happen. However, many other issues are likely to propagate throughout the pipeline that we know little about yet—the unknown-unknowns. For example, the values of one of the stocks are incorrect for a previous month due to errors introduced into the data during the CSV export. This problem will happen for at least one of your applications, and others like it.

Because of these unknown-unknowns, data observations mustn't be restricted to cover only predefined cases, but the applications must report as many observations as possible—with possible constraints on computation resources and time—to generate visibility about the anticipated or unmet situation. In this example, the distribution of the monthly stock values would be useful later for comparison with other months, and they could provide hints about whether the values are equal or similar.

The advantage of using low-level logging is having full flexibility over what you can generate as visible. Examples are custom metrics and key performance indicators (KPIs).

All jobs aren't equal; every company, project, and application has its own specific details. You're likely to control specific metrics, whether they are linked to consumed data or produced data. Such metrics, for a table, could be the sum of the number of items multiplied by the cost per unit minus the amount received from a web service, `count(items) * cost_per_unit`. The result must always be greater than zero. This easily can be added to the source code, but it has to be added by the engineer, as this constitutes specific metrics associated with the business logic (and the semantics of the columns).

Another reason for customizing observations is KPIs—the numbers stakeholders request that are important to the underlying business. KPIs are often reported periodically or computed on demand and used at random or fixed intervals. However, their meaning is so strong that stakeholders have high expectations for them, with little to no time to wait for corrections. Therefore, you must also create visibility about how KPIs evolve over time, because, if a stakeholder has doubts about it, time starts ticking the moment they ask you about its correctness. To increase responsiveness, you must generally know how the KPIs evolve, identify how they change before they do, and understand why they change based on their historical values and lineage.

As you might have anticipated during the `reporting` application update, defining the API—the model, encoding, and functions—isn't a task for each application. Rather, you must standardize and reuse it across applications. Standardization reduces the amount of work per application. More importantly, it enables the observations to be homogeneous, independently of the application, to simplify the observers' work in matching the behaviors of other applications that participate in the pipeline they are analyzing.

Standardization is also helpful for reusing entities across applications, such as the `assets_monthly DataSource`, which is the `ingestion` application's output and the `reporting` application's input. With the homogenous representation of the observations, you can consolidate the status of the entire pipeline by reusing the entities across applications.

Part of the architecture to support data observability must include creating an external system that aggregates the observations to build a global view, systematically. By having observers that rely on this aggregated view and act upon it, the system can evolve to perform some of the actions currently being done by the observers, which is where machine learning comes into play.

Conclusion

This chapter has provided a comprehensive exploration of data observability at the source and its significance in enhancing data quality and operational excellence. We delved into the concept of generating data observations within the code of data applications, highlighting the importance of incorporating observation generation code across various components of the application. These components include the application itself, the data being utilized, their relationships, and the content they hold.

Additionally, we discussed the creation of a data observability Python API at the low level, which offers a powerful toolset for developers to seamlessly integrate data observation capabilities into their applications. Through this API, practitioners gain the ability to generate data observations, track data flows, and ensure the reliability and accuracy of their data.

To reinforce these concepts, we presented a fully working example that showcased the transformation of a non-data-observable data pipeline written in Python into a robust and data-observability-driven pipeline. By leveraging the dedicated data observability Python API, we demonstrated how data observations can be generated, captured, and utilized to enhance visibility, identify issues, and drive continuous improvement.

As we move forward, the principles and strategies explored in this chapter serve as a foundation for incorporating data observability into the very fabric of data applications. By adopting these practices, organizations can ensure that their data pipelines are robust, reliable, and capable of providing valuable insights with a high level of trust.

Despite the hyper-customizability and flexibility of low-level logging, its adoption can be hindered by the initial effort required. This argument also applies to the adoption of tests. Therefore, it is crucial to simplify the usage complexity at this level. Additionally, we need to explore alternative approaches that complement low-level logging while promoting the widespread adoption of data observability across teams and individuals. The upcoming sections will delve into this subject, commencing with an exploration of event-based systems.

## CHAPTER 5

Automate the Generation of Data Observations

With the challenges of low-level logging introduced in the previous chapter, our focus shifts to exploring alternative approaches to enhance data observability and stream-line its adoption, via automation. In this chapter, I will introduce new possibilities and strategies for capturing and analyzing data observations, paving the way for a more comprehensive observability framework.

Abstraction Strategies

The previous chapter explained how to add data observability to applications that deal with data using a low-level API. This approach can become tedious, even for simple processes, leaving the task to the final user—the data engineer or practitioner.

Most of the work, such as the code instructions presented in Chapter 4, can be abstracted into a higher-level framework that reduces the amount of effort involved, as long as you dedicate enough time to defining it. Like other best practices, the pres-sure to reduce time to market can cause the generation of data observations to be skipped, even when the engineers know that they will deploy something in which they have little or no confidence.

To avoid falling into this trap, we can automate various best practice strategies or techniques—this is a classic optimization practice in other areas such as application observability, where most common observations are generated by default, such as the number of requests for a web service, the memory usage of a computation engine, the version of an application (cf. META-INF). Automation always comes with less flexi-bility because it addresses common tasks. However, you can combine these tasks by using the low-level API to extend to your specific needs.

These techniques are used heavily in application observability, for example, where they apply naturally. Players like Datadog, Splunk, and OpenTracing use them in the various agents they develop.

The first strategy—using event listeners—leverages events that the tools you use for your data work might trigger.

Event Listeners

Depending on the framework and tools you use to transform or manipulate data, you might encounter some, such as Apache Spark, that have implemented several concepts that allow their internal behavior to be reacted upon. When certain events happen, the technology enables you to register listeners to intercept and act depending on the information conveyed by the event. Understanding which behaviors can be intercepted allows you to create visibility about them in a more automated, systematic, and standard way.

In data observability, the events related to the model that represents the internal system explained in Chapter 2 are of particular interest. Such events are generally available for reading or writing a data source and running a transformation.

The components used to leverage these events are commonly named *listener* or *handler*. You can create and register them on the *event bus*, which is the system that propagates the triggered events.

Some technologies can trigger events that contain all available information at once, or enough information such that you can generate the model almost fully in a single line of log or action, such as with Apache Spark (covered in Chapter 6).

When possible, the event-based agents are powerful, as you can integrate them automatically at the framework level or in the tools' servers, publishing most of the information without involving much time.

Of course, this concept only works for creating standardized information. Any customization, such as metrics, algorithms, or descriptions, must be introduced by application or usage. The other types of observation that require involvement are the rules related to expectations. They leave little room for standardization while keeping their efficiency and performance. Generic rules apply to all cases and are too vague to capture custom or corner cases. Applications are different.

Logs as events are a special case of events that is interesting to consider as a fallback when the framework, application, or system you use doesn't provide the flexibility you need to create your goal for data observability. Those systems are called black boxes and include some legacy systems.

However, if those systems are closed, they are likely generating some logs, such as SQL executed or modules applied. The logs create some visibility about the system as part of application observability. However, they might eventually contain enough information to recreate part of the data observability out of context by patching the system externally, the way a Prometheus-compliant client can be attached to a Java application to generate logs about its execution context (version, runtime, etc.).

Aspect-Oriented Programming

The aspect-oriented programming strategy is somewhat similar to the event listener strategy, as the idea, put simply, is to react to some behavior to extend it. It's often used for configuration purposes because it enables components to be integrated in a more declarative fashion. Aspects are like triggering events when functions are going to be executed or have been executed. Figure 5-1 highlights the similarities and differences between event listeners and aspects, which are mainly related to where the injected code is running (e.g., a different thread) and how (e.g., via an event bus or injected).

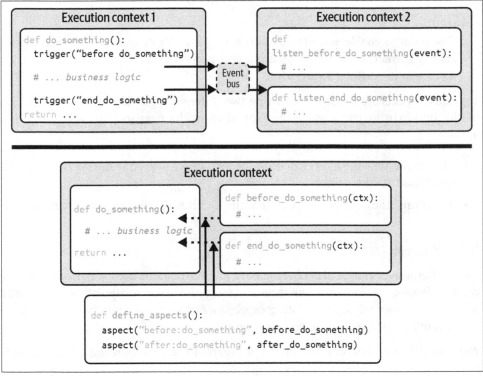

Figure 5-1. Event listeners (above) and aspects (below); similarities and differences

You can use this capacity to react before and after functions are executed to intercept behaviors and expose them as part of data observability. Examples include running a component to read a file or running an anonymization procedure.

Java application observability agents, such as OpenTracing for CDI/Spring applications, rely heavily on this approach. OpenTracing, for example, automatically captures access to an HTTP endpoint or database. In this case, the idea is to reuse as much as possible what already exists and is in place (see Chapter 7).

The components to be considered to apply this strategy are the following:

Aspect
> A dedicated behavior that spans several running classes, such as when a `DataObservabilityAspect` defines the behaviors to introduce data observability.

JointPoint
> The moment of a `pointCut` method or property, such as before access or after execution.

Advice
> The behavior to run at a `JointPoint`.

PointCut
> The point to enable and run an `Advice`. It's generally defined as a regular expression that matches the class, method, and property names to run the associated `Advice` at the defined `JointPoint`.

Typically, aspects are implemented using two different types of *weaving* to add capabilities into existing code, which we expand on in the next sections with two other options:

- At compile time the `Aspect` definitions help inject new code during the compilation phase. It's done once.
- At runtime the aspects update code while it's running. It's done at each execution.

Code enrichment

Other alternatives enable data observability in a more automated way from the code you are developing. The code enrichment strategy involves manipulating code to add behaviors without relying on existing capabilities introduced beforehand in the code (e.g., events, as in "Event Listeners" on page 124).

You can achieve code enrichment by using runtime manipulation or using code generation.

Runtime manipulation

Enriching the code at runtime enables the application to be extended with additional capabilities, such as data observability, when the application is run. This strategy is useful and efficient when adding generic capabilities that require few interventions or

---

customizations by your engineers. Nevertheless, the team deploying and monitoring the application can configure such customizations. However, the customizations aren't close to the application's business function but to its generic behavior.

You can update an application at runtime in several ways. One of the most popular dynamic languages is Python, which uses *monkey patching.*

Monkey patching. When your application uses dynamically typed languages, such as R or Python, instead of statically typed languages, such as Java or C++, the variables have types or structures that might be checked when the code is run.

You can apply monkey patches in the window where the types can be extended between the application start and the usage of the different types. The term monkey patch (*https://oreil.ly/ndWqw*) comes from *guerilla patch,* which refers to sneakily changing code.

Monkey patching doesn't require setting up the libraries to be used, such as installing a new version or updating the application code to generate the data observations, because those updates can be applied at runtime.

Currently, most data-related libraries haven't yet been conceived to generate data observations, offering little visibility into what they do. They'll likely be updated over time to add this capability. But, in the meantime, we must find workarounds, which are called *polyfills*[1] in web development.

Example 5-1 shows how to monkey patch a function in Python.

Example 5-1. The original non-observable code reading a csv file with pandas

```
AppTech = pd.read_csv(
    "data/AppTech.csv",
    parse_dates=["Date"],
    dtype={"Symbol": "category"},
)
```

Example 5-2 shows how to monkey patch the `read_csv` function.

Example 5-2. pandas read_csv monkey patched with data observability capabilities

```
import pandas as pd
original_read_csv = pd.read_csv  ❶

def read_csv_with_do(*args, **kwargs):  ❷
```

---

1 See Wikipedia's entry on polyfill (*https://oreil.ly/a_jwT*), and MDN Web Docs has a helpful entry (*https://oreil.ly/0qg4Q*).

```
    df = original_read_csv(*args, **kwargs)
    print("My monkey-patched code here")
    return df


pd.read_csv = read_csv_with_do  ❸

AppTech = pd.read_csv(
    "data/AppTech.csv",
    parse_dates=["Date"],
    dtype={"Symbol": "category"},
)
```

Example 5-2 shows how to:

❶ Save the original function

❷ Substitute the original function with a custom-defined one

❸ Define the function to be used as a substitution; in this case, we are calling the original function and adding an extra code

We need to generate data observations for the three activities. The first one is the reading activity. To illustrate what we need, we are using a well-known pandas library in Python that has many extensions for various data sources.

Imagine you have to read a CSV file that you want to make observable with monkey patching. Example 5-3 shows what you need to do.

Example 5-3. Data observable pandas.read_csv *function with monkey patch*

```
import pandas as pd
original_read_csv = pd.read_csv

class DataSource:[...]
class Schema:[...]

def read_csv_with_do(*args, **kwargs):
    df = original_read_csv(*args, **kwargs)
    file_name = args[0][0:args[0].rfind('.')]  ❷
    file_format = args[0][args[0].rfind('.') + 1:]  ❷
    ds = DataSource(file_name, file_format)  ❶
    sc = Schema(Schema.extract_fields_from_dataframe(df), ds)
    return df

pd.read_csv = read_csv_with_do

AppTech = pd.read_csv(
    "data/AppTech.csv",
    parse_dates=["Date"],
    dtype={"Symbol": "category"},
```

```
)
Buzzfeed = pd.read_csv(
    "data/Buzzfeed.csv",
    parse_dates=["Date"],
    dtype={"Symbol": "category"},
)
```

The monkey patch of the read_csv function is simply adding ❶, the data observability logo. For completeness of information, the file name and format are extracted
from the first parameter ❷.

For the writing activity, the code is pretty similar to the reading activity, as shown in
Example 5-4.

Example 5-4. Data observable pandas.to_csv function with monkey patch

```
import pandas as pd
original_to_csv = pd.DataFrame.to_csv

class DataSource:[...]
class Schema:[...]

def to_csv_with_do(self, *args, **kwargs):
    r = original_to_csv(self, *args, **kwargs)
    file_name = args[0][0:args[0].rfind('.')]
    file_format = args[0][args[0].rfind('.') + 1:]
    ds = DataSource(file_name, file_format)
    sc = Schema(Schema.extract_fields_from_dataframe(self), ds)
    return r

pd.DataFrame.to_csv = to_csv_with_do

AppTech = pd.read_csv(
    "data/AppTech.csv",
    parse_dates=["Date"],
    dtype={"Symbol": "category"},
)
Buzzfeed = pd.read_csv(
    "data/Buzzfeed.csv",
    parse_dates=["Date"],
    dtype={"Symbol": "category"},
)

monthly_assets = pd.concat([AppTech, Buzzfeed]) \
    .astype({"Symbol": "category"})
monthly_assets.to_csv( ❶
    "data/monthly_assets.csv", index=False
)
```

As you can see, the application code ❶ does not require any change.

For the transformation activity, some technologies don't prepare the transformation before applying it (called a *lazy evaluation,* as in Spark). Instead, they use a combo of *for-loop*s and manual manipulations. In these cases, keeping track of all transformations automatically from read to write can be difficult. But it's not impossible. And if it's challenging to do in an automated fashion, it's at least as challenging manually, and working on the automation must be done only once and by a few people.

Continuing with the pandas, if your application filters the data read and combines it with others, you can track these operations to make the whole transformation observable. Example 5-5 shows how to add data observability without the need to modify the application code.

Example 5-5. Make pandas.DataFrame data observable with DataFrame wrapper

```
import pandas as pd

original_read_csv = pd.read_csv
original_to_csv = pd.DataFrame.to_csv
original_concat = pd.concat

class DataFrameWithDO:❶
  def __init__(self, df: pd.DataFrame, ds: DataSource, sc: Schema,
               df_i: list[pd.DataFrame], ds_i: list[DataSource],
               sc_i: list[Schema]) -> None:
   #[...]
  def astype(self, *args, **kwargs):
    df = pd.DataFrame.astype(self.df, *args, **kwargs)
    return DataFrameWithDO(df, self.ds, self.sc, self.df_i, self.ds_i, self.sc_i)

  def to_csv(self, *args, **kwargs):
    r = original_to_csv(self.df, *args, **kwargs)
    file_name = args[0][0:args[0].rfind('.')]
    file_format = args[0][args[0].rfind('.') + 1:]
    ds = DataSource(file_name, file_format)
    sc = Schema(Schema.extract_fields_from_dataframe(self.df), ds)
    lineage = OutputDataLineage(sc, generate_direct_mapping(sc, self.sc_i))
    lineage_exe = DataLineageExecution(lineage, app_exe)
    for (df_l, sc_l) in zip(self.df_i, self.sc_i):
      ms = DataMetrics(extract_metrics_from_df(df_l), sc_l, lineage_exe)
      ms = DataMetrics(extract_metrics_from_df(self.df), sc, lineage_exe)
    return r
```

The class ❶ DataFrameWithDO involves a different concept, with the following implications:

- It acts as an "alternative" for the pandas DataFrame class; in fact, DataFrame WithDO is an enhancement of the default DataFrame with data observability capabilities.

- With this approach, the application code does not need any modification.

- `DataFrameWithDO` takes care of the lifecycle of a `DataFrame`, so it keeps track of the lineage from the input `DataFrame` and the final output.

- `DataFrame` methods for transformation and writing are overridden to add data observability capabilities to the original one.

- The `DataFrame` method for reading is monkey patched to substitute for the original behavior.

Now, we need a seamless way to substitute instances of `DataFrameWithDO` to instances of `DataFrame`. This will be done by injecting code in the pandas high-level functions that create instances of `DataFrame`, the functions `read_csv` and `concat`, for example, as shown in Example 5-6.

Example 5-6. Make pandas functions read_csv and concat data observable

```
def read_csv_with_do(*args, **kwargs):  ❶
    df = original_read_csv(*args, **kwargs)
    file_name = args[0][0:args[0].rfind('.')]
    file_format = args[0][args[0].rfind('.') + 1:]
    ds = DataSource(file_name, file_format)
    sc = Schema(Schema.extract_fields_from_dataframe(df), ds)
    df_with_do = DataFrameWithDO(df, ds, sc)  ❷
    return df_with_do

def concat_with_do(*args):  ❸
    df_list = []
    ds_list = []
    sc_list = []
    for i in args[0]:
        df_list.append(i.df)
        ds_list.append(i.ds)
        sc_list.append(i.sc)
    df = original_concat(df_list)
    df_with_do = DataFrameWithDO(df, None, None, df_list, ds_list, sc_list)
    return df_with_do
❹
pd.read_csv = read_csv_with_do
pd.concat = concat_with_do
```

Example 5-6 shows how to "inject" data observability in ❶read_csv, which ❷returns an instance of `DataFrameWithDO`. The function `concat` is following the same ❸pattern. These new functions `read_csv_with_do` and `concat_with_do` are then replacing the original functions, which would force us to use them instead. To avoid this, the lines in ❹ show how to substitute the original functions in the pandas module with the data-observable versions.

However, we now have another case we haven't handled yet, which is when the transformations are multi-threaded. In this case, we must maintain a correlation between the different operations that are happening asynchronously. We do this by tracing each step with a `correlation_id` that corresponds to the transformation that's being run. This tracing enables easier reconciliation later.

Bytecode instrumentation.   Dynamic languages offer a lot of flexibility, but that's not the case with other languages, such as Java. Types are checked at compile time, which generates the bytecode—an intermediate representation of the code—that the virtual machine runs.

In this case, the compiled code isn't something we can easily manipulate, because its representation isn't identical to the original code. Because allowing the code to be updated with polyfills is so convenient, you can use another technique that's a bit trickier than monkey patching.

This technique is called *bytecode instrumentation,* or compiled code manipulation. In Java, its low-level API is called ASM—a reference to Assembler—and has been used for decades to build tools such as test coverage analyzers or mock generators. With ASM, you can take any code running in Java and inject it with your own additional behavior. You can extend Spring Data, Flink, Spark, and the like at the bytecode level to generate data observations, without changing the original framework. ASM is low level; you can use a more convenient abstraction called *javassist* instead.

While the low-level bytecode injection is the most flexible, we don't go any deeper because most cases are possible with aspect-oriented programming (see "Aspect-Oriented Programming" on page 125). In reality, aspect-oriented programming is an elaborate version of bytecode, such as AspectJ. However, it's at a higher level of abstraction, to remove most of the complexities involved in injecting code, at the price of adding a new dependency to your application—the *aspectj.jar* file.

Therefore, you can apply something similar to monkey patching to inject the generation of data observations, and it will require fewer (guest) code changes because it happens in the background. In fact, Python also has a bytecode you can inject.[2] You can also implement what monkey patching enables at a lower level by injecting the compiled code without wrappers. For example, if you create a class to run SQLs, you can extend the methods that read, parse, and access columns and the like to trace the schema and the usage of the columns.

---

2 Reza Bagheri, "Understanding Python Bytecode," (*https://oreil.ly/qZa2C*) *Medium,* March 5, 2020.

Code generation

As introduced at the beginning of this section, you can generate data observations by using code generation. However, this strategy doesn't apply to enriching existing code from existing applications or libraries. Nevertheless, flexible alternatives are available to generate the code by considering new cases you encounter, or simply the code itself.

For example, say your application uses SQL to query and update database tables, with the ability to generate code. A piece of code can be generated to parse the SQL in place, which in turn generates code to run observations for each table that's touched, by, for example, generating other SQLs to gather metrics or metadata.

The following sections cover three options for generating code, starting with using an *abstract syntax tree* (AST).

AST manipulation.   Regardless of the language you use to process data, it goes through a series of steps that turn your code into forms until a processor can run it. The first two phases are lexical analyses, followed by a syntactic analysis. The latter phase generates an AST, which represents the structure of the code and encodes the execution of your logic.

An AST is a structure that allows you to manipulate it as long as you respect its rules before passing it to the code generator, which turns the result into machine code.

Most compilers and interpreters, such as Java, Python, and C#, can intercept and modify the AST, which you can change to include the instructions to generate the observations needed to make your application or framework data observable.

This method is illustrated in Figure 5-2, showing the AST of a subset of the code pan das.read_csv function.[3] Figure 5-3 shows the AST of the same code with additional instructions to generate additional logs (simulating the observations). You can see that the modified AST is not totally different from the original, but has "nodes" that were inserted where the new instructions have been added.

---

3 The figures were generated by the free online tool (*https://oreil.ly/MrB0D*), which supports most languages.

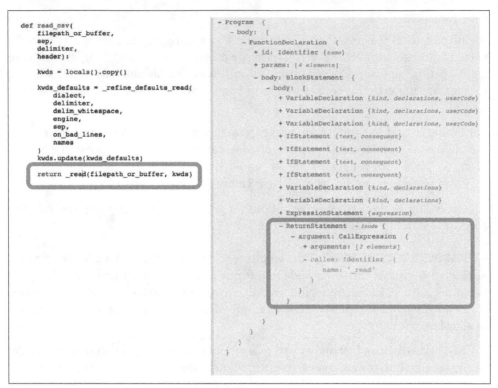

Figure 5-2. AST of a subset of the `pandas.read_csv` *code*

To do so, you can use a visitor pattern (*https://oreil.ly/hNOhO*) to navigate and act upon an AST that contains read, write, and transform operations and generate code blocks to create observations about those operations.

This code isn't limited to advanced programming languages like Java or C. You can also introduce it for any other high-level abstraction, such as SQL and its variations, or custom *domain specific languages* (DSLs). To do this, use the ANother Tool for Language Recognition (ANTLR) technology, which handles the language complexities and allows you to generate an AST or create your own representation.

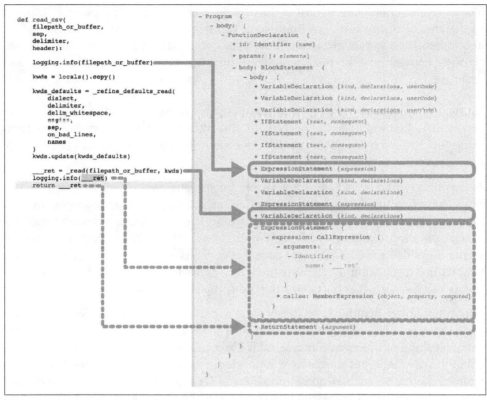

Figure 5-3. Updated AST of the `pandas.read_csv` *with additional instructions*

Annotations, decorators, and attributes.   Previously, we explained the possibilities of generating observations by using explicit logging, which requires your code to include all instructions to this effect.

A good programming practice is to decompose your code into smaller blocks without too many responsibilities or functions. You can label each function with its responsibility, such as merging datasets or updating a field with a computed value. The label is similar to a document that describes how the function will behave.

Because the label has a well-known semantic, you can use it to update the function's code with additional code that will generate observations about its behavior.

To leverage such capabilities, you can use a programming concept called *annotation* in Java, *attribute* in C#, or *decorator* in Python. These annotations are generally called *syntactic sugar* because they are removed from the generated machine code (or byte-code) after the compiler or interpreter processes them using plug-ins. For example, annotation can be a retention in Java at RUNTIME, enabling the runtime to access them using reflection.

The generated code handles most of the complexities based on the inputs and outputs of the annotated function. For example, it can infer the connections, create metrics about them, and extract metadata. In fact, the complexity of generating the observations is encapsulated in the annotations, making the code easier to reuse and maintain.

Macros.   The last strategy can help with avoiding rewriting most of the boilerplate and increasing adoption. Also, the quantity of observations is based on macro programming (*https://oreil.ly/OdMRs*) that enables code to be preprocessed and injects code in place at compile time.

Macro programming isn't always available for all languages. If all languages—even SQL—have functions, it is worth noting that macros might not be supported in your language. It turns out, for example, that Python is one of them, although there is a specification for it (*https://oreil.ly/RqWMo*). The key difference between a macro and a function is that a macro generates code that depends on the code it's applied on. In a way, it's metaprogramming, because the idea is to write code that takes code as arguments and generates it as output during pre-compilation phases.

You might notice that this is relatively close to the AST strategy. The idea is to use a code representation, manipulate it, and then generate the enhanced code with the extra capabilities, which, in our case, adds observation generation. AST happens outside the code itself, but macros are supported natively by the language and offer a simpler alternative, such as quasi quotations in R (*https://oreil.ly/jObzu*). The macros can process the lexical representation (tokens) or the abstract tree of the code, making it more capable.

Although it's also safer than other alternatives, such as bytecode or AST manipulation, you must first ensure the macros are hygienic to avoid capturing existing variable (term) names.

The advantage of a macro is that it runs faster because it's injected in the guest code and is supported by the language. Unlike annotations, which are added as function labels, macros are added within the body of the code.

High-Level Applications

Over the years, data management activities, such as data integration and orchestration, have been abstracted into higher-level solutions to lower the entry barrier and increase efficiency.

Such solutions hide most of the complexities involved in developing common tasks like connecting to a database or sequencing several tasks. Therefore, the level of control you have on such applications is much lower than when working on your own code base.

The main operations remain the same conceptually, meaning a data application has to read (extract, input), transform, and write (load, output). Abstracting them generally takes the form of dedicated components that share the same structure for each operation and are implemented to hide the specificities of each type of input (such as a file on S3), transformation (such as SQL), and writing (such as in a Kafka topic). The resulting application must be orchestrated to run and collect the results.

Today, such solutions don't yet fully embrace the data-observability principles introduced so far in this book. However, they can generate some visibility about how they operate. This capability gives us the opportunity to reconcile what's available and create global visibility across the different systems, but still, the task remains to complement what's not yet available. Such high-level applications aren't responsible for the entire end-to-end process but can be used to intervene as a step.

Let's look at the types of high-level applications for data engineering, which are categorized into low-code and no-code.

No-Code Applications

No-code solutions (e.g., Tableau) for data provide a user interface that enables users to manipulate data without having to use any programming. They're built to offer this capability to people with few or no programming skills.

While these applications currently lack full data observability, they boast a remarkable degree of flexibility. Consequently, the number of data accesses, transformations, and newly created data sources can rapidly expand. Regrettably, users are unable to manually generate the corresponding data observations or establish expectations. As a result, the utilization of such technology without a well-defined strategy for generating data observations carries significant and widespread risks.

Most of these systems operate as black boxes, meaning the code isn't accessible or generated as it is for the low-code ones described later. Therefore, we're limited in how we can fulfill our requirements. You can use the following workarounds until these applications embed the data observability features:

Logs to reconstruct observations
Like any applications, no-code applications have logs that include some information that you can use only to reconstruct—maybe only partially—some of the necessary observations. Of course, this covers the application part, but the lineage might also be present. However, metrics often aren't present.

Application or configuration files and APIs
Often, such applications store data pipeline configurations in files or make them available by using an API. This approach enables the opportunity to analyze the flow and generate the lineage and data sources from it, at a minimum. This information allows you to build an additional component to gather the data metrics.

However, the ability to notice when the pipeline is run is necessary in order to catch the right context of the usage.

Execution or logs control board
> Such applications also generally present an interface, or logs, to review what is being executed. They enable you to intercept the executions and combine them with previously presented options. Plus, you can develop an additional component to access the data sources at the same moment to gather their metrics.

External data observability platform
> Expectations are harder to introduce at this level. In general, an external data observability platform is preferred to leverage the observations gathered in previous steps. However, an alternative is to extend the pipeline defined in the tool with additional checks that are added, say, directly at the beginning and end, for example. This works if the tool has this feature.

Of course, no-code solutions don't provide much room to introduce data observability. But what was true for the frameworks you used in your code is also true here: the engineering team must also make data observable the results built by their users with their solutions. In the meantime, we are simply trying to go faster and complete what hasn't yet been implemented.

Low-Code Applications

Low-code alternatives require more technical skills than no-code systems and aim to help developers work faster on common tasks. This section addresses the data pipeline creation task, using code generation and workflows to define the processing steps.

Code generators

At a certain level, in a given environment, many tasks are often included in data pipelines, such as instances of the classic extract, transform, and load (ETL) components: the readers, transformers, and writers.

Low-code platforms offer engineers the ability to generate the pipeline code but keep them focused on the business logic rather than, say, boilerplate code. Although a software framework could also handle this, such platforms as Talend have gained a lot of traction thanks to the user interface (UI)-based environment.

The code generated by Talend is Java, and it can be handled like any other code base that can be revisited or extended. However, these platforms allow such extension beforehand with a system that gives engineers a way to define their own behavior and keep their focus on the business logic.

Because the code is being generated, we can use most of the strategies introduced in the first part of this section to give the platform the ability to create observations across the whole process. Over time, those building blocks will likely natively include the generation of data observations. Therefore, when we define this extension type for an open source platform, we can simply propose it as part of the original component instead of as a new one.

Workflows

Workflows might sometimes generate code, but it's not guaranteed you'll have access to it or room to extend it with data observability. However, describing a workflow in low code involves several steps when using templates that you can add in a JSON, YAML, or similar format to explicitly configure the read, transformation, and write functions.

We can customize these templates as long as they follow the workflow tool constraints. Therefore, we can add our own behavior by extending the existing templates that are available with data observability, and then register them as new ones. For example, `read_csv` can be `read_csv_with_do`.

For templates based on code, such as defining a Spark step, we can extend the underlying Spark component with the agent to create the observations. We can also extend the template to add the extra capabilities to compute specific metrics or introduce expectations.

Orchestrated SQL templates enable users to write SQL with additional configurations, such as database servers or credentials. You can adjust the template to intercept the SQL and use its configuration to build, for example, the lineage and data sources (tables), and compute metrics on the fly.

For APIs that handle user queries, such as those expressed in SQL, an alternative way to introduce data observability automatically is to introduce a proxy API, which mimics but also extends the original API. The proxy passes the query as is to the original API and returns the result with additional data observations, even though the generated observations might already be published.

The good news is a strategy is always available that enables us to retrieve some part of visibility and that has the flexibility to avoid falling into the trap of building data applications without control over the data.

Differences Among Monitoring Alternatives

Monitoring practices can be assimilated to data observability because they share the goal of monitoring data quality. However, they do not address the same process, because data observability aims to detect data issues and provide the necessary information to find the right solution.

We could reconstruct the context information by mixing data quality monitoring information with observations, such as about infrastructure and applications, provided independently by other systems. This might be an alternative for legacy systems in cases where it wouldn't be considered viable to update the applications with data observability. However, this only consists of a *best-effort* strategy that relies on the reconstructing system to have enough information at all times, and to reconstruct the internal data usage accurately.

Choosing this strategy to implement a long-term solution for data reliability is an anti-pattern of data observability. The practices introduced here don't involve all the different actors, such as data engineers, who are often outside the process or have potentially different goals.

This section doesn't detail data quality (monitoring) practices, because various materials are available that properly describe them, including DAMA-DMBOK2, as explained in Chapter 3. Those data quality practices rely on experts, such as business analysts or subject matter experts (SMEs), to define quality constraints (or rules in the domain) that consist of metrics (or KPIs) and controls. The constraints are then scheduled against the data sources to validate that the content matches them. They are expectations, although they're defined generally or independently of their usage. If that's not the case, a large number of constraints can satisfy the different needs. They come with management downsides, because over time, maintenance needs increase the program's total cost of ownership.

Setting up this battery of constraints can be relatively easy with the help of some open source systems, whether for the relational database or for files, such as Apache Griffin or AWS Deequ. However, the additional resources needed to install and manage this external system might be important. You must consider them before moving on this path. For example, AWS Deequ requires an Apache Spark cluster and a scheduler and orchestrator to configure for each job, which increases the cost of ownership, as they add resources to run, of course, but also to monitor and maintain, on top of what is already needed for the business jobs themselves.

Avoid Mismatched Discoveries

If you are monitoring only after you create or update the data (i.e., not in motion), the observations will likely lead to mismatched discoveries, as they are desynchronized with the real event—the real moment in time when the system deviated.

An evolution of these practices, recently coined as *augmented data quality*, softens the dependency on people's time or knowledge by introducing artificial intelligence (AI) into the mix. These practices still require resources and access to the data and its history. However, instead of sending predetermined metrics computations and controls, they analyze the data to perform the following functions:

- Discover rules that can be validated, meaning they're approved by the users of the same type as before.
- Pin data considered as anomalies, first statistically and eventually using machine-learning-based labeled anomalies.

With this information about the quality of the data, we're now aware of general data issues. To provide the necessary context for engineers to solve the issues, we need to rebuild this context using the information at hand to reverse engineer it. Luckily, we can use the observations generated by the following components, which follow the approaches covered in this chapter:

Operating systems
> These produce many observations through syslog (Linux). Many agents, such as Prometheus agents, are also developed to complement those native capabilities.

Filesystems
> They log many events through dedicated APIs that can be consumed. Such APIs include `inotify` in Linux, `kqueue` in FreeBSD, and `ReadDirectoryChangesW` in Microsoft Windows.

Most database servers
> They provide additional facets of data usage to extract observations partially. Two types of information can be considered:
>
> Audit logs: Extended Events Triggers in MSSQL, and log statements and triggers in, for example, PostgreSQL and BigQuery audit logs.
>
> Change data capture (CDC): uses monitoring events sent by databases, monitoring APIs, or supplementing tactics, such as triggers, to generate a stream of all changes in the server, from table creation or schema change to new entries or value updates.

Application log generation best practice
> Logs now generate large amounts of data—mostly untapped data. As recently as 2015, metrics and traces are also now regularly generated by using, for example, an open source solution such as open telemetry or Prometheus.

The next task is to consolidate all these sources of observations from different, unsynchronized periods to reconstruct the contexts as closely as possible to reality. You must also consolidate the information from which observations must still be extracted.

Log Standardization

Application logs are poorly standardized across applications and developers. The task of doing so is harder than we can imagine because there's no guarantee they'll be produced or enabled, even important ones such as debug logs.

In addition, the observations from these components don't cover the ones needed to observe the data behavior, such as of the application, the user, and the like. Otherwise, the applications are already data observable! That said, you might notice the following facts:

- The database or table used by the application is available in the traces of that application. The number of rows and columns might be available, but not the data itself, since the default intent is to control the application behavior.
- The SQL captured in the audit logs won't give much information about the metrics of the used or created tables—maybe about a few metrics, such as the number of output rows or the execution time, although rarely more. However, SQL systems should eventually change the way they function to provide more observability capabilities out of the box.

Restraining ourselves to the sole databases, we can also leverage change data capture. An open source implementation of this strategy, called Debezium (*https://oreil.ly/ 3iXan*), comes with the architecture shown in Figure 5-4.

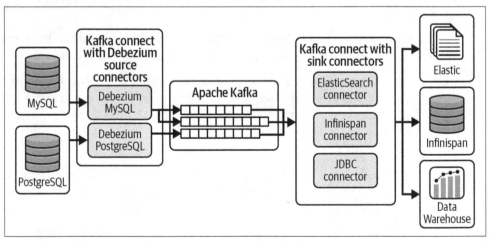

Figure 5-4. Debezium architecture (Source: Debezium)

CDC generates many new streams of information that can be turned into observations of the database server and its components, such as tables. It also requires some resources capable of handling potentially big and fast data points. Even though the captured information can be elaborate and helpful, such as SQL queries to extract lineage, they are decorrelated to the usage. Therefore, the context must still be reconstructed to find and address changes that lead to issues.

All in all, these strategies aren't suitable for really embracing data observability and its benefits, such as the prevention of data issues and ease of analysis of issues. Data observability can't work by only consuming what the system produces as is. Therefore, we need to find other alternatives to fill in the gaps, the most important, or most lacking, of which is metrics. We might be tempted to reuse an old data quality or data catalog pattern, called the *Kraken anti-pattern* (see Figure 5-5), which consists of crawling, defining service level indicators (SLI) or KPIs, and then scanning.

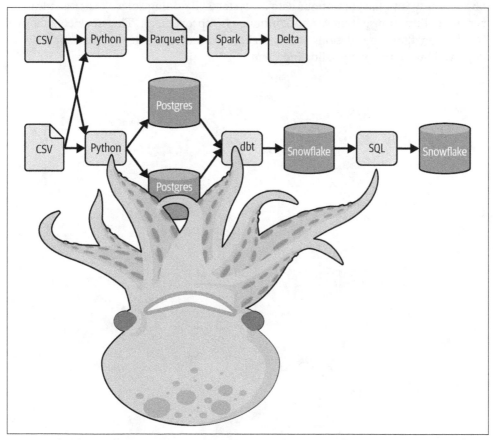

Figure 5-5. The Kraken anti-pattern used in an architecture implementing data observability for a data pipeline

Conclusion

This chapter delved into the realm of data observability, exploring various strategies to automatically generate data observations across different languages and systems. We examined approaches that enable the generation of data observations even for systems that operate as black boxes, providing insights into their internal workings. Furthermore, we emphasized the distinction between data observability and data monitoring, highlighting the importance of actively generating observations rather than passively monitoring data without contextual information.

As we move forward, it is crucial to embrace these strategies and incorporate data observability into the core of our data ecosystems. By doing so, we foster a culture of accountability, transparency, and continuous improvement. The next chapter will build upon these foundations to maintain a level of trust in the data applications deployed by continuously validating them.

## CHAPTER 6

Implementing Expectations

Like Chapter 2, we end this section on implementation with expectations. As data practitioners, expectations are key to the success of our data initiatives, especially their operational maintenance and keeping our stakeholders' trust. Introducing them in our applications is an important step in their development and maintenance, just as important as tests and documentation.

This chapter highlights moments of the application lifecycle where we must introduce expectations and the associated practices to discover and implement them. Expectations also represent pieces of knowledge or interpretations of the constraints based on understanding the context. They have their maintenance process just as tests and documentation do.

To conclude the chapter, we present two examples of overarching practices that combine the benefits of generating observations at the source and introducing expectations. But first, let's see how to define expectations and add them to our data applications.

Introducing Expectations

As mentioned in Chapter 2, expectations represent data constraints or usage that we must respect. If we don't follow them, we must be aware and take action. This section explains how to turn the expectations into rules—how to define and implement them—and the actions we need to take.

Before jumping in, let's see what a rule looks like. You can implement a rule as a function that takes observations as inputs and computes a Boolean condition in its simplest form. So, when you develop an application, you add instructions that use the observations and run the rule.

If you implement a pipeline where you're restricted in your code capacities, such as by a low-code platform, you have to implement the rules as an extension of the practices introduced in this chapter, likely in a declarative fashion.

The declarative approach is a good practice over implementing and running rule logic in the applications themselves. It enables you to give an external system this responsibility, which helps with standardizing, sharing, and notifying, for example. Also, this system can extend the usage of the observations to more use cases if it keeps the historical observations. For example, it can detect patterns in the observations and suggest new or updated rules.

You must also consider those expectations and have the opportunity to add them. Like generating observations, this best practice is one you must learn and master over time, often years. To help you, let's look at the opportunities that come naturally or that you can establish as part of the development process.

Shift-Left Data Quality

As your organization has grown, it's likely to have initiated a data quality process, or program, you can use to nurture the data observability process. In most cases, data governance initiatives drive data quality programs. These initiatives are often led by chief data officers who are closer to the business, have knowledge about how the data is used to make decisions, and therefore have important expectations based on their business knowledge and experience.

Over the years, data quality programs have leveraged this knowledge to introduce in-house or existing data quality tools, data validation points, or data control points. These controls access the data to compute metrics and apply checks. The computations or checks might fail, or in some cases the data is reported wrong.

But in most of the cases, these programs are detached from the data engineers. They're meant to be used by less technical people, which creates a distance from the knowledge and lowers the opportunity for data engineers to use it. Data governance programs have tried to close this gap by introducing a dedicated role—the data steward. This role has many responsibilities, such as maintaining data quality and streamlining communication between the different actors who use it.

Because these practices happen farther downstream, it's often too late when failures are discovered, as mentioned in Chapter 1. You can break this pattern and communicate with your stakeholders or use the tools mentioned previously to integrate metrics and controls earlier in your work. This notion is referred to as *shifting left*.

You can shift left by introducing a step in the data project to capture existing data expectations from downstream users. Or you can review the existing controls and implement them directly in your applications, making them closer to, and synchronizing them with, the data usage. You can think of shifting left as functional tests in software development that determine whether the business functions are working as expected. However, in data observability, shifting left consists of production validations based on the observations generated and validated as the application runs.

The shift-left step at the beginning of your project might not be enough. Often, additional cases are discovered after application deployment, for which observations aren't yet generated. In this case, you can use the data quality tools described previously to define new control points if you can't fix or update the application in a timely manner.

However, you must communicate this need properly. This way, when you or someone else is tasked with "fixing" the application, you can implement the controls as observations and expectations. We say "fixing" because the application might not be seen as having a bug, and instead you might have to deal with a corner case that requires extra cleaning or business logic. Consequently, you can remove the controls from the data quality tools, reducing the number of dedicated resources to validate the data and maintenance of the orchestration.

Shifting left isn't a one-time action to capture all the knowledge or migrate the data quality tools toward data observability. Rather, it's an ongoing process and collaboration.

Corner Cases Discovery

Data application development entails choosing the data to connect and creating the transformations to apply, such as data selection, filtering, grouping, and joining. These choices aren't random but are the result of analyses, explorations, trial and error, and tests performed until satisfaction is reached.

All these activities generate knowledge about the data and the outcome, which conceptually is a large graph of interconnected information. This knowledge is mainly the result of assumptions we've accumulated during these activities, such as data completeness, available fields, and data freshness.

Because the data graph is so large, you have to keep in mind the following considerations:

- It's an incomplete representation of reality.
- It's impossible to implement the code needed to handle all corner cases.
- You'll forget about it over time when it is deployed in production and you moved to another application.

The first point indicates you might have made false assumptions that led to a misunderstanding. It also means you haven't seen some cases because they aren't represented in the datasets used during development. This is the case with *data drifts*, where the data values change over time so much that the business logic is no longer appropriate, or worse, there is a risk of bias influencing the data. The bad news is these situations are hard to anticipate because they are classic unknown-unknowns. However, when you generate enough observations by default in your applications, not necessarily only those linked to known cases, you increase the probability of having some visibility when those cases occur.

The two latter points give you more to think about because they represent your known-knowns and known-unknowns at the time. However, they tend to fade away over time if you don't do anything to persist them as expectations right away. Adding expectations in the applications gives someone else—such as a maintenance team—the opportunity to deal with these cases, so you can focus on your work, instead of having to jump back on this one to fix it.

Why isn't it always possible to implement the code to validate all cases? Well, there isn't any good and valid reason, other than the value of time and the level of laziness inherent to each of us. The reality is that adding code to handle all those corner cases can be boring. Also, because their probability is low, we want to demonstrate the fastest possible solution, so we focus on the main cases and leave those apart. If this weren't true, null pointer or similar expectations would never be thrown, because everyone would be checking that all values aren't null.

In addition, adding code for each case considerably increases the complexity of the application. Therefore, it'll increase its maintenance requirements, or even the probability of needing to rewrite the whole thing the next time someone—even yourself—looks at it.

Consider this example. You read a table with an `email` field that's highly important for the customer-360 table you're building. But your application logic returns an error if some values are null because you extract the domain from it by using a substring. You notice the number of null values is really low when you develop your application. You assume that's the case, because you have so much data, so you decide to drop all rows with a null email and move on. Instead, you could have issued a query to another table that represents the customers' business information, such as their employers, which would help you discover the domain with extra logic. However, it's quicker and simpler to just drop them—"for now at least," you think.

The point here is: "okay fine, fair enough." But you must add an expectation that this number of nulls cannot increase dramatically or should stay below a certain percentage. This approach will save you countless hours of dramatic debugging sessions.

Lifting Service Level Indicators

When creating and maintaining trust in the data and associated applications you have deployed, you must conceive of this trust as a combination of your own with the trust of your producers and consumers. Trust doesn't happen in isolation. Rather, it's a team effort, because your work is part of a larger picture that involves other people's work with multi-layered dependencies.

This concept isn't specific to data applications but is well-known in IT and other contexts, such as the food chain, where trust must be continuous along the entire chain. Considering the importance of this trust, contracts are discussed and signed to create the notion of accountability, which should lead to greater respect and consciousness to stay within the contract's acceptable boundaries.

These contracts provide a way to create a relationship between the contract constraints and the cost associated with ensuring them. Consequently, it helps to create an environment where trust isn't infinite—well, as long as the available money isn't infinite. You must build the number of controls that must be respected so it's viable and known by all parties. Without this type of contract, consumers will expect that everything is always 100% perfect.

In IT, these contracts are called service level agreements (SLAs), with their sidecars—the service level objectives, a sort of contract with yourself. SLAs translate easily into the data world because they determine rules based on arguments, called service level indicators (SLIs), as input. For data observability, SLIs are nothing but observations.

If you've already defined SLAs, the associated expectations are available in a limited, finite amount. If not, introduce them as early as possible. To help define them, use the available observations to propose to your data consumers (and data producers) a panel of observations you can choose from to create the first set of SLAs. This concept is referred to as *lifting observations into SLIs*.

Using Data Profilers

When starting a new data project or application, a common issue is the lack of a priori confidence about what to expect from the input or output data. This situation can result from:

- A lack of knowledgeable people, such as business or domain experts
- The usage of newly acquired internal or external data
- Various factors about the data, such as its speed and size
- Little input is available on what expectations can help you, including rules in your work. This case presents something of a *cold start* issue.

Fortunately, data profilers can be a source of a priori expectations. You're likely to use them anyway during the exploration phase, as mentioned in "Corner Cases Discovery" on page 147.

A data profiler, which is often mixed with a data quality tool, "[examines] the data available from an existing information source (such as a database or a file) and [collects] statistics or informative summaries about that data."[1]

It's a lighter version of the process we introduced when we explained how to create data metrics. However, in this case, the data profiler is an independent tool. Leverage data profilers when possible, even to produce data metrics within your application when it is in production.

Examples of data profiler tools include Talend Open Studio, OpenRefine, Apache Griffin, or AWS Deequ. However, we recommend Great Expectations, which performs statistics and includes learning processes to discover rules, instead of only anomalies. You can use this tool at the beginning of your work on a data source or after creating your own new data; it will generate rules for you to review that you can accept or reject.

Be Careful with Auto Accept

Why you don't want to auto accept rules: You might wonder why you can't accept all rules automatically. Well, those rules will become one of the main sources of qualification of your work and how others see it. You don't want to use rules that you don't clearly understand the reasons for, consider as a representation of the current data, or anything else that would complicate the maintenance of your work in production.

Maintaining Expectations

The practices described in the previous sections to introduce and implement expectations in your work rely heavily on the status of the knowledge and data at a point in time. However, because data changes, the world changes, and knowledge improves, you must consider expectations as artifacts that require maintenance and reevaluation of their accuracy.

Consequently, you need to review the rules that could lead to an update process, like any application logic that might not match the reality of the business. You need to know when such maintenance is required, by introducing a periodic review process of the status, based on the observations, to make the update process data-driven and less subjective. Without this review process, you end up having to do a post-mortem analysis of cases raised due to missing or inadequate rules upstream, or when unknown-unknowns issues are encountered.

---

1 Theodore Johnson, "Data Profiling," in Ling Liu and M. Tamer Özsu, editors, *Encyclopedia of Database Systems* (Springer, Heidelberg, 2009).

Having rules defined in a declarative way and stored in a separate system comes with additional benefits. You can make the update simply when reconfiguring a configuration file or updating the rules in the external system.

Overarching Practices

As explained, introducing rules in your applications has many benefits. However, you can also benefit from other corollary practices.

Fail Fast and Fail Safe

Fail-fast and fail-safe practices are efficient ways to increase confidence and keep maintenance costs under control.

A fail-fast system follows an Agile methodology paradigm, where the system fails as fast as possible to avoid pursuing a flawed process. As quickly and early as possible, the practice is to move on and run the application with pre-established control points in place that highlight whether the process reaches the expected level of quality or requires improvements. Following this practice, and making it clear to everyone, removes any stress or fear associated with deploying your project live, because you expect the first versions to fail…fast.

Moreover, finding the cause of a failure is easier in a fail-fast system because the system reports the failure with as much information as possible as close to the time of failure as possible (*https://oreil.ly/9JXSk*).

Therefore, expectations and their rules are key to turning your application into a fail-fast system. The iterations enable you to improve your applications and their results and tune the expectations as you progress. Plus, implementing the observations and rules "at the source" makes it easier for you to find the cause of the problem.

Similarly, a fail-safe system can also stop the process as early as possible, focusing on preventing the whole system from crashing (although you can still use it) and minimizing the effects on the other components.

For the data application part of the pipeline, introducing expectations as preconditions to execute logic or write (update) their results has the following effects on failures:

- Stops their behavior early.
- Provides enough observations to identify the reason.
- Avoids "garbage in-garbage out" from invading the remaining pipelines.

However, the application might still be up and running and accept other tasks, because the failure was inherently due to the situation it ran into, not its behavior.

Simplify Tests and Extend CI/CD

After reading about expectations and the introduction of rules, a sense of similarity might come to your mind. You might think of rules as unit or functional tests, because they usually represent examples of situations based on sample data and validate an implementation against its results. A test validates two types of outcomes: a thrown exception (or the code that errored) or a match of the expected value.

With expectations and associated rules, we haven't deviated from the test behavior and function. They were introduced to validate that the observations, which represent the status (by definition of data observability), match the expected values or behavior.

Therefore, making your application data observable by introducing those rules is similar to data testing in production, not data testing alone. But we're not really testing in the sense of how testing is conceived in engineering, which is why we prefer to use the concepts *validating in production* or *continuous validation*.

There's a big advantage to leaving the rules in the main production code versus creating tests with the validation logic running against sample datasets (or pre-production data dumps). That is, by nature, the rules in data observability test the intrinsic logic, and not only the implemented logic, which can be correct for certain predefined cases but still flawed intrinsically.

The other advantage of having the rules within the application is that it's collocated with the logic. Therefore, when reviewing the implementation, you don't need to jump between test cases and the logic to understand how it should work or to update a wide range of tests. Of course, when the logic changes, you must refactor the rules, but you don't have to refactor the "test," which is conceptually different.

Another advantage of this practice is you can't deactivate the tests. Period.

Nonetheless, you still need tests. If we focus on the ones related to data observability, they can be largely limited to testing a single type of outcome in a situation where the rules are throwing exceptions. For this reason, tests are much simpler because most, if not all, of the test logic is in the main application source.

Consequently, in CI/CD, continuous integration means everyone saves their code in the main code base, and then tests and builds it. Continuous deployment refers to when the built deliverables are deployed automatically in several environments until production. This practice requires a certain level of commitment by your engineers (especially for testing) and can be extended with continuous validation.

Conclusion

By implementing the practices described in this chapter, data practitioners can experience several advantages.

Introducing expectations helps maintain data quality and build trust among stakeholders. Shifting left allows for early detection and resolution of issues, reducing the impact on downstream processes. Utilizing data profilers and service level indicators provides insights and metrics for monitoring and improving data applications.

In addition, employing fail-fast and fail-safe practices ensures prompt identification of failures and minimizes their impact. And lastly, integrating continuous validation into the CI/CD pipeline enhances the overall efficiency and reliability of data systems.

These practices collectively contribute to a more robust and trustworthy data ecosystem.

You're now ready to shift another gear up and see some of the methods presented in this chapter in action for several frameworks, languages, and tools you are using (or similar ones). Let's get our hands dirtier.

Data Observability in Action

## CHAPTER 7

Integrating Data Observability in Your Data Stack

In the previous chapter, you learned about the three components of data observability, and how to apply data observability in your day to day data work. In this chapter, we will get our hands dirty and put these concepts to work.

The goals of this chapter are to provide recipes that will help you integrate data observability in your pipelines, provide technical materials to up-skill your capabilities to make your frameworks and applications data observable—then, as a good chef would do with any recipe, you will personalize it, extend it, improve it. I will explain the proper steps to follow, the purpose of each step, and how it works. Spoiler alert: it will get pretty technical from time to time—almost nerdy—but trust me, it's worth it.

To give this chapter a logical flow, I will follow the data engineering lifecycle introduced by Joe Reis and Matt Housley in the *Fundamentals of Data Engineering* (Figure 7-1).

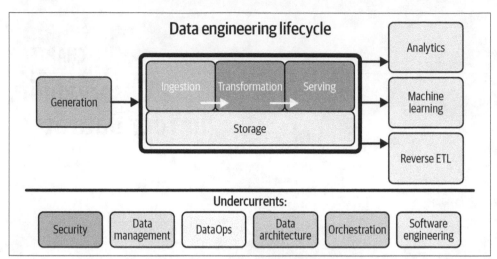

Figure 7-1. The Data Engineering Lifecycle[1] (Courtesy of Joe Reis and Matthew Housley)

Data observability resides in the undercurrents of data engineering, as part of DataOps. To generate the values discussed in Chapter 2, the data observability platform must be present in both the data architecture and the undercurrents layer. While I won't discuss the *generation* stage much, I will cover *ingestion, transformation*, and *serving*, and provide examples of how data observability supports their operations.

Data observability extends quite naturally to what the data engineering lifecycle produces, and the responsibility to satisfy consumers is inherent to the mindset I have presented so far in this book. Therefore, I will also cover the data products built upon the served data, especially analytics (e.g., reporting) and machine learning.

Let's start with the ingestion stage.

Ingestion Stage

The ingestion stage consists of moving data from the source, where business applications are deployed and used. Data engineers have the least control over the applications, data, and the teams generating it. At times it's similar to working with third-party vendors. So, ingestion is moving data from one system to another where we do have control over it.

---

1 Joe Reis and Matt Housley, "Chapter 1," in *Fundamentals of Data Engineering* (*https://oreil.ly/GkOBU*) (O'Reilly Media, 2022).

Therefore, ingestion is the first line of visibility, as this is where most downstream issues originate. Ingestion is, in fact, the stage when you can anticipate most *datastrophes*[2] and prevent dramatic propagations (aka *data cascades*[3]).

The first step in ingestion is connecting with external or siloed data sources. At this stage, the data team loses full control over the process. To regain its influence and more control, the data team must create higher visibility to clearly communicate their requests, backing them with facts such as metrics, trends, etc. Otherwise, the other party is likely to turn down or deprioritize all requests, thus leaving the data team in a situation where the data must be continuously "cleaned," instead of fixing the issue at the source.

As represented in Figure 7-2, ingestion is the first line of defense, but it is also where there is less knowledge about what must be validated, as the purpose of the data pipeline is to refine, combine, and generate more advanced insights. Moreover, the number of impacts fans out, as the data moves downstream toward many usages, which implies that data cascades starting here have greater impact (butterfly or snowball effect). Therefore, because root cause analysis will often stop here, ingestion must be checked and updated regularly. Catching events in ingestion can avoid about 85% of the issues downstream, if not more. But because of a lack of knowledge, or because it is hard to anticipate all use cases in advance without exploding the number of checks, good ingestion practices usually evolve as a consequence of post-mortems or because some metrics tracked anticipatively are already capable of highlighting anomalies. For example, an ingested data source could have one field used as a filter in some transformations, split into several groups to perform segmentations, and aggregated with another field from another data source to compute a business KPI. This list of usages can go on and on, and thus the chances to implement all related checks at the very beginning (ingestion) is daunting, if not impossible; actually, I would almost say that it is so unlikely as to be irrelevant.

---

2 Andy Petrella, "Datastrophes: Il Buono, il Brutto, il Cattivo," *Medium*, March 2, 2021, *https://oreil.ly/OT6xl*.

3 Nithya Sambasivan, Shivani Kapania, Hannah Highfill, Diana Akrong, Praveen Paritosh, and Lora M. Aroyo. "'Everyone wants to do the model work, not the data work': Data Cascades in High-Stakes AI." In proceedings of the 2021 CHI Conference on Human Factors in Computing Systems, 2021, pp. 1–15, *https://oreil.ly/Hs6MX*.

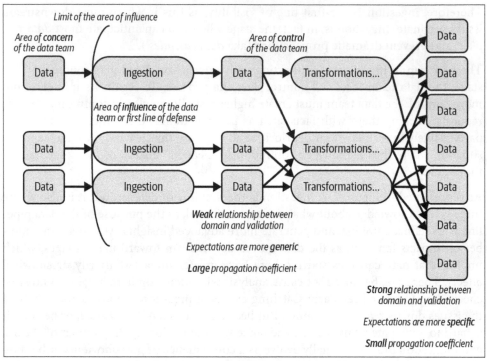

Figure 7-2. Ingestion is the first line of defense

Adding anticipated metrics so early may be considered useless, though, because the data is quite raw and little semantic knowledge is attached to the information ingested. For example, one may be tempted to produce for each field in a JSON file a bunch of metrics such as `min`, `max`, `stddev`, `mean`, `quantiles{1, 5, 25, 50, 75, 95, 99}`, `unique count`, `null values`, `skewness`. So, with 14 metrics for each field to be computed and observed, for a JSON structure with 100 fields in its schema, this will yield 1,400 metrics, and so 1,400 timeseries as the pipeline runs. Consider that the pipeline uses 10 data sources like this, and you end up in 14,000 timeseries, which can seem daunting and can overload the data observability platform with much information that may never be used. However, in my opinion, the individual "expected value" of these metrics is still huge in the event of an issue associated with the corresponding field.

Therefore, defining the semantics and usefulness of observations is a challenge, and so is the cost of producing, storing, and analyzing them. This challenge decreases in importance as we move down in the pipeline toward the business output, as the data gains in semantic and contextual usage; therefore, it becomes easier to generate observations from the outcomes (e.g., KPIs) as the number of options also diminishes.

Consequently, it is often preferred to start with a minimal set of observations (especially metrics) and increase them over time. This is mainly due to the associated cost and management overhead. If observations are reduced to a negligible amount (as will happen over time), their majority will be produced, and discovered, at ingestion time. Nevertheless, this shouldn't be surprising, as when a software goes to production, engineers tend to decrease the level of logging from DEBUG to WARN but can then increase it during troubleshooting.

In the next section, I will cover some technologies to ingest data into the data platform and discuss how data observability capabilities can be added to each of them. I will also cover what may have been provided by the technology to prevent users (us, in this case) from extending the capabilities ourselves.

Ingestion Stage Data Observability Recipes

In this section, I will highlight the Airbyte technology that performs ingestion by copying sources to destinations. Airbyte's core engine is implemented in Java, and I will use an approach to make it data observable based on Java capabilities such as bytecode injection. This approach can be reused easily for any other technologies based on the JVM, such as ingestion, Debezium,[4] Kafka Connect, or Apache Flink. However, ingestion is not limited to JVM technologies; for example, the Python ecosystem is rich in options (e.g., Airflow, Singer (*https://oreil.ly/Rkapm*)). In fact, for Python, the approach I will use in this section can be adapted to the Python capabilities to achieve the same results, which I will introduce in the dbt section.

Airbyte Agent

Airbyte (*https://oreil.ly/3X7cH*) is an open source Java-based data integration platform that replicates data from the long tail of APIs, databases, and files to data warehouses, lakes, and other destinations. Airbyte comes with a protocol to extract and load (EL) data in a serialized form (JSON messages), which is already available as open source connectors for many data sources. While ingesting data, you can also normalize the messages using the embedded dbt (covered in the next section), which will, for example, linearize the deep structure in the ingested JSON messages (e.g., {"name" : {"first": …} } normalized as name.first). Moreover, Airbyte has developer kits to easily and rapidly implement new connectors (or customize them).

The transfer of data between the source and the destination implements the Airbyte protocol (*https://oreil.ly/xbr0r*), which describes a series of standard components and all the interactions between them in order to declare an ELT pipeline. All messages are passed across components via serialized JSON messages for inter-process

---

4 Also used by Airbyte (*https://oreil.ly/i-7gP*) to perform CDC.

communication. The processes run inside *workers*, between which the data is transferred using `stdin` and `stdout`.

Figure 7-3 shows the architecture involving the workers and their interactions with the Airbyte scheduler that takes care of their lifecycle via the temporal service. Thus, the JSON messages are exchanged between the *source* (e.g., PostgreSQL) and *destination* (e.g., Snowflake) workers.

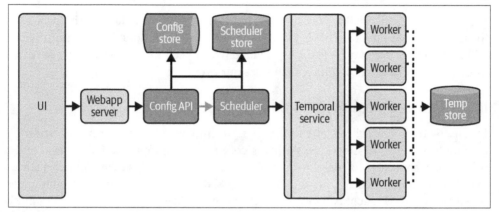

Figure 7-3. Airbyte architecture overview (https://oreil.ly/xbr0r)

Airbyte makes available some data observations via its API (*https://oreil.ly/1qCz5*), such as:

Get a connection
Application and lineage

Get information about a job
Application execution and lineage execution: At the time of writing, Airbyte includes data observability capabilities via the MessageTracker (*https://oreil.ly/c94x5*), which is a Java class that accumulates information (observations) about the execution of a connection between a source and a destination, such as:

- Get the overall emitted record count.
- Data metrics for the input data source (source).
- Get the overall committed record count.
- Data metrics for the target data source (destination).

We could also consume data from the logs combined with API calls to create some observations. However, that would only partially cover the model introduced in Chapter 2, and we'd miss important information; thus that method does not provide the value we expect from data observability.

This is true for all technologies I cover in this chapter. For the time being, while Airbyte is not yet supporting data observations (which will most likely happen over time), let's extend it to cover the missing pieces.

Because you likely already have Airbyte jobs (connections) deployed and running in your platform, the work needed to change all jobs to generate data observations could be daunting. So in this section, to minimize those efforts, I am showing you a strategy that will inject data observation generation capabilities at a lower level, the Airbyte core, as shown in Figure 7-4.

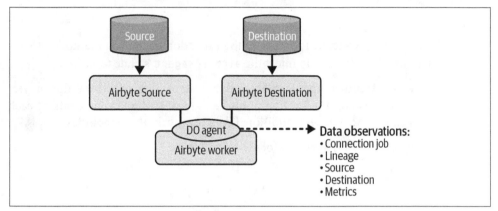

Figure 7-4. Airbyte data observability agent extending the Airbyte core engine

As explained in the introduction, Airbyte has a component called a *worker*, which is responsible for the execution of the replication jobs. The worker's code is in Airbyte's GitHub as a module called `airbyte-workers`.

The worker executes the jobs configured in Airbyte, the replication and the normalization. The first replicates the source into the destination (the extract and load parts of ELT) and the latter transforms the raw data created by Airbyte in the destination into the required form. If normalization has not been configured, the raw data will be replicated as is to the final destination table.

The normalization step is not covered here, as it will be covered in the next section, so I will concentrate on replication jobs in this section.

Replication is defined in a Java interface called `ReplicationWorker`, which mainly contains a run function using a `StandardSyncInput` (replication configuration) to produce a `ReplicationOutput` (summary information of the process). Both objects are defined in the Airbyte `config-models`—the model objects of the Airbyte protocol defined using the Open API standard.

Because we want to enable data observability for the replication job, generating observations about the source, destination, lineage, and metrics is a good starting point.

We'll use bytecode injection (see Chapter 5) to avoid changing, recompiling, and redeploying the Java code.

The code for this agent is available in the book's repository (*https://oreil.ly/BE1Y1*) and is composed of two Java projects:

`airbyte-agent`
> Implements the generation of data observations. The `airbyte-agent` initializes the client that logs the observations, extracts metadata from the source and destination, and computes metrics for them.

`airbyte-instrumentation`
> Implements the `javaagent` to intercept the execution of the `run` method before it is loaded into the JVM and to inject the `airbyte-agent`'s code to it.

> If you need to extend another Java-based data system such as Airbyte, this project combination gives you the starting point. Let's look at the key elements of each project to extend Airbyte with additional data observability capabilities.

The Airbyte agent project defines the following concepts:

Agent Factory
> A factory that can generate new data observability clients.

Agent
> The agent is performing most of the actions, such as extracting metadata using the processors and complementing them when data is read (`handleMessage Read`), mapped (`handleMessageMapped`), and copied (`handleMessageCopied`)—including the generation of data metrics. In addition, the agent is initialized with project information, so the application and related entities of the core model can be generated.

Processor
> A processor can be defined for the source and destination. It is responsible for generating metadata (data source, schema) of the data sources being replicated.

While the Airbyte agent isn't in the code base, this project extends Airbyte's capabilities by using its internal concepts, and we can inject it there.

We need to look at the Airbyte instrumentation project to inject this code, which produces a JVM-Agent capable of executing code before the application's `main` is executed. To do this, it uses a JVM capability, called the `Premain` class.

Supporting Data Sources in Airbyte

You will see this pattern often in the data engineering tools ecosystem, and I'll come back to it often in this section. The source and destination in Airbyte are an abstraction that allows the tool to be extended and support new data sources; therefore, it defines a contract (API) to read and write to them. For the agent to support exhaustively all types of data sources (e.g., CSV, BigQuery, MySQL, Snowflake, etc.), it needs to be updated to support each of them, which can seem complex, especially as new data sources are continuously added to the Airbyte catalog. Alternatively, if this responsibility is introduced in Airbyte's abstraction layer (*source* and *destination* contracts), then data observability would be implemented by design, and you wouldn't need the information in this section about the agent.

The `Premain` class (*https://oreil.ly/gehi_*), provided by the jar attached to the Airbyte worker JVM using the `javaagent` property, is a class that is supposed to be executed before the `main` class, as its name suggests (premain). The `Premain` class is a special class; the JVM knows that it must call its static method `premain` before the `main` one. This gives us the opportunity to inject the Airbyte agent code into the `Replication Worker` before it gets used.

Example 7-1 shows the signature of the `premain` method.

Example 7-1. Signature of the JVM-Agent's premain method

```
public static void premain(String agentArgs, Instrumentation inst)
```

The `Instrumentation` argument passed to `premain` by the JVM is used to transform the bytecode as it is loaded. To achieve this, we can use its method `addTransformer`, to which we're providing an instance of a `ClassFileTransformer`. The JVM will pass all loaded classes to this transformer, including the `ReplicationWorker`, that we can intercept as shown in Example 7-2.

Example 7-2. Intercept a class using JVM-Agent Premain

```
public byte[] transform(ClassLoader l, String name, Class c, ProtectionDomain d,
                        byte[] b) {
  // The class to be injected
  if(name.equals("io/airbyte/workers/general/DefaultReplicationWorker")) {
    // [...]
```

As shown in Example 7-2, the `transform` method is also provided as an argument (the variable b), with the bytecode for the class as a `byte[]`, that we can transform with the Airbyte agent code before returning it. This can be done with the ASM library discussed in Chapter 5, using four classes:

ClassReader
> Reads the bytecode of the class into the structure that can be visited by a ClassVisitor.

ClassWriter
> Writes a provided structure from a ClassReader and writes it as bytecode (byte[]).

ClassVisitor
> Wraps a ClassWriter, which will delegate to the ClassVisitor's visiting methods (e.g., visitMethod, visitCode) the information from the ClassReader so that it can transform them before being written.

MethodVisitor
> Instantiated by a ClassVisitor's visitMethod, it has its own set of visiting methods to transform the contents of methods.

The ClassVisitor is the most important piece of code to analyze to understand how to turn the Airbyte process into a data observable one. Even though the instrumentation is relatively simple and straightforward, its code is quite long. Therefore, I will focus only on the key aspects.

The instrumentation implements a ClassVisitor for the ReplicationWorker that intercepts its run method by overriding the visitMethod. When the run method is intercepted, it uses ASM to include a call to the AgentFactory (from the airbyte-agent project) and instantiate a new agent for the replication work.

To do so, the instrumentation defines an instance of a MethodVisitor which intercepts the three main steps of the replication process for each message, which are the following:

- Its read from the source: by intercepting a call to the function attemptRead on the Source object and calling the agent's handleMessageRead to generate observations about the source.

- Its mapping to the destination format: by intercepting a call to mapMessage and calling the agent's handleMessageMapped methods to maintain the information about the lineage.

- Its write into the destination: by intercepting a call to accept and calling the agent's handleMessageCopied method to complete the lineage and generate observations about the destination.

With this in place, the replication process is fully observable, and data metrics are accumulated to the source and destination from each message that is read, mapped, and written.

Using bytecode injection helped us add data observability capabilities to existing Airbyte servers. However, we'd prefer that Airbyte itself exposes its data observations, to allow a data observability platform to consolidate them in the global picture. This is what we discuss next.

Transformation

The ingestion stage provides the first line of defense against incoming data, and its inherent responsibility is limited to moving data from A (e.g., an operational data store (*https://oreil.ly/oyHqQ*)) to B (e.g., a data lake). However, the complexity doesn't come from what is done with the data, but from the lack of control we have over the incoming data.

The transformation stage, however, is dedicated to manipulating the ingested data into as many forms as needed for downstream usages such as analytics or machine learning, or more generally, data products. Therefore, what is important to create at this stage is visibility about how the transformations are behaving, including their interactions, along pipelines. This is because, assuming that the data is somewhat under control at the ingestion stage, issues happening in the transformation stage are most likely associated with inappropriate transformations that could be due to misunderstandings: about business needs, time-related expectations about the data, and other larger issues.

Consequently, in this section, I will focus on how to create data observations about the manipulations of the data, and which observations are interesting to generate and can handle issues more easily. For this, I will use two different technologies, Apache Spark, then dbt.

Transformation Stage Data Observability Recipes

In this section, I will explore recipes for making data observable in two major technologies commonly used for data transformation: Apache Spark and dbt. These technologies play crucial roles in large-scale data processing and transforming data within data warehouses, respectively.

By following these recipes, you will learn how to incorporate data observability practices into your Apache Spark workflows and dbt transformations. I will provide step-by-step instructions, best practices, and code examples to guide you through the process of generating data observations, integrating them into your workflows, and leveraging the power of data observability in these technologies.

Whether you are already using Apache Spark or dbt, or if you are considering adopting these technologies in your data pipeline, these recipes will serve as valuable resources to enhance the reliability, quality, and trustworthiness of your data processes. You will gain insights into how to monitor and control your data transformations, identify and address issues, and ensure that your data workflows are operating as expected.

By embracing data observability in Apache Spark and dbt, you will be able to unlock the full potential of these technologies and empower your data teams to make data-driven decisions with confidence. Let's dive into the recipes and explore how data observability can improve your data transformation workflows.

Apache Spark

Transforming data at scale has historically challenged data engineers, until Apache Hadoop popularized MapReduce. However, Hadoop was not straightforward to set up and use. For example, after installing several projects, when you wanted to test your first project, you had to create a Maven project, create a few Java classes with your business logic decomposed into a `Map-phase` and a `Reduce-phase`, and finally combine those. It was not easy for big data to become mainstream (i.e., usable by many more people), as the entry barrier was too high. Eventually, this is what Apache Spark succeeded at doing, as a consequence of these two things:

- Using Scala as the programming language, leveraging the functional approach pre-Java8 and the Scala interactive shell.
- Introducing a new paradigm to implement `MapReduce` jobs called Resilient Distributed Dataset (RDD), the functional alternative to the `MapReduce` classes implemented at the `Collection` level.

As Spark became the de facto standard for manipulating data, it embraced the Data-Frame API, which follows relational principles and therefore offers SQL-like capabilities. This introduction expanded the scope of Spark, which had been limited to Scala users, to include the Python and SQL communities.

We'll see in this section how we can leverage one of the core aspects of Spark to accurately generate many data observations through automation. This approach uses directed acyclic graphs, or DAGs, resulting from using RDDs to compose functional (descriptive) computations.

The DAG is not a unique Spark concept per se, but it has been further popularized by Spark. For example, DAGs have been embraced by the Google ML library Tensor-Flow (*https://oreil.ly/KftBj*) as well as by high-level tools like open source orchestrators (e.g., Prefect, Airflow), which will be covered later in this chapter.

A DAG is key to supporting data observability in Spark, similarly to any DAG-based framework. It provides the support to generate important observations on how data is composed, as this capability is natively available in its structure. Each vertex in the graph represents a function applied to the incoming input to generate outputs that will be, in turn, consumed by other vertices. Hence, by making each vertex data observable, the whole graph becomes one, because data is only moving from one vertex to another. In other words, each vertex represents a micro application, a micro-transformation on data in flight (not stored on physical storage; for example, see Figure 7-5). It is worth noting that a DAG is the theoretical representation of a programming paradigm, called dataflow programming (*https://oreil.ly/Zsqw9*), dedicated to solving computing issues with sequential programming that requires the (data) state to be managed by the developer in a distributed environment. Spark is one of the libraries that follows this paradigm.

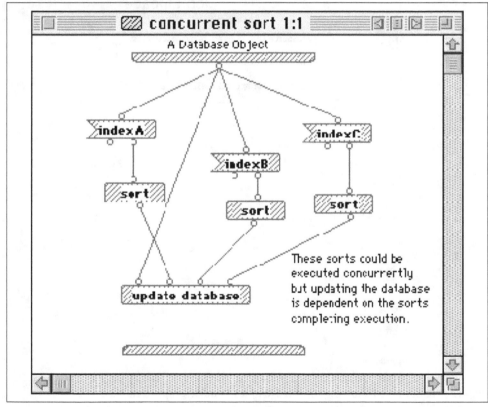

Figure 7-5. A database sorting operation implemented in Prograph (https://oreil.ly/k0k0j) in the 1980–90s

Because Spark is deployed at scale in many organizations, some efforts have been made to extend its capabilities with data observability, such as the Spline project.

Spline

Spline (*https://oreil.ly/eq2fP*) is an external component that generates observations about data applications, data source metadata (location, schema), lineage, and execution information.

Adding Spline to a Spark job involves adding the Spline agent to the Spark classpath and installing the Spline server (and the associated ArangoDB database) to aggregate the observations that will be presented in the Spline UI, as shown in Figure 7-6.

Figure 7-6. Spline UI showing the lineage of a Databricks Spark application

The Spline Spark agent can be initialized in a codeless fashion by adding the configuration to the job shown in Example 7-3.

Example 7-3. Spline agent codeless configuration

```
--conf "spark.sql.queryExecutionListeners=za.co.absa.spline.harvester.listener. ⌁
SplineQueryExecutionListener" \
--conf "spark.spline.lineageDispatcher.http.producer.url= ⌁
http://localhost:9090/producer"
```

From the configuration, we can see that this agent will use the events generated by Spark to create visibility about some situations, such as writing to a data store.

For this, Spline uses a component that Spark has already exposed, the QueryExecu tionListener (*https://oreil.ly/n5XrP*), which defines this method: onSuccess(func Name: String, qe: QueryExecution, durationNs: Long). In fact, Spark triggers many SparkListenerEvents (*https://oreil.ly/j21sn*), and these can be used to generate observations such as the data lineage and data metrics. The onSuccess function, however, intercepts mainly the events related to the job after successful completion. Therefore, when a job is successfully executed, Spline can extract data observations from the QueryExecution object provided to the function.

The QueryExecution is key in this scenario because it contains a reference to the LogicalPlan that represents the DAG of the executed job. Hence, by traversing the graph of computation encoded in the LogicalPlan, Spline can extract references to the data sources used by the job, as well as their schema and associated lineage.

At first glance, this is all fantastic, as it seems Spark combined with Spline implements a lot of what we have described in the first chapter. Nevertheless, one notable downside is that Spline's architecture is fundamentally Spark-centric and highly coupled to its own server and UI. We want to allow the data observations to be used across technologies to provide a holistic view of the data system, and therefore accelerate tedious operational processes such as root cause analysis.

Therefore, we need to intercept the observations generated by Spline and convert them into the core mode (at least), and allow them to be made available to a data observability platform. To accomplish this, we can use the CompositeLineageDis patcher provided by Spline, which allows us to dispatch the observations to the original Spline server but can also be adapted to use alternative endpoints, such as files or another HTTP server.

Several patterns can be implemented to achieve this conversion and redispatching, like sending the observation to the data observability platform, which converts them into the core model (cf. Chapter 2) or implementing a dedicated LineageDispatcher (*https://oreil.ly/7_EXr*) that performs this conversion into the model itself.

The latter option allows the observations to be manipulated and linked, following the core model, directly in the agent, instead of arriving disconnected to another service that will have to reconsolidate the graph. This is significant, as we are talking about

HTTP communication and could potentially be dealing with the need to order the observations by arrival time.

Example 7-4 shows a skeleton of what such a custom dispatcher could look like (in Scala).

Example 7-4. Spline custom dispatcher

```scala
class FODOLineageDispatcher(conf: Configuration)
      extends LineageDispatcher with Logging {
  type DataObservationBase = Any
  type Observations = List[DataObservationBase]

  // Create client to publish data observations using configuration
  val client:Any = ???

  // Navigate the plan to convert it into the core model
  def convertIntoDataObservations(plan:ExecutionPlan):Observations = ???

  // Send observations to a platform, a file, or anything collecting them
  // Use client to publish
  def reportDataObservations(obs: Observations):Unit = ???

  override def send(plan: ExecutionPlan): Unit =
    reportDataObservations(convertIntoDataObservations(plan))

  override def send(event: ExecutionEvent): Unit = ()
}
```

To use this dispatcher, you will need to build it in a jar, put it on the classpath of your Spark application, and configure Spline to use it, as shown in Example 7-5.

Example 7-5. Configure the custom dispatcher

```
spline.lineageDispatcher.cust.className fodo.ch4.transformation.FODOLineageDispatcher
spline.lineageDispatcher cust
```

This way, you will skip the Spline server (installation and usage) but use your own data observations collection strategy. Nevertheless, if you want to keep both options, there is also the possibility of using the *composite dispatcher*.

Using the strategy presented so far, we can leverage the information gathered by Spline in the ExecutionPlan to generate the observations, as presented in Chapter 2. Here is the information available in its JSON representation:

name
> The name of the application that ran the job (e.g., Databricks Shell)

operations
> Contains the information about the job's structure, including:
>
> - write: Information about the data source created or updated by the job. This contains the location of the data source (e.g., file path) and its format (e.g., parquet). It also embeds an extra field that can be used to attach additional information (see next section)
> - reads: Information about the data sources used by the job to generate the data written. This is an array of entries having the same information as in write for each data source used.
> - other: Information about the operation performed (e.g., joins, subquery).

expressions
> Contains information about the functions and constants used in the job.

attributes
> The entries in operations and expressions refer to columns or fields used by the job to generate the output. Those are detailed in this array, which contains an entry for each with information about the name and a reference to its type.

extraInfo
> Additional information that can be extended also typically contains:
>
> - appName: Can be changed to match the application name, instead of the job name introduced earlier.
> - dataTypes: Provide information about the data types for the attributes.

We can see that Spline generates a lot of information that will help us generate a big part of the core model. Spline was primarily created to support compliance requirements (e.g., GDPR, BCBS239), so its capabilities are well adapted for those use cases. In Figure 7-7 you can see which part of the core model you can cover from Spline.

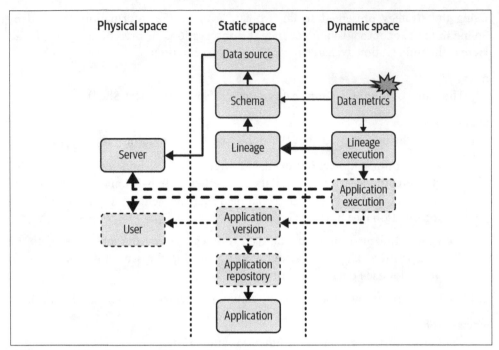

Figure 7-7. Spline's core model coverage and its extensions

Figure 7-7 shows that a big part of the model can be extracted from Spline information (represented by the solid lines).

Here is a further breakdown of the information available and how it relates to the core model:

Application
: Using `name` or `appName`.

Data source
: From `write` and `reads`.

Server
: From `write` and `reads` we can extract where the data resides. But we don't have information about the server executing the application.

Schema
: From `attributes`, as referred from `operations` and `expressions`, combined with `dataTypes`.

Lineage
: By interpreting the `operations` and `expressions`.

Lineage Execution

The job completed with the plan, or the ExecutionEvent can be used.

Next, we can see that Figure 7-7's dashed lines represent the information that can be generated from the application's runtime during the interception of the plan:

Application execution

This can be extracted from the runtime (e.g., System.currentTimeMillis to retrieve when the application is running).

Server

We can use local code to extract the information about the server (or cluster) running the Spark job.

User

The information about who is running the application can be fetched from the runtime (e.g., $USER). However, it is trickier to know who developed it.

The last part of the model covered by a Spline-based agent is shown by the dotted lines and must be retrieved by integrating it with the environment that built the job, such as the SBT project definition, for example. The idea is to generate information such as its application repository (e.g., git URL), application version (e.g., git tag, or version defined in SBT), and user (e.g., git committer) at the build time, and make it available at runtime, for example in a *manifest* file. Note that this can also be added as a continuous integration step.

As stated, some capabilities of data observability are missing in Spline, namely data metrics. Let's see how we can take Spline to the next level in the next section.

Going beyond the compliance use case

At the time of writing, Spline is focused on collecting data observations from the static space, such as the data source, schema, and lineage. The other kind of observations, taken from the dynamic space, that Spline collects is pipeline metrics, which are part of application observability (in this case, a subset called pipeline observability). However, with just these pipeline metrics, we miss an important part of the dynamic space of the core model, the data metrics to control the behavior of the data during its usage or creation.

In this section, I will provide the key elements that allow you to extend Spline with this capability. Because the full implementation can get pretty complex, I will present a high-level picture of the code. However, the book repository contains a good starting point to work on the agent you can add to your projects (or you can use an existing implementation such as the one provided by Kensu (*https://oreil.ly/kBVgZ*)).

We want to create additional visibility about the data going in and out of a job, not just where it is, but what it looks like, from the content perspective. That way, if something goes wrong, we have many observations at hand to explore the issues, or, if we want to detect something, it can be done during the execution of the job. Execution provides us with the last chance to address issues before falling into the garbage in-garbage out scenario (again), or failing the job after "write" has happened due to incorrect data having been written. So we want data metrics.

To do that with Spline, we can use an extension mechanism called "filter." A "post processing filter," in fact, which gives us hooks to update some parts of the Execution Plan used in the previous section to generate the model. These hooks can apply to five cases:

- Data read
- Data written
- Data operation executed
- Execution plan available
- Execution event (more general)

The cases we are interested in the most are when the data is read and written,[5] as they allow us to generate observations about the data involved in the job.

To do so, we have to implement a post-processing filter by extending the Abstract PostProcessingFilter (*https://oreil.ly/ivWUM*) (default empty implementation), adding it to our agent, and then configuring Spline to use it. The skeleton of such a filter is available in the book's repository. Here are a few things to keep in mind:

Generating metrics
    To generate metrics on the data read or written, we can leverage Spark itself. To do this, we can browse the LogicalPlan provided by the hook, which can be turned into a DataFrame with a trick that is hidden in the Spark code base: Dataset.ofRows(spark, plan). Using the returned DataFrame, we can easily generate many observations by design (automatically) such as the amount of data (count), distinct values, null values, or even statistics (e.g., min, stddev, or skewness).

Making metrics available
    Because metrics are not defined in the Spline model, we have to use the extra Info to save the generated data metrics for each data source. This is not very convenient, as we lose the types or the structure of the object given to us, but it is a convention that can be used easily and shared with the dispatcher (introduced in the previous section) that will encode them in the model.

---

5 Nevertheless, the operation executed could be extremely interesting as an extension of the core model.

Another Approach

For the sake of simplicity, the example in the repository relies only on the ExecutionPlan, not on the reads and writes of the data. However, the same approach can be applied by decoupling the work across the different events instead of only when the plan is available.

For Spline to apply this filter, it simply needs to be in the same jar as the dispatcher on the classpath, and those configurations must be added to the job:

```
spline.lineageDispatcher.cust.className fodo.ch4.transformation. ⤶
FODOLineageDispatcher
spline.postProcessingFilter fodo-filter
spline.postProcessingFilter.fodo-filter.className …FODOPostProcessingFilter
```

The configurations define which filter needs to be applied (fodo-filter) and which class is implementing it (fodo.ch4.transformation.FODOPostProcessingFilter).

For completeness, it is also worth noting that since its version 3.3, Spark has started to introduce "observations" as this book defines them. In fact, there is now an "observe" function provided directly by the DataFrame interface that allows additional metrics to be computed alongside the Spark job. Therefore, the engineer developing the job can "instrument" it directly with them, and they will be available in the filter, so that they can be added to the extraInfo before saving them contextually with the other observations. This is a nice way to introduce "custom metrics" as opposed to the default metrics that are generated automatically by the agent. Such custom metrics are generally extremely important, as they are based on domain knowledge instead of being generic. They can be quite complex (e.g., multiplying fields, or even involving several data sources).

This section shows how an existing agent can be extended to generate additional information about a technology such as Spark. Over the years, one of these agents will proliferate for most technologies, so it is worth keeping an eye on them (such as those provided by Kensu). Also, as discussed, the data technologies will likely embrace them directly by requiring external agents, as Spark started to do with the "observe" method. Next, let's look at another data transformation tool that can be extended from its Python core, this time to generate data observations—namely, dbt.

dbt Agent

dbt is an SQL-first transformation workflow facilitating best practices such as modularity, testing, and documentation. dbt has gained popularity over the years by leveraging SQL to simplify the work of building data models without necessarily requiring coding skills (e.g., Python or Spark).

Given that dbt is responsible for transforming data sources, it must also be data observable, and some aspects are already available out-of-the-box. In this section, we will see what is available, then show how a system such as dbt can be extended with additional data observability capabilities.

When defining a model in dbt, the engineer builds an SQL query that will rely on either *seed* or other *models*. In their simplest form, a seed is a file that will be loaded into a model, and a model is a relational database table. Along the lifecycle of a dbt project, the system will generate observations about the job, which are available in the following artifacts as JSON files generated by dbt commands (e.g., `build`, `compile`, `run`, `test`)[6]:

- *Manifest:*[7] Contains much information, such as models and lineage.
- *Catalog:*[8] Contains the metadata of the data (e.g., schema, location).
- *Run results:*[9] Contains the results of commands, including the tests.

Another artifact is the *sources* that contain a specific type of check performed by dbt itself: the freshness test. This test provides metrics (and associated checks) about the data at the moment of its usage.

Other Approaches With dbt

The good news is that dbt already embraces data observability, as most of the observations of the core model are produced. Nevertheless, collecting them requires extra effort, to combine the information coming from all these files, which may not even be produced in certain circumstances (e.g., failures).

Therefore, an agent for dbt that produces the observations in the core model along with the process could be invoked by adding an external component that would collect the information from those files when they are ready. This can be relatively easily achieved. However, it would probably have to run outside of the "box," which is contrary to the notion of "Observability" on page 79 as defined in Chapter 1.

Such as the external listener provided by the open source data catalog, DataHub, which connects to the dbt HTTP endpoint or s3 to retrieve, parse, and process those files to create data catalog entries.

---

6 You can read about dbt artifacts on the dbt Developer Hub (*https://oreil.ly/bJiTq*).

7 dbt Developer Hub has more information about the Manifest JSON file (*https://oreil.ly/5sHcw*).

8 See the dbt Developer Hub to learn more about the Catalog JSON file (*https://oreil.ly/w0rZS*).

9 See the dbt Developer Hub to learn more about the Run results JSON file (*https://oreil.ly/ljfaT*).

Moreover, as in the Spark case, the data metrics aren't exposed in the JSON file. We could consider using the data metrics generated by the dbt tests, which means that the *test* also needs to be run in production. However, we need to consider only invariant tests instead of conditional tests, which are valid only given predefined testing datasets. Therefore, data metrics could be provided by dbt if tests are well defined as expectations under any conditions, and the dbt test command is set to always be run in production.

Now, I will propose another approach that consists of extending the dbt-core module (the central engine of dbt) with additional capabilities, which can leverage the information used to produce the artifacts but can also add more capabilities, such as the generation of data metrics for the seed and models.

For this, I will guide you on how to extend an existing Python application such as dbt-core, to introduce the data observability directly in the engine. This agent will use a technique introduced in Chapter 5, the AST-based transformation of the code at runtime.

---

dbt-cloud versus dbt-core

The term dbt-core refers to the dbt framework that can be cloned from GitHub or cloned from Python repositories. This avoids confusion with dbt-cloud, which is the SaaS version of the framework.

To use this strategy, we need to dig deeper into the dbt core code available on GitHub (*https://oreil.ly/0gBrP*) to analyze where we can ingest, as we did for the Airbyte agent, the needed functionality that will intercept or generate the observations.

First, when dbt runs, it will run a task. A task is implemented as a class called `Model Runner`. This class is responsible for running what was developed by the engineer, and therefore what we want to make observable by default.

A `ModelRunner` can mainly[10] represent a seed task or a model itself, and an instance of that class contains all the observations or will give us the opportunity to generate what is not provided by default. This happens in its execute method (*https://oreil.ly/n_c8t*), defined in Example 7-6.

Example 7-6. dbt ModelRunner.execute method signature

```
def execute(self, model, manifest):
```

---

10 It can also represent a Snapshot, which generates information about the changes over time. I didn't cover this part, as it is a practice to control what happens on data, not to build data.

As we can see, this method has the knowledge of the model to be executed but also the *manifest,* which gives us access to the artifacts introduced earlier, as in Example 7-7.

Example 7-7. Generate dbt context (artifacts)

```
context = generate_runtime_model_context(model, self.config, manifest)
```

This will give us the information about the job (name, sources, etc.). Therefore, this is a good place to initiate the collection of observations. Because it is not really an option to change the code of the installed dbt,[11] I will explain how to inject it similarly into Airbyte. Let's see how we can achieve this, and then I will address the next part of the generation of the observations related to the data involved in the task.

The approach is to inject additional Python code at runtime by intercepting when the `ModelRunner.execute` method is called and when the context is built. To do this, we'll use a Python capability called site (*https://oreil.ly/u0yjZ*), which allows us to define a "site-specific configuration hook" by running a specific file named `sitecustomize`.[12]

When this file is made available on the `site-packages` path that Python will use to load modules, the Python runtime ensures that it will always be executed before anything else. Therefore, this script can be used to run additional code that will be injected into the dbt runtime before the `ModelRunner.execute` is loaded and executed.

Thus, the `sitecustomize.py` script will use another module called `ast`, which allows us to parse Python code into its AST and modify it. This is how we'll inject our agent code to generate the observations. In the following, I will provide additional details on how this can be achieved. However, you can refer to the book's repository to see the full code.

There are two steps to inject code:

1. Intercept when a module and its functions are loaded, and parse it.
2. Modify the parser AST of the module to inject the code that will generate the data observations.

The first step is achieved by using the `importlib` package, which is nothing but the package that implements `import`. This package provides two classes:[13]

---

11 Well, because Python is not compiled...we could, but that would involve another level of nastiness.

12 Or `usercustomize` at a lower level.

13 More information about these low-level mechanisms of Python can be found in the New Import Hooks specification (*https://oreil.ly/bpoAA*).

`importlib.abc.MetaPathFinder`

A class with a `find_spec` method to find a module to be imported. This method returns a `importlib.machinery.ModuleSpec` that contains the import-related information used to load a module. `MetaPathFinder` instances are found on the `sys.meta_path`.

`importlib.abc.Loader`

This abstract class is used to (re)load and execute a provided module (found by the `Finder`). It comes also with the `exec_module` method which executes the loaded module.

Example 7-8 shows how to combine these two classes, starting with the `ModelRunner`.

Example 7-8. Intercepting a module load with importlib in sitecustomize.py

```
class DBTAgentPathFinder(MetaPathFinder):
  def find_spec(self, fullname, path, target=None):
    # [...]
    if fullname == "dbt.task.run":
      return ModuleSpec(fullname, DBTAgentLoader(fullname, p))
    # [...]

class DBTAgentLoader(Loader):
  def __init__(self, fullname, path) -> None:
    # [...]
    source = Path(path, module_file).read_text()
    tree = parse(source)
    # TODO new_tree = ???
    self.code = compile(new_tree, 'exec')

  def exec_module(self, module):
    exec(self.code, module.__dict__)

sys.meta_path.insert(0, DBTAgentPathFinder())
```

The key elements to notice in Example 7-8 are the following:

`fullname == "dbt.task.run"`

Intercepts the file *run.py* containing the `ModelRunner`.

`ModuleSpec(fullname, DBTAgentLoader(fullname, p))`

Returns a `DBTAgentLoader` for this intercepted module.

`DBTAgentLoader.__init__`

Reads the module (*.py*) file and parses into its AST tree, using `ast.parse`. This tree needs to be modified in the second step:

```
self.code = compile(new_tree, 'exec')
```

Compiles the new tree that will be executed:

```
exec(self.code, module.__dict__)
```

Implements the exec_module method of *Loader* to load the self.code, that is, the code that was modified using ast:

```
sys.meta_path.insert(0, DBTAgentPathFinder())
```

Ensures that the new finder we have defined is located on the meta_path where finders are searched for by Python.

The second step is to modify the parsed tree. To achieve this, we'll use the mechanism that comes with ast called NodeTransformer. A NodeTransformer is a visitor with corresponding visit_XXX methods that can be overridden to intercept and modify the visited node XXX. In our case, the two interesting node types are these:

ClassDef
: The definition of a class (e.g., ModelRunner).

FunctionDef
: The definition of a function (e.g., execute).

Modifying the code is, in reality, much simpler than we might anticipate. Example 7-9 shows what it looks like to inject the data observability agent in the execute function's code after the context has been initialized.

Example 7-9. Define a nodetransformer to modify ModelRunner.execute

```
class DBTTransformer(NodeTransformer):
  CURRENT_ModelRunner = False

  def visit_ClassDef(self, node):
    if node.name == "ModelRunner":
      DBTKensuTransformer.CURRENT_ModelRunner = True
    # [...]


  def visit_FunctionDef(self, node):
    # [...]
    if DBTTransformer.CURRENT_ModelRunner:
      if node.name == "execute":
        new_node.body.insert(1,
          ImportFrom(
            module='fodo_dbt_agent,
            names=[
                alias(name='dbt_agent', asname=None)
            ],
            level=0,
          )
```

```
        )
    new_node.body.insert(2,
        Assign(
            targets=[Name(id='__fodo_agent', ctx=Store())],
            value=Call(
                func=Name(id='dbt_agent', ctx=Load()),
                args=[
                    Name(id='context', ctx=Load()),
                    Name(id='model', ctx=Load()),
                ],
                keywords=[],
            ),
            type_comment=None,
        )
    )
    # [...]
```

In Example 7-9, you can see how we start injecting the data observability code, starting with the initialization of the agent that uses the `context` and the `model` variables to create observations about the application, the data sources, and even the lineage defined by this dbt model.

Here are the key steps:

1. `if node.name == "ModelRunner"`: because the tree represents the whole *run.py* in this case, several classes may be defined in it, and we're only interested in Model Runner. This code allows the transformation to be active only for this class.

2. `if node.name == "execute"`: when visiting the `ModelRunner` class, we are only interested in the `execute` method, so we can extend its code. This is the starting point.

3. `new_node.body.insert(1,`: this is where we start inserting code into the current function's parsed tree—we add a new node after the very first one that, in the case of `execute`, is initializing the `context` in which we need to create observations.

4. `ImportFrom`: builds an *import* AST node, with the module name `fodo_dbt_agent` that needs to be imported, as it will contain our data observability agent code.

5. `Assign`: a variable assignment node, following the import, that will create a variable `__fodo_agent`, to be initialized with the data observability agent.

6. `Call`: an AST node representing a function call; in this case, it will call the `dbt_agent` function with the `context` and the `model` as parameters. Those variables are provided by the `ModelRunner.execute` local variables.

At this point, we have all the mechanics to intercept and change any aspect of a Python-based system such as dbt. What remains to be done is to create the agent itself, the module `fodo_dbt_agent`. This code is provided in the book's repository and is quite long, as we must generate a lot of observations. However, I'll drive you through the important parts that are related to what is missing from dbt-supported observations; the data metrics, as pretty much the whole core model, can be generated from the `context` and `model`.

To generate data metrics observations for the data sources involved in a `seed` or `model` task, we must first understand how they are used. dbt works on top of a templating system called Jinja. dbt provides Jinja templates to allow the engineer to manipulate data sources, via *adapters*. An adapter (*https://oreil.ly/zUehh*) is a contract that must be implemented to support a new data source (e.g., Snowflake, Delta tables, MySQL), so it can be implemented independently of the dbt core by the community. The adapter instances are created by dbt core and made available to the Jinja execution context.

The instantiation of adapters and the execution of the Jinja task defined by the engineer is executed in the `ModelRunner._build_run_model_result`. However this method only calls the Jinja engine. The adapters do most of the work to access, read, and process the data sources.

We are looking for a handle to the data sources used in a task, so we must also intercept the work done by the adapters to generate the data observations.

Before giving you the solution to how to do this, it is worth pausing and noticing again that the responsibility to generate data observations must be given to the teams who are creating the tools used by engineers, natively. Because each data source will have its own complexity and behavior (hence the adapters), it is more challenging for a generic data observability agent to handle them all. Of course, the agent will come with abstractions such as adapters to allow its own extensivity, although it would have been more convenient if the dbt adapters had already provided this capability.

In other words, the dbt adapter contracts should evolve to also expose data observability capabilities, such as data metrics. This is already the case for the metadata.

To close this section on dbt agent, here are two recommendations to generate observations about the `seed` and the `model` run by dbt.

The `seed` task is a specific Jinja template that reads a file (e.g., CSV) into an *agate* table. *agate* is a Python package that performs data manipulation, which also provides an SQL-like API on top of files loaded as `Table`. dbt will load the seed file into an agate table using the `ProviderContext.load_agate_table` method, where the `ProviderContext` is what feeds the Jinja with the context, and `load_agate_table` is the method that reads the file into the table.

Therefore, the way we can intercept and compute observations of the loaded files can be to add another interceptor for this method in the *sitecustomize.py*.

For the `model` task, however, this is where adapters come into play, and we must extend our coverage to all of them to be fully data observable. This can be achieved if we intercept a method defined at the adapter level, such as `BaseAdapter.execute`. But we also have the opportunity, for the SQL adapter, to intercept `SQLAdapter.add_query`. Nevertheless, all adapters must also implement a `connection` that provides a handle on the data source. Therefore, we can simply intercept the `SQLConnectionManager.add_query` and use the provided `connection` to execute additional queries on the data source, such as computing the number of nulls, the distribution of all columns, etc. For an example of such implementation, please refer to the *kensu_postgres.py* file in the book's repository.

In this section, we saw that data transformation systems have been partially implementing data observability and probably will continue to align with what we have covered in this book so far. However, because we need it now, you have in hand the strategies that can be used to augment those capabilities.

Let's move to the next phase of the data engineering lifecycle, where the data is served to the next users, and see what can be done to support data observability.

Serving

At this stage, the data is ingested and transformed, yet it has to be made available, most probably in a continuous manner, for consumers, as described in "Recipes" on page 186. In this section, I will first address how data can be made available without breaking the data observability chain in a data warehouse such as BigQuery. Then, I will address the second point, which is how to ensure the data is continuously available using an orchestrator responsible for running the pipeline according to the consumers' expectations (e.g., freshness).

The serving stage is the last frontier wherein data engineers have influence, and therefore, it is the last line of defense to ensure data observability. Consequently, it is also the first line of defense for the next group in the lifecycle—the analytical group.

This shared frontier means that making data production and consumption observable, and thus transparent and controllable, constitutes a communication medium between two groups of people working hand in hand toward the same goals with different practices and, probably, tools. Therefore, making the serving stage data observable is four times as valuable as elsewhere, for the following reasons:

- Data engineers can gain insight about their own work.
- Consumers can be aware of produced data behavior.

- Data engineers can understand better how data has changed and impacted their consumers.
- Consumers can provide explanations about the expected behavior.

In other words, making data observable in the serving stage is a step toward the definition, update, and respect of SLOs and SLAs, with mutual acknowledgment of each party's constraints and capabilities.

Recipes

As served data is traditionally exposed with queryable systems, for example relational databases with SQL, those systems typically hide the complexity of the data transformation in their engine—and this process is not yet data observable.

A solution could be to create agents to extend the capabilities of such databases to become data observable, by generating from the engine all lineages of the tables used in the queries and their destinations, and even more interestingly, generating metrics of those tables along the way.

Although this work would generate a ton of fun, it won't be enough; unless the protocol between the application and the database is also made data observable, we need to have information also about the applications working with this data, and this kind of information is not made available to the database. Again, this is an idea to explore using practices such as distributed tracing, but the database would need to support that. We're not there yet.

An alternative that will work, though, is to consider that an application always provides the SQL queries executed by databases (see Figure 7-8), which must be data observable. Therefore, an agent in this application would also have access to the SQLs thrown at the databases and could use them to generate the data observations that the databases should have generated.

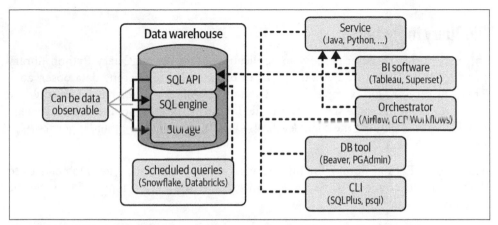

Figure 7-8. SQLs are just character strings sent to an API by applications, always

We will look at two types of applications for one type of database in the following recipes. The applications are:

- Python applications creating the SQLs
- Orchestrators capable of sending SQLs to databases (in a no-code or less-code manner)

The chosen database is Google BigQuery.

Before jumping into the recipes, caution must be taken regarding the cons of this practice that will generate the data observations on behalf of the database. As we need to generate metrics about the data (in and out), the applications will have to execute additional queries to the databases, which is going to increase the load of the database (and cost), and also introduce a slight latency between the time when the data is used in the query, and when it is "observed."[14]

Nevertheless, this trade-off is acceptable, considering that blindness would have a cost of another magnitude on the business (remember the 1-10-100 rule).

---

14 The quotes are there because the metrics observed here do not fit exactly the definition in Chapter 1, because additional queries are hitting the database to compute metrics. Therefore, it is intrusive to the experiment.

BigQuery in Python

In this section, I'll describe how an application using the BigQuery Python library provided by Google in a Python script can be extended to become data observable. This will serve as an example, as most Python clients for other databases could be extended using the same strategies provided in this section. Also, the overall strategy to intercept the SQLs at the client level can easily be extended to other languages (e.g., Java JDBC driver).

The Google Python library for BigQuery provides `Client` and `QueryJob` classes to define how to connect to the server and execute SQLs. Two types of jobs can be executed:

One-way
> These jobs aren't meant to retrieve data returned to the Python script but to update the data in BigQuery. Examples include creating a new dataset, updating or deleting rows in a table, etc.

Roundtrip
> These jobs are typically queries that the BigQuery servers will execute to prepare a dataset to be serialized back to the Python script, which can, in turn, manipulate them (using pandas, for example).

It is important to understand both types because, in the first case, the lineage connecting inputs and output is fully included for one-way jobs. However, for roundtrip ones, they initiate only the lineage, as there is no output yet defined in them. The outputs of the lineage will depend on how the data will be used by the script afterwards.

To describe how the agent can be structured, we will separate what it will do, and how to do it, in Python using delegation and monkey patching, illustrated in Figure 7-9.

In Figure 7-9, we see how the two jobs interact with Google BigQuery through its API to send SQLs. In the rounded boxes are highlighted the components that should be made data observable, and will allow the Python application to be data observable natively. Because they are not, I will introduce the agent in the Python application, which will take care of it (see Figure 7-10).

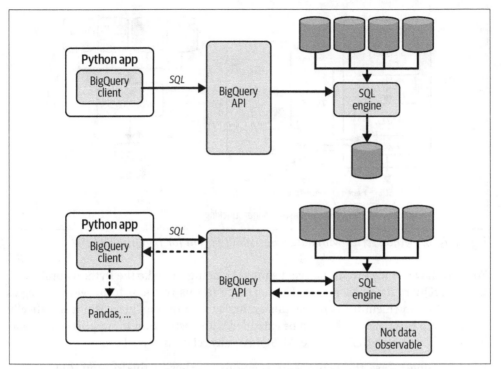

Figure 7-9. Python script with BigQuery Client sending two types of job

The agent, described later in this section, is loaded into the Python application and acts as an interceptor of the jobs sent to the BigQuery API. With this information, the agent can extract the lineage using an appropriate parser or simply using the plan of the query (*https://oreil.ly/rOLAE*),[15] which in fact offers the closest thing to data observability functionality, as it returns the operations performed in a query and one metric, the number of data written (in the one-way scenario). Over time, the plans will eventually evolve to return more data observations to complete the picture that must be made observable by the application. Meanwhile, let's fix it.

When the lineage includes the table references used in the process, this provides the opportunity to retrieve the metadata and compute metrics on them, using dedicated SQL queries executed against them by the agent.

Those two steps are summarized in the bottom of the Figure 7-10.

---

15 For example, see *https://oreil.ly/YLX4p*.

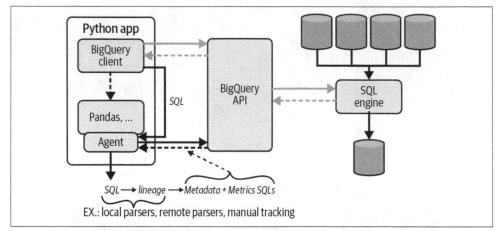

Figure 7-10. Python script with data observability agent for BigQuery jobs

You now have an idea what the agent should be doing to make the Python application using BigQuery data observable. The next step in this recipe is to provide strategies for how to implement it. As noted, this example based on BigQuery is not specifically dedicated to this database but can be extended with abstraction to support other databases such as PostgreSQL, Oracle, MySQL, or any relational database.

We are going to use the two classes mentioned earlier in this section, `Client` and `QueryJob`, to make our Python script data observable by implementing the extra steps we just covered. To support this work, Example 7-10 shows how BigQuery is used:

Example 7-10. BigQuery Python scripts—examples

```python
from google.cloud import bigquery
# Connect the client.
client = bigquery.Client()

# 1. Perform a query.
QUERY = (
    'SELECT name FROM `bigquery-public-data.usa_names.usa_1910_2013` '
    'WHERE state = "TX" '
    'LIMIT 100')
query_job = client.query(QUERY)  # API request
rows = query_job.result()  # Waits for query to finish
# Waits for query to finish
# And create a DataFrame with the data returned
df = query_job.to_dataframe()
# Store the data locally (this is bad)
df.to_csv("/tmp/iwillforgetaboutthis/important_data.csv")

# 2. Update a table.
table_id = "<destination id :: TODO>"
```

```
job_config = bigquery.QueryJobConfig(destination=table_id)
sql = """
    SELECT corpus
    FROM `bigquery-public-data.samples.shakespeare`
    GROUP BY corpus;
"""
# Start the query, passing in the extra configuration.
query_job = client.query(sql, job_config=job_config)  # Make an API request.
query_job.result()  # Wait for the job to complete.
```

In Example 7-10, you can see that the `client` is the `Client` instance created first to connect with the underlying credentials the developer had to provide. Then, this `client` is used to execute (query) a `QueryJob` that can be created from a simple QUERY string or a `QueryJobConfig` that contains the destination corresponding to where the result of the query must be stored, and therefore not returned to the application runtime.

I won't detail the agent completely, as you can find it on the book's GitHub repository; however, here is an explanation of the concepts.

First, we need to extend the `client` with tracing capabilities, as it will initiate computations with its methods `query` and `load_from_uri` (where the latter is loading a dataset from a URI into a table). In fact, each of those methods needs to create or retrieve an existing agent logger to track the data sources (URI, file, tables) and compute the observations.

To achieve this, we'll use another strategy described in Chapter 5, runtime manipulation, to override the `Client` class with data observability capabilities, as we did for the pandas `DataFrame` class. Because we want to reduce the number of changes for non data observable script, we will limit it to only changing the module path from `google.cloud.bigquery` to `fodo.google.cloud.bigquery`. It is very simple to execute. I simply need to create a folder structure that starts with *fodo*, then recursively add *google* and *bigquery*. In this last folder, I have to create the *client.py* where the delegation with data observability capabilities will be performed for the `Client` class.

It is important to add *__init__.py* files in the folders created but also to add imports to those in the folder where delegations are done to load all other non-delegated classes to be exposed in this prefixed module path. For example, in the *fodo/google/bigquery/__init__.py* file, because the *client.py* is overridden, it must contain the line shown in Example 7-11.

Example 7-11. Load all content of a Python module in a prefixed module

```
from google.cloud.bigquery import *
```

Now that the structure is prepared, the delegation can be done as follows:

- Define the class `Client` by extending the Google one.

- Override the methods to be made observable; for example, *query*.

- Retrieve the `self` instance of the delegated class (`super`) to allow the original method to be called without creating interferences with the delegated action (in other words, execute it as it would have been executed without our extensions).

- Execute the original method to ensure the original result is computed.

- From the method's parameters, intercept the variables that can be used to compute the data observations such as the `sql`, the loaded data (`uri`), or the `QueryJob` `Config`.

- Generate the data observations as explained before.

- Return the result of the original method.

In the listing, I return the original result as is; however, for the roundtrip case, this result can be used to retrieve the data in memory (using pandas, for example) to perform further transformations and actions. Therefore, this result must be paired with data observability capabilities.

To explain this part, I will focus on the `Client.query` that returns a `QueryJob` and its `result` method that retrieves the data. So, the `QueryJob` instance is created by the `Client.query` method. If we want to reuse the delegation pattern, I need to change its code using *ast* for *dbt* or copy-pasting its code in our delegated `Client`.[16]

However, there is a simpler way, using monkey patching (introduced in Chapter 5), to beef up the method of the return `QueryJob` with data observability capabilities. This will consist of replacing the methods directly in the instance using the `patcher` function, as shown in Example 7-12.

Example 7-12. Python patcher function

```
def patcher(o, f_name, f_patch):
    # 1. Keep a reference to original non-patched method
    orig_f = getattr(o, f_name)
    # 2. Define the patching function.
    def monkey(*args, **kwargs):
        # 3. Executing original non-patched code to get the result
        res = orig_f(*args, **kwargs)
        # 4. Patch the result
        res_patched = f_patch(res)
        # 5. Return the patched result
        return res_patched
```

---

16 Noooooooooooooooooooooooooooooooooooooo

```
# 6. Inject the documentation of the original function (for intellisense)
monkey.__doc__ = orig_f.__doc__
# 7. Reassign (patch) the original method with `monkey`
setattr(o, f_name, monkey)
# 8. Return the patched object
return o
```

The patcher function shown in Example 7-12 takes three parameters:

- The object holding the method to be overwritten
- The function name to be overwritten
- The function code to overwrite with

This function is used between steps four and five of the delegation listing presented, so that the returned QueryJob by *query* is data observable.

Finally, let's see how patcher can be used to overwrite the to_dataframe method of QueryJob, which returns the data as a pandas DataFrame. The returned DataFrame has to be data observable then too, which can be achieved with the same patterns as explained in this section—using, for example, the Python module kensu that is provided with such a data-observable DataFrame wrapper.

In Example 7-13, we see an excerpt that implements this agent using those techniques.

Example 7-13. Python BigQuery agent simplified

```
class Client(client.Client):
    def query(self, query, ...):
        gclient = super(Client, self)
        job = gclient.query(query)
        generate_data_observations(query, job)
        return patch_to_dataframe(job)

def patch_to_dataframe(job):
  def to_dataframe_with_do(df):
    # Check on the `kensu` package
  return patcher(job, "to_dataframe", to_dataframe_with_do)
```

With this agent at hand, the changes required to make all of Example 7-13 data observable consist of one single modification, as shown in Figure 7-11.

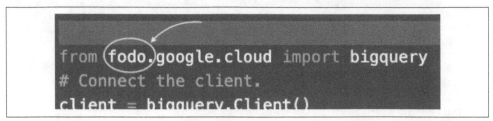

Figure 7-11. The change required in BigQuery Python script to make it data observable

This seems to be quite some work to make a script data observable; however, it is setting the foundation for higher-level systems to be data observable with less effort. The next section will demonstrate how this works when SQL is configured as part of an orchestrated pipeline.

Orchestrated SQL with Airflow

As seen with dbt, the trend in data tools is to simplify most of the data engineering tasks (e.g., DataOps). This includes the empowerment of SQL over coding scripts and the definition of pipelines wherein tasks, such as executing an SQL query, are combined in a straightforward manner, using tools called orchestrators, such as Airflow.

Airflow provides a simple-to-use domain specific language or API to create the DAG of data operations running as atomic tasks, which are as simple as Python functions, or can be created from templates called operators (*https://oreil.ly/OmVI1*). Using such an orchestrator considerably reduces the boilerplate needed to create pipeline-based composable tasks, operate them, and track successes and, especially, failures, to eventually prevent the remaining pipelines from being executed.

Such a task can be an SQL job in BigQuery that loads a dataset into a table or performs a query stored in a new table. The pipeline is defined with the code shown in Example 7-14, which is a simplified form of what you can find in the book's repository.

Example 7-14. Airflow DAG operators for BigQuery

```
etl_bigquery_external_table_task = BigQueryCreateExternalTableOperator(
    task_id=f"bq_load_external_table_task",
    table_resource={
        "tableReference": {
            "projectId": PROJECT_ID,
            "datasetId": BIGQUERY_DATASET,
            "tableId": "loaded_dataset_external_table",
        },
        "externalDataConfiguration": {
            "autodetect": "True",
            "sourceFormat": "JSON",
```

```
        "sourceUris": [
            'gs://bucket/tripdata'],
        },
    },
)
CREATE_BQ_TBL_QUERY = (
    f"CREATE OR REPLACE TABLE dataset_table\
    PARTITION BY DATE(some_date) \
    AS \
    SELECT * FROM loaded_dataset_external_table;"
)
bq_create_partitioned_table_job = BigQueryInsertJobOperator(
    task_id=f"bq_create_dataset_partitioned_table_task",
    configuration={
        "query": {
            "query": CREATE_BQ_TBL_QUERY,
            "useLegacySql": False,
        }
    }
)
```

Example 7-14 shows how two BigQuery operators, namely the `BigQueryCreateExter` `nalTableOperator` and `BigQueryInsertJobOperator`, can be combined to load a dataset and create a new table from an SQL statement. The two operators define the steps that are executed in sequence to create a partitioned table as the final result served for analytical purposes (see "Analytics" on page 197).

Each step must be made data observable, as it represents the execution of a lineage, taking some data as input to generate outputs that other steps will use. So, the whole DAG is a pipeline that will be made data observable, because each individual step will be and they can be combined using the lineage, which is where data sources are stitched together.

The good thing is that each of those steps is nothing but Python code executing Big-Query jobs using the Google Python library, and thus, if the agent explained in the previous section is added to the project, it is already data observable. Consequently, we don't have much to do, because data observability came by default. The foundations have embraced good practices and can be relied on by higher-level layers and abstractions, such as an orchestrator. This is much like how a program using a tested library doesn't have to test the library but does test its usage. As long as the usage is appropriate, this in turn should be asserted by the library itself during its execution, thus leading back to the concept of expectations introduced in Chapter 2.

Therefore, Airflow can be made data observable by overloading its operator classes for BigQuery, as presented in Figure 7-12, using the same strategy as per the Python agent.

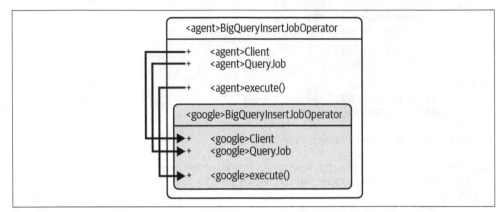

Figure 7-12. Using the BigQuery agent to automatically make the Airflow operator data observable

Therefore, the original Airflow DAG descriptor can remain the same. However, imports must be adapted to import the data-observable ones from the agent library, similarly to what was presented in Figure 7-12.

In Figure 7-13, I present examples of such modifications for BigQuery operators but also for other types of operators, such as bash or Python. You'll find the corresponding agent code in the kensu-py library (*https://oreil.ly/lf63p*).

```
from airflow.operators.bash import BashOperator
from airflow.operators.python import PythonOperator
from airflow.providers.google.cloud.operators.bigquery import
BigQueryInsertJobOperator
from airflow.providers.google.cloud.operators.bigquery import
BigQueryCreateExternalTableOperator
from airflow.providers.google.cloud.transfers.gcs_to_gcs import GCSToGCSOperator
```

```
from kensu.airflow.operators.bash import BashOperator
from kensu.airflow.operators.python import PythonOperator
from kensu.airflow.providers.google.cloud.operators.bigquery import
BigQueryInsertJobOperator
from kensu.airflow.providers.google.cloud.operators.bigquery import
BigQueryCreateExternalTableOperator
from kensu.airflow.providers.google.cloud.transfers.gcs_to_gcs import
GCSToGCSOperator
```

Figure 7-13. Changes to make a complete Airflow DAG data observable (bash, Python, BigQuery)

Airflow Support for BigQuery

Note that Airflow has a mechanism available via the classes SQLCheckOperator (*https://oreil.ly/QqWLu*) and its extended variations to support BigQuery. Those components can be used to include extra steps in the Airflow DAG (which could also be run at given intervals). Data engineers can use those to generate data observations (especially DataMetrics) and at the same time check expectations (e.g., rules). This is handy, although it comes with limited capabilities with regard to what data observability offers, such as using the history of metrics to validate the current data state. Also, additional and repetitive work is required to add it to the DAG, which includes its maintenance, still disconnected (desynchronized) from its usage in the other components.

Analytics

Developing and using machine learning models is a key goal for all data organizations to make decision-making processes more autonomous, or to leverage data from multiple sources.

With business intelligence, business stakeholders are the most exposed and involved, expectations are high, and trust about the whole data program depends on the success or failure of business intelligence analytics results.

Analytics is where trust can be destroyed with the highest impact. As distrust spreads among stakeholders, the question of budget allocation for data activities may be placed on the table, as data teams receive budgets from the business to create data products for their domain. Without trust, business stakeholders are less likely to count on data teams to drive some of their goals.

Therefore, we'd better make sure that any data used for analytics is observable, to allow for fast reaction and prevention of issues coming from inappropriate data, data drift, and behavioral changes. Analytics and data applications require data observability to expose aspects of the information that will qualify their behavior, whereas other areas, such as application observability, bring other facets.

On top of that, analytics, and especially ML applications, need to extend their observations to other data observability areas specific to their operations; namely, analytics observability. The purpose of this combination is to link the behavior of the data with the behavior of the machine learning or business intelligence "queries" models.

With this capability enabled in analytics applications, it is possible to detect if and when anomalies are happening in the analytics process and rapidly identify whether the responsibility lies in the data or the analysis (or both).

In the Machine Learning Recipes and Business Intelligence Recipes sections, I will give some examples of how data observability agents can be leveraged to generate observations at the intersection of both areas, data and analytics, for different scenarios in machine learning and business intelligence.

Machine Learning Recipes

To illustrate how data and analytics observations can be generated altogether in a machine-learning environment, I will use a common Python library called scikit-learn.

In the machine learning ecosystem, scikit-learn is one of the first successful open source Python libraries. Because it is also in Python and well-coupled with pandas, which we encountered already in the section about BigQuery, it will give us the opportunity to leverage mature techniques introduced before, as well as available agents.

The typical process to train and use a model with scikit-learn is presented in Figure 7-14 with two pipelines, training and prediction.[17]

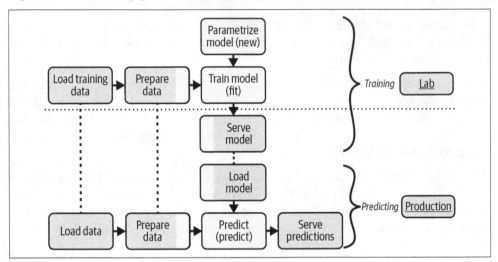

Figure 7-14. Machine learning process involving scikit-learn

In Figure 7-14, the machine learning steps involving scikit-learn alone are marked in a lighter color:

- Choosing and parametrizing the model: create a new instance of a classifier class; for example, `sklearn.svm.SVM`.
- Training the model: executing the `fit` method on the model.
- Predicting: executing the `predict` method on data.

However, the pipeline has other steps that will play a role in the final results, and they must be data observable too. Some of them rely on some functionality of scikit-learn, but the biggest parts will be done using dedicated libraries:

Loading (training) data
   This step can be assimilated to the ingestion phase in the data engineering lifecycle, and in the case of scikit-learn, you would use a library such as pandas.

---

17 Keep in mind, though, this process is quite similar for any other machine learning library.

Preparing the data

Data preparation is the transformation phase in the data engineering lifecycle, and in fact, it can also be handled as a data engineering step, to create a data mart. Nevertheless, it can also be accomplished simply, with another pandas manipulation in a Python script to make sure the data matches the model contract. Or, the data can simply be shaped (creating the matrix of numbers with the right dimensions) using the *numpy* library. It is worth noting that the preparation of data can also involve some machine-learning-related tasks, such as scaling the data, which are available in scikit-learn; therefore, the data observability agent has to work across technologies.

Loading and serving the model

These crucial steps are similar to the serving phase of the data engineering lifecycle. They can be easily done using libraries like *joblib* or *pickle*. Same as for loading (training) data, the storage and load of a model involves some functionality of scikit-learn, and thus interoperability must be also preserved here.

In Figure 7-14, I added the environments where the training and prediction pipelines would run.[18] Consequently, key artifacts such as data sources, library versions, or the infrastructure may differ across the environments. But some constraints must be respected across environments, such as:

Loading the data

The connection should be similar between each environment, or different scripts must be created (and aligned).

Preparing the data

The preparation step must be identical in production to that performed in the lab, if the data sources are similar; otherwise, the data must be prepared differently to align with the requirements of the `predict` method of the model.

Serving and loading

The model must be stored and loaded with the same library to ensure compatibility at the binary level and with the rest of the pipeline.

As you can imagine, the whole system is somewhat fragile, especially if steps are decoupled from each other and assigned to several people or teams. Even a small change in data source, schema, content, parameter, versions, or anything else may generate wrong predictions.

---

18 When online training is applied, the diagram needs to be slightly more complicated; however, in that case, there is still work being prepared in the lab before moving to production. The minimum step needed would be to validate how models are going to be built. Even if we use an autoML, there is still some work to be validated in the lab.

Because most steps, such as loading or preparing the data, are related to the ingestion and transformation stages of the data engineering lifecycle, I will consider them as covered. Thus, I can concentrate on the characteristics specific to where scikit-learn is involved, the model training and prediction steps.

Without getting too deep into analytics observability (cf. end of the section), what must be done for scikit-learn to be made observable is to track the data used to train a model (including the location, schema, metrics, etc.) and link it to the fitted model stored and served for predictions. Indeed, a model stored and served can therefore be considered as anything but a data source, with a schema and even metrics. In fact, a model *is* data; a linear regression model, for example, is rebuilt by reading the fitted weights, and, thus, additional metrics could be computed on those weights, such as the number of zeros, the min and max, etc.

Continuing with models, we could think of generating observations about the model behavior, or performance. This is done with `estimators` (e.g., r2). Although we can technically use them this way, I don't consider them to be data source metrics. Such information is not intrinsic to the model; rather, it reflects. Since they reflect the model performance related to the data during the training phase, they are more specific to machine learning, and therefore should be associated with the trained model using an analytics extension to the observability core model introduced in Chapter 2.

Then comes the prediction phase. We must make the generation of those predictions observable by linking the model and the observations (the data) to them.

To accomplish this, because scikit-learn is also a Python library, we can apply the overload pattern used before and overload, for example, the `LinearRegression` class, as proposed in the (pseudo)code excerpt in Example 7-15.

Example 7-15. scikit-learn's `LinearRegression` extension for data observability

```
import sklearn.linear_model as sk_lm

class LinearRegression(sk_lm.LinearRegression):
  def fit(self, X, y, sample_weight=None):
    # 1. call the `sk_lm.LinearRegression` first to compute the fitted model
    model = super(LinearRegression, self).fit(X, y, sample_weight)
    # 2. Compute for the `model`.
    # E.g., the number of `parameters`, the min/max of the returned `weight`, etc
    metrics_for(model)
    # 3. Link the `model` to the input data `X` and `y`
    lineage_for(_in=[X, y], _out=[model])
    # 4. Include analytics observations
    # E.g., fetch hyper parameters, execute estimators, ...
    # 5. wrap `model` to ensure its usages will also be observed, and return
    return do_wrap(model)
```

```
def predict(self, X):
    # 1. Compute the predictions first
    predictions = super(LinearRegression, self).predict(X)
    # 2. Wrap the `predictions` to make it data observable
    do_wrap(predictions)
    # 3. link `predictions` to the `model` and the data `X`
    lineage_for(_in=[self, X], _out=[predictions])
    return predictions
```

In Example 7-15, you can see the key steps to follow that will turn any `LinearRegres` `sion` model training and predictions into fully data-observable applications. Because we can rely on the other libraries that have followed (or have an agent for) the data observability principles, the amount of work is relatively small, but it is also straightforward, as it consists mainly of linking the inputs to the outputs.

With this agent added to your data science environment, the code changes in your analytics scripts are limited to what is shown in Example 7-16, as they enable the agent, which will collect all observations defined by default (see the code repository for a full working example).

Example 7-16. scikit-learn's data-observable LinearRegression usage

```
# Prefixing the module package with our agent name "doagent" for example
from doagent.sklearn.linear_model import LinearRegression

regressor = LinearRegression()
regressor.fit(x_train, y_train)
```

As stated before, we also have the opportunity to introduce analytics observations. By joining those capabilities from data and analytics observability, it becomes possible to detect issues and analyze them across the analytical parts. Possible benefits include the ability to engineer observations even when a model has biases, or when a model is no longer appropriate for the population it originally reflected.

Business Intelligence Recipes

Business intelligence, especially considering its visualization tools, such as reports and dashboards, is directly related to business decisions taken by stakeholders. It is probably the last line of defense to prevent issues from happening, or to solve them quickly when they arise. Therefore, in addition to considering stakeholders as individuals—their skills, their power, and their availability—it is crucial to demonstrate a high level of maturity and accountability when delivering BI, as any issue or lack of confidence can generate a storm of consequences for the whole data organization.

In this section, I have chosen to demonstrate how data observability can be introduced in two kinds of applications that decision makers will likely use. First, we'll look at notebook technology that can be deployed in production with presentation capabilities, as this has become a common practice over the years (though still controversial). For this, I'll use Databricks, one of the main actors who can make this practice an easy-to-apply reality.

Then, I'll follow up with a more traditional data tool, a dashboarding software used to present business facts in a single view connected to data sources, generally the data warehouse or data marts. For this, I'll use an open source product called Superset.

Databricks

Databricks is a company built around the distributed computing library Apache Spark we covered earlier in this chapter. However, over the years, the company has developed notebook and SQL capabilities (among others, such as DataOps) to better support business intelligence requirements.

In this section, I will focus on the presentation aspects, which allow users to define analytics and present them as a sort of report.[19] Notebooks also support data storage or work on machine learning models, but this part was covered in earlier sections.

Databricks is a low-code platform, where queries can be added directly to notebooks and the results presented immediately. Therefore, it massively simplifies the work that makes this possible. The machinery behind the platform is hidden from the outside world; hence, adding agents directly at that level is allowed.[20] Nevertheless, we can still do it at a higher level, where Databricks provides access: for example, the cluster running the analyses defined in the notebooks.

But before explaining what this integration would look like, I'll go through what we would do to make data observable in a Databricks notebook. A notebook for reporting will likely execute the following tasks:

- Connect to data sources
- Perform analytics
- Present the results as tables or charts

So, no real output is stored, but they are visually served to the final users. Consequently, to conceptualize the lineage, we need output data sources to represent the tables and charts. This is why, for a reporting notebook, we have a kind of split brain between data source and application, because such a notebook is both of the following things, at the same time:

---

19 But they're not limited to analytics, in this specific case, as this is powered by Apache Spark.

20 I have to qualify this statement with "at the time of writing," because it is likely that Databricks will make their system data observable, given that they are also the same people who introduced observe in the Spark library.

- An application: because it is a script that will run to produce results.
- A data source(s): each table or chart is a visual storage for the underlying data.

Moreover, we can connect to the user receiving the information, as we can create a user entity for them that will be linked to the application execution entity, created out of the necessity for the notebook to execute to present the information. This way, we can fully observe how a report is being consumed and intercept signals from that process.

Figure 7-15 describes this scenario, which will help us understand how the agent can be integrated, and what it generates.

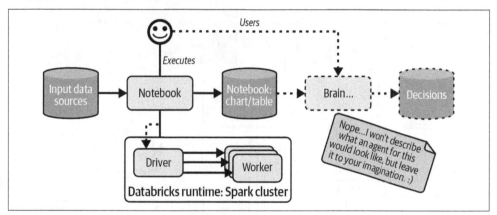

Figure 7-15. Databricks notebook's usage flow

In Figure 7-15, you can see that the notebook relies on the Spark cluster that it is connected to; therefore, as long as this environment is data observable, we've almost covered the whole scenario. However, three peculiarities coming from the Databricks notebook may remain:

1. Capturing the user
2. Capturing the notebook name or path to qualify the name of the application
3. Capturing the Databricks visual components as data sources

Luckily, Spark is compatible; we covered its reference implementation earlier in this chapter. So, these three points that need to be connected to the data observations are already collected by the Spark agent.

For the two first pieces of information, we have to use some internals of Databricks, the class `com.databricks.dbutils_v1.DBUtilsHolder`, which comes with the following fields:

- `userName`: the connected user name

- `notebookPath`: the path to the current notebook

Then, there are several ways to create the visuals: a common one is to use the `display` function. The `display` function runs Spark jobs to organize and collect the data to be presented in the frontend. Here, again, most of the work is done by the installed Spark agent, as it will generate data observations about the collected data; that is, when one of the Spark functions `collect, take`, or others are used. Consequently, we could create a data source for the `notebookPath` and attach the schema of all data collected, alongside with the statistics returned. The data observations will look like Figure 7-16.

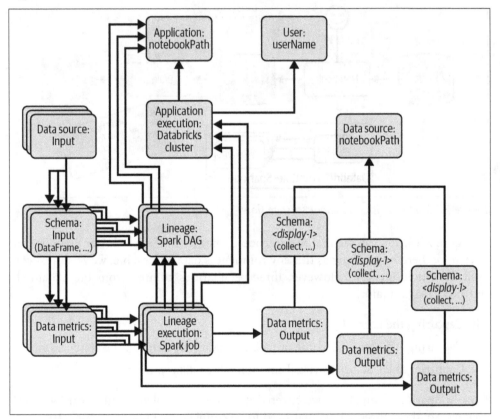

Figure 7-16. Excerpt of the observations generated by Databricks agent[21]

---

21 And that's why it can't reasonably be done manually...

Hence, enabling data observability for any Databricks notebooks executed on a cluster and generating the data observations showcased in Figure 7-16 can be achieved simply by adding the agent (the jar) to the cluster's configuration classpath. This can be done through the Databricks cluster configuration page.

Superset

Superset is an open source reporting and dashboarding solution that supports many types of data sources. Superset is implemented in Python and can be installed from Docker or from the source code.

Superset offers a low-code or no-code interface for analysts to query available datasets using SQL directly, or via the wizard that simplifies the exploration of the dataset to generate table or chart visualizations. Actually, it is quite close to a combination of writing a query in a Databricks notebook, then using the visualization to manipulate the results further with `display`. The table and charts can be added to dashboards to make all important information available in one glance.

It is therefore easy for the user to access and define dashboards using the wizard, resulting in a lot of information to be observed. Superset must therefore be made data observable with a high degree of automation, as it is not practical for users to have to go through many steps for all the information they generate so easily.

Making dashboards data observable has the potential to solve a common challenge that comes with reporting tools: the management of their reliability. However, another challenge to consider is the management of their lifecycle, their deletion. As reporting tools allow their users to quickly and easily create dashboards, many are created to perform some explorations of a situation. However, after the exploration, those dashboards aren't generally deleted, as, for example, the situation may return at a random time. From the data observability standpoint, those dashboards are still using the linked data sources (via the lineage). Hence, the frequency of access to those dashboards is a good indicator for the data producers to use to estimate the risks associated with an observed change in the data or a data migration.

Adding the data observability capability to Superset will, among other things, make transparent how the dashboards are created, how they are run, how often, and, with data metrics in place, their reliability.

It turns out that enabling this capability is straightforward and requires few changes, yet will cover a wide range of cases. This is because a chart in Superset is always accessing the data using SQL queries and returning the results as `pandas.Data Frames`. Therefore, since we have already discussed `DataFrame` in regard to the transformation phase of the data engineering lifecycle, I won't go into detail here, other than to explain that the agent can leverage the existing agents in a modular fashion and then focus on the specifics of Superset.

In Figure 7-17, you can see where an agent has been added to enable, by default, data observability for charts and what it would look like.

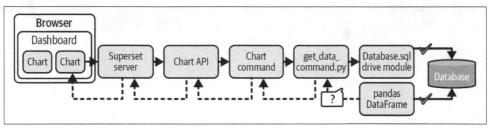

Figure 7-17. Superset chart refresh flow

You can see that most of the process touching data is already covered. Consider, for example, the database to be BigQuery. We can use the agent introduced in the Serving section to make this part data observable. Then, we apply the command to get the data and wrap the result into a DataFrame. However, as with Databricks, the data is not written in a storage medium but is transformed into JSON and returned in memory to the browser for presentation.

Therefore, the agent specifics for Superset are essentially to intercept in the file *get_data_command.py*, when the SQL is executed and the result retrieved, then enrich the data observations generated by the SQL and pandas agent with the information about the dashboard and the chart that will present the data.

This will be accomplished by intercepting the two following objects:

- The `QueryContext` contains the information about the dashboard and the chart.
- The result of the execution of its method `get_payload`, which contains the resulting `DataFrame`.

The agent has this information if it is embedded in the `run` method of the `ChartData Command` class defined in *get_data_command.py*. This class has a field `_query_context` and the `run` method looks roughly like what is shown in Example 7-17.

Example 7-17. Superset ChartDataCommand.run logic

```
try:
    payload = self._query_context.get_payload(
        cache_query_context=cache_query_context, force_cached=force_cached
    )
except CacheLoadError as ex:
    raise ChartDataCacheLoadError(ex.message) from ex
```

As Example 7-17 shows, we have all the information we need to create all data observations, and so we can simply add two lines after payload is returned, as shown in Example 7-18.

Example 7-18. Superset's agent interception

```
from superset_agent import generate_data_observations
generate_data_observations(self, payload)
```

To do so, we can reuse what was done for dbt and inject the AST representation of calling `generate_data_observations`. The generation of data observations relies on existing data observability capabilities from underlying modules, but it does one special thing to represent the output data source, which is the chart, shown in Example 7-19.

Example 7-19. Create data source entity observations for Superset chart

```
qc = chart_data_command._query_context

from superset.charts.dao import ChartDAO
chart_id = qc.form_data["slice_id"]
chart_slice = ChartDAO.find_by_id(chart_id)
chart_name = str(chart_slice) # returns the name of the slice

from superset.dashboards.dao import DashboardDAO
dashboard_id = qc.form_data["dashboardId"]
dashboard = DashboardDAO.find_by_id(dashboard_id)
dashboard_dashboard_title = dashboard.dashboard_title

name = f"""Superset:{dashboard_dashboard_title}:{chart_name}"""
_format = "Superset:Chart"
location = f"""/superset/explore/?form_data={{"slice_id":{chart_id}}}"""
```

In Example 7-19, you see that we can extract the dashboard and chart ids, which, when reusing the data access objects (DAO) for both classes, allows the agent to retrieve their names and titles. So a data source can be generated with a name containing the dashboard and chart, quite similar to what was achieved for Databricks' notebooks.

Note that the chart's location can be precisely generated as well, that is, the data observation that uniquely identifies where the chart is available and can be accessed is generated.

Installing this agent into an existing Superset environment ensures that the link between a chart and the datasets can be observed, including when the lineages were executed and by whom. This addresses the previously mentioned challenge and because both agents, for SQL and pandas, are generating data metrics, the reliability of the charts is also made observable.

Conclusion

This chapter delved into the technical aspects of data observability, providing a comprehensive guide to making data observable in various languages and technologies. We explored numerous tricks and techniques that can be implemented at different stages of the data engineering lifecycle, ensuring that every practitioner can adopt data observability practices and start benefiting from them today. By covering end-to-end pipelines, we ensured that data observability is not limited to specific components but rather permeates the entire data ecosystem.

The chapter presented practical examples that can be easily translated into other technologies, allowing readers to apply the concepts and principles in their own data environments. By providing these working examples, we aim to empower data practitioners with the knowledge and tools needed to make their data observable and gain valuable insights into the behavior and quality of their data.

The next chapter will address the challenge of introducing data observability in opaque systems. These systems, characterized by their limited transparency and visibility into internal processes, present unique obstacles to achieving data observability. We will explore strategies and approaches to overcome these challenges, enabling practitioners to bring data observability to even the most opaque systems.

## CHAPTER 8

Making Opaque Systems Translucent

In previous chapters, when I covered low-code no-code solutions, I enumerated some outside-of-the-box strategies that can be used to generate data observations until those solutions evolve to become natively data observable.

Other, often familiar, systems are similar to those solutions, as they have the same characteristics: the data usages happen in the engine under the hood. It is neither efficient (cost and time effective) nor recommended to open it.

Significant risks are associated with systems that do not provide clear visibility into their engine or usage of data. The main problem is that users cannot access the system to analyze if there are any issues that may cause problems. This lack of transparency means that users are unable to identify the root causes of issues, which forces them to patch downstream systems instead of addressing the upstream problems. Another issue with these systems is the loss of knowledge about their internal behavior.

While people may have configured or developed them successfully in the past, very few still have the internal knowledge to understand what they do. As a result, the strategies covered in Chapter 4 and Chapter 5 for achieving data observability may not apply. However, this chapter introduces strategies for these opaque systems, which allow users to get closer to data observability without necessarily satisfying all its principles.

These strategies will make the systems partially data observable or "data translucent," allowing users to understand their internal behaviors better.

Data Translucence

Imagine you have a steel safe with a bright light behind it. All you can see is the outside of the safe—the contents are hidden. That's an opaque system. Now imagine a box made of frosted glass in front of the light. You still can't see exactly what's inside the box, but you can see its shape. Maybe the shadow looks like a mechanical clock. Now you know you can listen for a tick-tock to see if the clock is working as a clock should. Data translucence represents the data observability capability added or natively supported by partially data-observable systems.

In Chapter 2, I defined the principles of data observability as foundational to generating and leveraging its value. To review, a data-observable system generates data observations synchronously and contextually, and continuously validates its expectations.

Therefore, a data-translucent system falls into one or both of the following categories:

- At least one data observability principle is not respected.
- At least one data observability principle is only loosely supported.

Let's look at some examples to illustrate this concept.

Lagged data observations
> An application generates observations about its data usage context and validates its expectations, but the metrics about the data it consumes are not synchronized with its runtime because it uses pre-computed ones (e.g., in a previous step). One of the problems that can occur is if the validation it performs fails. The application stops running because it estimates it will generate garbage. However, the metrics are computed every two hours, and resolution procedures are applied in the meantime. In this situation, the continuous validation would generate false negatives.

Partial context
> An application generates data observations omitting some elements of the context, such as reporting its current version. This will lead to problems when a new version of the application with updated data transformations and validations is developed. You can see it coming; the production environment could have both versions operating simultaneously, or the old version had not been deployed appropriately (i.e., it doesn't work, but there were no errors during deployment), leading to cases where the data sources are either inappropriately considered valid, or the validations fail. On the other hand, you might think a new version has been deployed. Hence, you would look at the wrong places (e.g., the data or the new application version) to understand situations that arise.

You might wonder why you should bother with such systems if they cannot be made fully data observable. Fair enough. My answer is that the number of cases where there will not be enough data observability to be useful is far smaller than the cases where data translucence will save you time, money, energy, and trust (i.e., `number of "not enough" << number of "good enough"`). However, since you know these systems are not fully data observable, you will incorporate extra precautions when utilizing the insights gained from their exposed information—this awareness helps decrease the probability of making inappropriate decisions, like in the lagged data observation and partial context examples.

Perfect Is the Enemy of Good

Law: it's much better than nothing.

Fact: it is better to know that the system does not know that something you know influences what it knows than to know that it doesn't know anything, so you must know everything it doesn't know.

Data translucence is a term I made up. Its destiny, I hope, is to fade away rapidly. I am picturing its lifetime as in *The Curious Case of Benjamin Button*, where it feels like it is born old and loses maturity over time as its usefulness decreases.

But, to avoid confusion, we needed a dedicated term to distinguish between data-observable and partially data-observable systems. Confusion would lead to incorrect expectations and, therefore, diminish the importance and value generated by data observability. Data translucence is a capability that can be added or used to strengthen systems. In the following section, I'll introduce the types of systems that are good candidates for it—the opaque systems.

Opaque Systems

An opaque system is a system (an infrastructure, an application, a pipeline, a solution, etc.) that, from the perspective of the user or the team in charge of its maintenance or operation, is acting pretty much like a closed system.

It doesn't mean those systems are black boxes! But they must be considered as such. Picture the motor of a car under the hood, where each component is covered by opaque plastic (i.e., most new cars). It is like this because most car makers don't expect drivers to get their hands in there, especially as the motors become more and more complex.[1] However, if you are skilled, passionate, or simply a DIY person (or you are curious), when there is an issue, you can get a screwdriver and get the cover off, or connect an electronic diagnostic tool; however, from now on, everything you do falls under your responsibility.

---

1 OK, there is a business component; you get it, I get it.

In IT, there are at least three categories of such systems.

SaaS

Software as a service (SaaS) is a common way of developing and commercializing solutions, most often deployed in the cloud versus on-premises.

Even if they are the enterprise version of an open source solution, these services are meant to be usable out of the box and focused on specific use cases, verticals, and user experiences. They usually provide limited access to their internals. Otherwise, it becomes almost impossible for the operations, support, and maintenance teams of the SaaS provider to handle hundreds, thousands, or even millions of users.

Therefore, if these solutions are not natively data observable, the consuming team will have limited (but not null) freedom and options to circumvent this fact. However, as a customer, you have the power to provide feedback to the vendor, the product team, or the project manager about their solutions' lack of data observability and demand it as part of the negotiation and feature request procedure. As this is becoming part of the table stakes of solutions and a catalyst for customer adoption, chances are that existing technologies will become data observable soon, or that new technologies will be launched as data observable by default. As of this writing, many technologies and companies are dedicating their development forces to creating features going in that direction. Examples include Databricks, dbt labs, Fivetran, Matillion, Talend, Upsolver (and many more) starting to expose data observations in what are called *system tables*, similar to *information schemas* in database servers (the tables mainly expose the metadata, such as data source and schema). Those system tables aim at exposing the metadata of the applications, which, therefore, are mixing infrastructure, application, and, of course, data observations. We're getting there.

Yet, some solutions may already be partially data observable or generate alternative information which, with some creativity, can help us, the users, turn them into data-translucent systems.

Don't Touch It; It (Kinda) Works

I am pretty sure you are familiar with these systems. They are not old-fashioned or fully closed. Theoretically, you can access their internals or update them.

The last word explains it all. It works. The system is running in production, used by many users, and, most of the time, does not present many challenges. But, and there is a but, maintaining this level of trust for the users is extremely expensive or cumbersome. When something goes wrong, and something will inevitably go wrong over a long enough time period, it will cause your team a good deal of stress and extra work.

Just like that, the lack of confidence in the system generates a high dose of anxiety when considering introducing a new capability, such as data observability. The anxiety often comes with fear of being responsible for the system breaking down, so no one feels brave enough to get their hands dirty and turn the capability on.

Note that the fear is not linked to the complexity of introducing data observability. The task will be complicated, and the amount of work and the time needed to do it can be limited. But this sensation is induced by the system itself; it possesses a certain aura, and that's all there is to it.

Sometimes, the system or the framework's footprint can be the blocking point—"it's everywhere." Hence, thinking about changing it even a little feels risky and stressful. However, with an appropriate project plan following a thorough analysis of the system, and a correct phasing with achievable expectations, the doubts fade quickly, replaced by the excitement about the foreseen benefit. Also, it is fair to realize that the *minimal stuff needed to cover most common cases* (Pareto principle (*https://oreil.ly/j-zHK*)) must be respected with such systems.

Therefore, the task is to consider as many strategies as possible that can turn the opacity into translucence, and which feel *doable,* with minimal risk but high return (even if not maximal at first).

A last note on those systems—like SaaS, they can become data observable in the long run. Still, the path to get there goes through the generation of trust in the process and outcome, which is the purpose of this chapter.

Inherited Systems

The last opaque system I want you to consider for data observability is systems you don't even think about. Those systems have been inherited and have been there *forever,* and it feels like they always will be. Sometimes you just don't see them anymore. They are kind of doing their thing. In fact, you probably don't know what they do exactly, and you are not alone.

Those who know are no longer around. The knowledge is distributed across people and time, or the technology is not supported; in the worst-case scenario, the vendor no longer exists. In large corporations, you'll see one person coming at a random time in the year, sitting down in the corner of the open space, and there is a machine there, likely running an old Windows distribution, and it is noisy (sometimes not only the machine). Curious, you look over their shoulder,[2] and you notice that this unknown character conscientiously deletes files here, goes through a list of 23 opened *cmd* windows, kills some processes, and restarts others. After a couple of hours, the phone rings, and the person picks up and says, "Everything is back up, the project continues." A second later, the seat is empty. A magician.

---

2 Please don't do that.

Don't get me wrong. I am not saying those systems are rare. They are everywhere, and they are running the most critical business processes, but they shouldn't be the main focus of starting your data observability implementation project in your organization. Even new applications and systems are introduced without touching them, and they are built around them, often working around them or simply trying to replicate some part of their processes.

In a sense, this is one of the reasons why data integration and ingestion are so prominent in the data space—because nowadays, data is considered a first-class asset and must be brought into the foreground instead of hidden in the back service.

> "The things I know about yesterday today,
>
> are not the same things I will know about yesterday, tomorrow."
>
> —Adi Polak, Data Engineering Keynote, Data Day Texas 2023

For most of those systems, data translucence is almost the best you can expect, and you must choose goals carefully, such as the following key ones:

Knowledge recovery
Automatically generating a portion of the contextual observations about the applications and lineages (even high-level, omitting the field-level one).

Prepare a migration (full or partial)
Inherited systems are robust; they have passed so many edge cases in their lifetime that the migration to another system is fraught with risk. Running both systems in parallel, with the inherited system providing information about the generated outcomes that can be compared with the new one, is key to generating trust.

Improve the status quo
Because the maintenance cost generally increases in such a system, limiting the assessments and reducing the time to recover, are key objectives for CIOs or CDOs. Therefore, increasing the visibility of such systems can come with a cost that can be easily justified, as the amount of money saved from it is much greater.

It's time to cover alternatives to the strategies discussed in the previous chapter, which targeted systems assumed to be relatively open. The strategies that I will discuss in the following sections can also be applied immediately to conceive solutions for the systems you are using or maintaining every day and will impact the reliability of the insights and projects you deliver.

Strategies for Data Translucence

In this section, I will introduce several strategies that you can use with opaque systems to make them more transparent than they are naturally. Each strategy will bring its own set of observations that can be used to generate, likely partially, the data observability core model introduced in Chapter 2. This aggregation is discussed in the second part of this section, in which I will follow up with an example of how a SaaS technology leverages a combination of several strategies.

Strategies

As with any combination of technological skill and creativity, we end up with hacks that turn existing features or capabilities of a solution into doors for new practices, usages, and outcomes.

As you have read several times in this book, the practices under the implementation of data observability are continuations of practices already embraced in other areas, such as software engineering. So we'll see what we can reuse to generate data observations. We'll also look at some concepts that cover management requirements—even legal requirements, when applicable.

The other strategies are slightly more technical and will likely require acting outside of the systems as sidecars to generate additional information to be turned into data observations.

I don't mean to say that the following strategies are exhaustive; this is why I started this section by mentioning *creativity,* as I am sure other strategies can be applied to uncover additional data observation generation processes.[3]

Data governance APIs

I will not repeat the importance of data governance and how critical it is to implement it at scale; most companies have embraced this already, and this will not stop. We can see this with the proliferation of data governance-related APIs introduced in technologies that are not centered on data governance (such as data cataloging or metadata registry).

At the time of writing, data governance is still influenced by regulations such as the California Consumer Privacy Act (CCPA) and the General Data Protection Regulation (GDPR). However, the idea that data must be under good management and governed appropriately is also becoming part of the culture. Therefore, many data warehouses, data integrations, or data transformation tools expose the data they are using or generating and how they are being used or generated.

Hence, when you are confronted with an opaque system that is not yet offering data observability capabilities, the first step is to look out for such APIs, which will generally provide you with access to the following information:

---

3 Please, reach out to me when you have those ideas; I'll be happy to discuss them.

Data lineage

This is the very first one you should look for, as it is often required to comply with privacy regulations. It will give you instant access to understand the data flow and thus the data sources in use.

Structure Metadata

Generally speaking, these technologies will also offer APIs on the data they generate or manage, which you, the user, access. You can consider those as control outputs for the system. Therefore, the APIs expose the metadata such as the schema, the underlying technology (e.g., database), and its location.

Content Metadata

The information about the data type, data category, and data definition used in the applications can be exposed in the form of a semantic layer linked to data usage, especially for produced data. This may not be as common as the other two, but it is worth checking out, as it provides great insight into the usage of the data.

Therefore, these APIs can be used with regular HTTP (or other protocols such as gRPC) clients consuming the information regularly, or it can be that the solution is providing a subscription mechanism or even a push notification to receive information continuously.

Log analytics

Logs are the most common source of information allowing solutions to be monitored and maintained. Therefore, although logs don't contain all information of the data observability core model, or don't fully respect the three data observability principles (synchronous, contextual, and continuous validation), logs likely contain some portion of it. Logs the system creates in production are necessary to handle errors, for example. Therefore, because data issues are not new, you can expect that some logs will contain some information you need.

A log analyzer is software that consumes logs for the (potentially distributed) application that will extract relevant information useful to generate data observations.

Of course, many dimensions of information are found in logs. For our needs, there are five dimensions you will want to chase:

- SQL queries
- Data sources' read and write operations
- Exceptions and retries
- Execution start time and end time
- Coarse-grained metrics about data (e.g., the number of rows)

Logs are meant to be recorded line by line, and the information about, say, a transformation, is likely spread across multiple log lines, which need to be reconstructed by a log analyzer. That said, if the application supports open tracing standards for those logs, the log analyzer can leverage this to accumulate multiple logs (spans) to rebuild the context. This takes on another dimension when the context is distributed across machines, such as Spark, where the logs must be centralized and reconsolidated to extract the observations representing the state of the system.

Also, the content of the logs is often in freeform and considered a document data type; therefore, the logs analyzer will have to master string parsing to extract the subset of the logs to turn them into usable information. In fact, this is quite close to any feature extraction process for a natural language processing (NLP) process. Of course, some solutions will have their logs follow a custom standard, simplifying the analyzer's work.

That said, another source of logs is useful to consider: the data source logs—especially from databases. A database is also an application, and therefore generates its own logs, which, for the purpose of data observability, I'll split into two categories:

Audit logs
These logs contain information on how the database is used, including queries.

CDC logs
These logs provide internal input about what changes are occurring in the database.

The interesting thing about these logs is that they are centralized to each data source and therefore easy to consume and even parse. However, they usually come without usage context; namely, the application issuing the queries or performing the changes is not known. We'll see then how log sources, applications, and data sources need to be combined to get closer to the three principles.

Usage Observations Included in the Consumption Protocols

If those data sources (distributed files, databases, etc.) allow operations to be *tagged* with the application issuing them, then the task of constructing data observations will be more straightforward.

Code and binary analyzers

In previous chapters, I focused on the application code, as it is the best place to generate data observations respecting all the principles of data observability. However, in those chapters, I have assumed the following:

- The code is available
- The code is understandable
- The code, in some cases, can be modified

However, as discussed in the first section, this may not always be the case with opaque systems.

There are two practices to handle this: code analysis and reverse engineering; I will discuss them briefly, as it is outside the scope of this book to cover them in detail. The purpose of these practices is to create systems capable of generating data observations landing in the static space, mainly the lineage and the data sources.

Let's start with reverse engineering, which, in software engineering, is the process of generating the documentation (e.g., diagram, flow chart, and so on) and/or the source code of an application. Reverse engineering can apply techniques such as decompiling or disassembling, which are meant to turn machine language or byte-code into code instructions. Those may not exactly be the source code itself; however, as compiling optimization may have been used during compilation, they are functionally identical.

Many solutions exist, depending on the languages and runtime of the application. For example, one can use javap or JAD to decompile bytecode in Java. For binary applications, I recommend looking at IDA Pro even though it is not free. Of course, the amount of code generated will likely be significant, and it can be challenging to analyze it and generate the expected information for data observability.

System Refreshment

Such work is generally linked to a big project, such as migrating from an inherited system to another. Therefore, it is worth mentioning that data observability will not be the only outcome of such a project.

Next, the other component of this section is static code analysis, which performs an analysis of software without running it. It is a technique widely used in code security analysis to identify code weaknesses and risks. Static code analysis is also used in test coverage tools that highlight poorly tested code, and even for optimization by detecting unused branches, libraries, etc.

Solutions like SonarQube already offer many functionalities and extension mechanisms, such as language visitors, to leverage their internals. As covered in Chapter 5, most code is represented as a tree (AST), which can be analyzed to reconstruct, for example, the traces between two execution points. I'm not saying this is an easy task. My point here is to highlight the fact that the data transformations can be extracted from the code and used to publish the associated data observations.

Data scanning

I will close this section on strategies with a practice used for decades in data quality and data governance, the use of data scanners (aka data harvesters, crawlers).

This practice is straightforward; it consists of regularly scheduled visits to the data sources to retrieve the data quality dimensions introduced in Chapter 1. They will take the form of SQL queries, returning metrics such as the number of null values and the number of rows, or they can be tailored with an appropriate mechanism (e.g., UI, DSL) to compute KPIs. Overall, this is quite similar to the collection of the data metrics covered in Chapter 4 and Chapter 5 but this time from an external point of view (e.g., a data catalog), not from the applications themselves.

Recently, other technologies have emerged around the term *augmented data quality*, which is meant to detect issues directly either AI or by leveraging internal information about the data structures (e.g., foreign keys) to check the integrity of the data.

However, I don't distinguish between those practices and the queries mentioned before, as they work hand in hand to produce metrics and insight about the data, which can be incorporated into data observations.

As I noted when discussing data source logs, the common way this practice is applied is decoupled from the data usage context. This is especially true when the scans are scheduled independently of the usages (the application runtimes). However, I will present an architecture in the next section to help recover information about the data usage context.

The Data Observability Connector

Now that I have covered several strategies to capture parts of the data observability core model, we'll develop them into a starter kit to make translucent the opaque systems in your ecosystem. In this section, I will demonstrate how to combine those strategies into a compelling solution that you can freely adapt to your situation.

I call this a *data observability collecto*r, as it is meant to be implemented at the data observability platform level (or close to it) instead of being a capability of the system itself. Its role is to connect to as many systems as possible to apply all strategies introduced in previous sections, collect the information, extract the data observations, and organize them in the data observability core model.

A collector is better represented as an architecture, as presented in Figure 8-1. It sits between the data platform (showing a data application only, here) and the data observability platform.

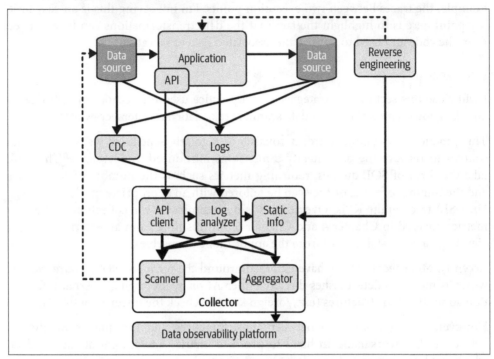

Figure 8-1. The collector's place in the data architecture

And you can see, Figure 8-1 represents the strategies introduced in the collector component, which comes with an additional component called the *aggregator*. The aggregator's role is to bring together the data observations produced by the other components and turn them into the data observability core model.

The aggregator is necessary, as the data observations coming from the different sources must be linked together, often asynchronously. For example, take a look at the following process:

1. The API client will check regularly (let's say every day) to see if there is a new version of the application that will yield the observations: code base, code version, and perhaps the user (developer).

2. Next, the *reverse engineering* component extracts the lineage from the new code version. This will generate the data lineage and could also generate the data source and schema.

3. Then, the *log analyzer* receives logs from this version and generates the observations about the application and lineage execution, and likely the user and server.

4. When logs about the application execution are consumed, the *log analyzer* can trigger some *scanners* on the data sources involved in the execution to retrieve data metrics.

All of this happens without direct synchronization (time-wise) or necessarily being orchestrated. Data observations come from different places and need to be consolidated, which can be done with an appropriate identification mechanism for each data observation entity (e.g., an ID such as those introduced in Chapter 4). For example, if a data source can be uniquely identified using a database connection string, then the log analyzer and the reverse engineering components can use this identifier to create the same data source entity and send it to the aggregator, which can connect the data lineage, data lineage execution, and users with that data source asynchronously.

Because this is too complex to describe with words only, Figure 8-2 shows which entities are generated by each component of the collector and how they link back to the aggregator.

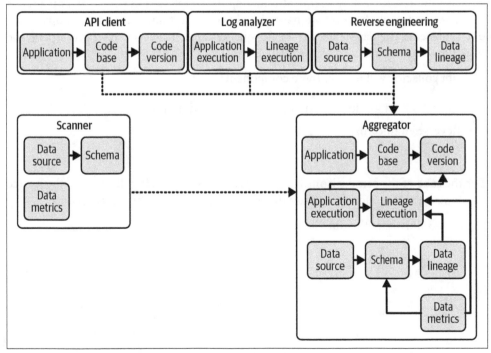

Figure 8-2. Collector components producing data observations aggregated by an aggregator

Because all data observations will likely arrive at different times, we can see that the role of the aggregator is to keep the model consistent by linking the incoming (dashed arrows across components) subsets of the data observability core model. For example, the contextual principle is respected, as the data metrics (coming from the scanner) are linked to the lineage executions (coming from the log analyzer), which themselves are linked to the application (coming from the API client).

In this example, the aggregator works in memory, retaining all data observations until the whole model is complete. Of course, this can be implemented differently. For example, you could have the data observability platform capable of handling partial data observations and serving them back to the aggregator for completion. That's more like an implementation detail, though, which is beyond the scope of this book.

Nevertheless, as this seems quite abstract, let's dig into an example using a technology covered in a previous chapter to explore the pros and cons of using one strategy or the other.

Example: Building a dbt Data Observability Connector (SaaS)

Because the collector may seem intimidating, let's look at a concrete example using dbt. I've chosen dbt because we have already covered it and can make comparisons. dbt represents the SaaS category of opaque systems. However, it's fairly open, and thus allows us to build a collector relatively easily.

The dbt collector will rely on these components:

- An API client for dbt Cloud or log analyzer for dbt-core
- Reverse engineering
- Scanners

For the sake of the comparisons later in this section, I am using dbt Cloud, the hosted version of dbt. Therefore, I will use the API client instead of the log analyzer.

Figure 8-3 illustrates the dbt Cloud collector.

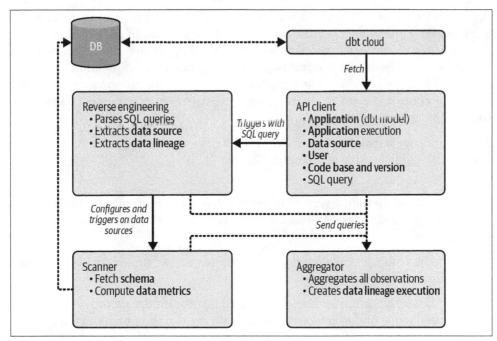

Figure 8-3. dbt Cloud collector's components

As you can see, dbt Cloud has an API that delivers information about the dbt models running on the platform. Several pieces of observations are available, such as the data source (the tables, files, etc.) but also the location of the dbt model in GitHub. One key piece of information provided by this API allows the collector to capture more information than that: the SQL query generated by dbt that is used to fetch and create the model.

This SQL query is the primary information that will be reverse engineered to reconnect the data source with its usages (the lineage). However, the observations about the data content itself, the data metrics, are missing. Therefore, the scanners are leveraged to fill this gap and issue metrics collections queries or computations on the data sources.

All observations are consolidated in the collector as they come. Most of the tasks are relatively fast (unless you consider congestion of the services, of course), but the collection of the data metrics may take longer (depending on the number of metrics), which is why the collector asynchronously integrates that information. However, because the reverse engineering component doesn't get the information about the execution context, the collector must create the data lineage execution observation itself.

That sounds great and doable, but let's see what we may have gained or lost in the process compared to using an agent (cf. Chapter 7).

Pros:

It works for the cloud version where there is no opportunity to add an agent unless the vendor agrees to add it, or it has the functionality (which is not the case here).

It doesn't require installation if the collector is installed on the data observability platform or close to it.

Continuous validation can be implemented if the scanners are provided with the tests defined in dbt, which can be turned into metrics computations and expectations at the platform level.

It's likely easier to maintain, as the API evolution is part of the SLA, while the agent might be impacted by code change (if the AST method is used).

Cons:

It requires authentication tokens for the API.

It requires authentication and authorization to connect to all data sources involved in the dbt models.

The metrics are likely to be disconnected from the context, unless the queries are parsed to extract the business logic and retrieve metrics of the involved subsets of the data instead of the whole dataset.

Continuing with the same example, the metrics are desynchronized from the moment when the data is used and consumed, and thus could lead to misleading results.

If the API is not real time, then delays are introduced between the collection time and the execution time.

Circuit breakers cannot be implemented, as the dbt models have run already and the API is disconnected from the runtime.

Conclusion

Inherited systems can pose a significant challenge when it comes to achieving full data observability. These systems are often opaque, and updating them is not as straightforward as with modern systems.

However, we have explored an alternative approach that can help turn these opaque systems into translucent ones, where we can recover as much data observability values as possible, using collectors.

We have covered several components that can make up a collector, providing the tools to fill the gaps of those systems and relieve any associated anxiety.

In the Afterword, we will dive into the future of data observability and explore the potential advancements that can be made as more tools and systems embrace the principles and strategies outlined in this book. From new technologies to emerging best practices, we will explore what lies ahead for the world of data observability and how you can stay ahead of the curve.

Afterword: Future Observations

Imagine a world where data is everything. All engineers come together to explore the principles and strategies for achieving data observability. They work tirelessly to implement these practices in their systems and tools, striving for complete visibility and control over their data. And finally, after their success, the underlying principles and strategies become second nature, and all tools in the data ecosystem embody them.

Now, we are looking to the future. We're in a world where data is no longer a source of anxiety but rather a source of power and innovation. A world where the principles and strategies engineers have developed are not only best practices but are also widely accepted norms. A dream world where engineers no longer have to struggle with opaque and difficult-to-maintain systems but instead can focus on creating and implementing new solutions that advance their organizations and the world at large.

It is time to unleash their imagination from the chains of the present and envision a future where the principles and strategies of data observability are the cornerstones of all data systems. And so, they set forth on a journey to explore this brave new world, eager to discover what possibilities await them.

Let's take a short walk into the probable observable future we'll build together.

Unification of Processing

The future of data observability is inextricably linked to the broader evolution of data in society and the systems we build. As data-driven decision making becomes increasingly ubiquitous, the processes underpinning these decisions must be transparent, explainable, and trustworthy. Furthermore, with more and more people relying on data-based systems without necessarily understanding their underlying processes, the need for observability and transparency is greater than ever.

As such, the future of data observability will be shaped by our ability to develop tools and strategies that enable us to track, contextualize, and continuously validate data at scale while also integrating them with a wide range of other tools to capture as many observations as possible. Ultimately, the goal of the data observability platform will be to accelerate innovation with data efficiently and with complete trust, empowering users to make informed decisions with confidence.

In sum, a wide deployment of data observability, as a control layer in data management, is essential to prevent the whole system from collapsing as it goes out of control.[1] Let me introduce the main supports of this claim.

First, *data* has traditionally been considered an independent entity, with an acceleration effect in the 2010s marked by the emergence of Big Data, followed by data teams. Second, in the 2020s, data resurged as a significant strategic component that empowered the whole organization and, therefore, the economy. Data culture is spreading.

Therefore, as the data ecosystem continues to expand and evolve, it becomes imperative to address the absence of data observability. While data solutions have flourished, the lack of observability has raised concerns among stakeholders who seek to leverage data to drive their business processes, as discussed in Chapter 1.

To sustain the growing importance of data within organizations, it is crucial to instill confidence in the usage of data, similarly to what has been done in software development. Data observability shares many characteristics with other concepts in software development and serves as the next evolutionary step in the data landscape.

Observability is currently gaining traction across various domains, including DevOps, DataOps, and MLOps. Organizations investing in these practices have multiple objectives in mind.

First, they aim to establish comprehensive operational oversight to monitor data usage, particularly within business processes. This serves as a natural step toward achieving optimized business operations and efficiency.

Second, organizations adopt observability practices through the lens of FinOps, which focuses on optimizing the total cost of ownership (TCO). By identifying the costs associated with data usage and quantifying the generated value, they can justify additional budgets and resources.

Third, observability practices foster collaboration among different communities, including software engineers, system engineers, and analytics professionals. By sharing common principles and philosophies, these communities can break down silos and align their objectives. This convergence of practitioner cultures and collaboration across teams is becoming more prevalent.

---

1 Let's avoid the 0th law, okay?

Overall, observability is not only a technical concept but is also a cultural shift that encourages cross-functional collaboration and alignment. By embracing observability, organizations can enhance their operational efficiency, optimize costs, and foster a collaborative environment among various engineering teams.

Moreover, technological trends are playing a significant role in driving the convergence of online transaction processing (OLTP) and online analytical processing (OLAP), bringing them closer together. One such trend is the emergence of complex cloud systems that abstract the complexity of the data flow between different systems. These systems facilitate the seamless integration and interoperability of transactional and analytical processes, breaking down the traditional barriers between OLTP and OLAP.

Additionally, unified business intelligence systems are becoming the central operating layer for organizations across various industries, including manufacturing, banking, and health care. In this evolving landscape, OLTP and OLAP are no longer seen as separate entities but are intertwined and interconnected. They are united by shared cultural behaviors and a common goal of optimizing business operations and leveraging data analytics. This integration and collaboration between transactional processing and analytical processing can be referred to as the unification of processing.

The unification of processing represents a shift in how organizations leverage data and analytics. It signifies a departure from the traditional view of OLTP and OLAP as distinct and isolated components. Instead, they are now seen as complementary and interdependent, working together to drive actionable insights and enable informed decision making.

As organizations embrace this merging of OLTP and OLAP, they are better positioned to leverage the full potential of their data. By adopting unified systems and fostering a culture of collaboration between business operations and data analytics, organizations can unlock new levels of efficiency, agility, and innovation. The unification of processing paves the way for a more integrated and holistic approach to data-driven decision making, transforming the way organizations operate and thrive in the digital era.

Consequently, the concept of data-observable systems introduced in this book will be embraced across the board to maintain, in coordination with governance, a high level of trust in operational systems as well as analytics departments, along with their technologies and objectives.

Practitioners will gain confidence in the systems deployed as the feeling of complexity decreases, because the amount of data observations is sufficient to handle most, if not all, situations. The availability of data observations, by default and by design, will enable practitioners to concentrate on the duties linked to adding more precise expectations and validating them. As a normal evolution, already witnessed in software development, practitioners will raise a certain level of awareness and discomfort when putting into production a system without guard rails, ensuring a minimal set of continuous validations. This fact would naturally lead to the emergence of a set of practices that can be fully (or only even partially) followed by what I call data-observability-driven development (a fitting, if odd, name) as a subset of what would then be observability-driven-development.

Although all these concepts really deserve their own books, for starters, I'll refer you to Charity Majors, Liz Fong-Jones, and George Miranda, who dedicated the 11th chapter of *Observability Engineering* (O'Reilly, 2022) to introduce this idea.

Generative Milestones

At the time of writing, generative pre-trained transformers (GPTs) are extremely popular. They allow you to generate content based on prompts, such as text, images, or sounds. In sum, a piece of content can be generated as the most probable next item in a sequence of a given content. For example, the next item for a question is an answer, and the most probable is the answer that addresses the topic and follows the structure requested in the question.

Hence, with enough data, GPTs can accelerate imagination and creativity processes using guided questions to reveal potential connections between as-yet unrelated concepts and can continue until finding a niche (a relatively small subspace of potential responses). In a sense, one could say that a GPT can be creative by replicating structured–creative thinking, but it won't do it on its own; it will need prompts that contain the needed spark of creativity.

So, GPTs are used to generate structured content such as code snippets (e.g., SQL), and they give extra powers to practitioners to develop code much faster, especially with, but not limited to, repetitive or common tasks.

Therefore, as the generated snippets may not necessarily be fully understood,[2] the generated code can't be deployed without being data observable, to give control over its behavior, which is the quality of the output given some inputs (the topic of the given prompt).

In fact, the generated snippet represents only the most probable code the developer would have implemented, based on the actual knowledge and data available, so the model cannot guarantee that it will always return the correct outcome as the context and data change in unknown ways.

---

2 This is already the case with Stack Overflow's Oriented Programming.

To circumvent this, the generated code must be data observable, and, as it is becoming a best practice, it could be already. It will be available in most code known by the model, and therefore, you may prompt the mode, "Okay, sounds good, now make it data observable, and include a data metric for the uniqueness of the returned data."

However, GPTs and similar strategies will also benefit the establishment of expectations. If we consider that they are meant to model the generative process, we can suppose that this can be applied to transformations and algorithms.

This capability would lead to the generation of expectations themselves in addition to the data observations. Let's consider that you have created a SQL, a data transformation code, or an algorithm, and you give it as a prompt to the model, likely alongside the connection to the input data and perhaps also the output. You then could use the prompt "What are the expectations encoded in the code I need to validate in production?" This will extract the expectations you are somewhat aware of (known-known and known-unknown), but it also will discover unconscious expectations (unknown-known) or generate unanticipated ones (unknown-unknown).

For this to happen, of course, we need data. The data we need is the data observations, the expectations, and the associated deliverables. This is another argument for the unification of processing.

Future practitioners will also benefit from combinations with other types of information, namely, the data issues resulting from not meeting expectations and the information related to their resolution process. For this, the data observability platform itself plays a significant role, as it centralizes the information and actions on the data, such as the trigger of the issues, the root cause analysis performed, and the resolution actions taken.

The platform concentrates the data that can feed a generative model and allows the users to prompt it with "From this data quality alert I just received, what would be the next thing I should look at to resolve the upstream data, the code, the server?"

As we feed the system with more cases of issue detection, troubleshooting, and their resolution (or no resolution), it will gain other capabilities, such as the detection of false positives, the maintenance of expectations, making code change recommendations (including branching), and even automated remediation (including, again, branching).

In other words, a self-healing system, *boom*.[3]

---

3 Mic dropped.

Trustable Expanded Creativity

Data observability aims to ensure that any system using data can be observed by default easily, intuitively, and independently of the observers. The observers are free to elaborate their own results based on the available data observations. Data observations feed data practitioners' creative process.

One of the aspects of creativity I appreciate the most is the capacity to think outside the box, which means to see, find, or *create* relationships between uncorrelated, a priori unrelatable events, facts, or assets.

Because data observations and expectations are meant to describe data usages, including their purpose, context, and behavior, creative processes will undoubtedly leverage this information to elaborate theories to apply (proven right) practices to totally different situations. This could lead to discovering a solution to manage the spread of a virus in colonies of endangered species, leveraging analytical practices that have been employed to control customer churn within subsegments.

Over time those creative discoveries, if encoded and retained by the data observability platform, can become a new learning dataset for the elaboration of not only generative processes but (close to) creative processes.

Based on data observations and the evidence of the adaptability of specific patterns to other contexts, algorithms should be able to be trained to generate a valid next step, which could be, for example, "Hey, why don't we try this marketing thing on medical data? Like *this* for example. Does that make sense to you?"

Okay, I have used the medical context on purpose because it is scary, but, wait; by the time my prediction comes true, systems will be (data) observable and, therefore, controllable. That is, trustable.

Conclusion

The future of data observability holds immense potential for transforming our world. As engineers come together to explore and implement the principles and strategies outlined in this book, we envision a future where data is no longer a source of anxiety but rather a source of power and innovation.

The widespread adoption of data observability practices will ensure transparency, explainability, and trustworthiness in data-driven decision making processes. It will unify processing across various domains, enabling accelerated analytics and decision making closely aligned with business needs.

Integrating generative models, such as GPTs, will enhance creativity and problem-solving capabilities, while data observability platforms will serve as a central hub for tracking and resolving data-related issues. As practitioners embrace data observability and expand their creative thinking, they will uncover unexpected connections and solutions, revolutionizing fields such as health care and conservation.

With the assurance of data observability, trustable systems will emerge, empowering us to navigate the complexities of the future with confidence and innovation.

Each of us has a crucial part to play in advancing the data community. It begins by taking action today to make existing technologies data observable while fostering the development of new technologies that inherently support this capability. By harnessing the power of data observations within a comprehensive platform, we can effectively gather evidence and demonstrate the value of monitoring and control. This, in turn, will encourage our users and stakeholders to engage in expressing and discussing their expectations actively. Together, we can create an environment that stimulates collaboration, reassurance, and a shared commitment to data observability.

I hope you enjoyed those predictions as much as I love thinking about them. In fact, whether you like them or not, let's chat on my Discord (*https://discord.gg/ xeuxtmpVBT*).

Index

A

abstract syntax tree (see AST manipulation)

abstraction strategies, 123-136

    aspect-oriented programming, 125-136

    using event listeners, 124

accountability

    ease of access versus, 64

    how data observability helps with, 75

active learning, 61

adapters (dbt), 184

Advice, 126

agent factory (Airbyte), 164

agents

    Airbyte, 161-167

        agent concept, 164

    BigQuery agent, using to automatically make Airflow data observable, 195

    Databricks, excerpt of data observations from, 204

    dbt agent, 177-185

    example dbt data observability connector versus an agent, 224

    Python BigQuery agent simplified, 193

    Python script with data observability agent for BigQuery, 189

    Spline Spark agent, 170

    Superset agent interceptions, 207

aggregators

    aggregator component in data observability collector, 220, 223

    collector components producing aggregated data observations, 221

AI (artificial intelligence)

    data team evolving toward use of automated decision making with AI, 11

    disruption in usage caused by accessibility to the public, 22

    lack of understanding of AI benefits and uses, 22

    scaling AI roadblocks, 20

Airbyte, 161-167

    agent, 161-167

        concepts defined in, 164

        intercepting a class with, 165

        signature of premain method, 165

    architecture overview, 162

    supporting data sources in, 165

Airflow, 96

    orchestrated SQL with, 194-196

        Airflow DAG operators for BigQuery, 194

        overloading DAG operators for BigQuery for data observability, 195

    support for BigQuery, 196

alert fatigue, 62

analytic/data scientists, 9

analytics

    analyses performed on data metrics, 53

    in data observability, 30

    log, 216

analytics engineers, 9

analytics observability, 28

    lineage and, 46

analytics stage, 197-208

    business intelligence recipes, 201-208

        using Databricks, 202-205

        using Superset, 205-208

rules, 55-60, 145
    advantages of having them within the application, 152
    assisted, 58
    auto accepting, care with, 150
    best practices with, 150
    connections with SLAs/SLOs, 59
    explicit, 57
    insights need to create, 56
runtime manipulation of code, 126

S

SaaS (software as a service), 212
    example dbt data observability connector, 222-224
Scala programming language, 168
scaling, 79
schemas, 42
    data metrics linked to, 53
    information schemas in database servers, 212
    Schema entity class, 106
    Spline information on, 174
scikit-learn library (Python), 197-201
scope and quality of data, 22
SDLC (systems development life cycle), 8
search trends, 5
security
    how data observability helps with, 72
    observability of, 28
    and privacy in data observability, 30
security/privacy concerns, barrier to AI implementation, 21
seed, 178, 184
self-healing systems, 231
semi-unsupervised learning, 61
server (observations model physical space), 40
servers, 29
    Spline information on, 174
service level agreements (see SLAs; SLAs/SLOs)
service level indicators (see SLIs)
service-level objectives, 59
    (see also SLAs/SLOs)
serving stage, 185-197
    BigQuery in Python, 188-194
    loading and serving ML model, 199
    orchestrated SQL with Airflow, 194-197
    recipes, 186
    value of making data observable in, 185

shifting left, 146
silent failures, 97
    in ingestion application of Python data observation pipeline, 97
    in reporting application of Python data observation pipeline, 98
"silent killer (data as)", 19
siloing, 11
single-state-based rules, 56
site-packages path (Python), 180
sitecustomize.py script, 180
SLAs/SLOs (service level agreements/objectives), 149
    accountability, how data observability helps with, 75
    connections to data observability rules, 59
    considerations in establishing SLA for data, 60
    definition at the data product level, 87
    serving stage and, 186
SLIs (service level indicators), 60, 143
    lifting observations into, 149
SMEs (subject matter experts), 75
software and operation engineers, 9
software as a service (SaaS), 212
    example dbt data observability connector, 222-224
software engineering, 82
SonarQube, 218
source and destination workers (Airbyte), 162
spans (traces), 35
Spark (see Apache Spark)
SparkListenerEvents, 171
Spline, 170-177
    core model coverage and its extensions, 173
    custom lineage dispatcher, 172
    data lineage tracking and visualization, 170
    downside of Spark-centric architecture, 171
    going beyond compliance use cases, 175-177
    leveraging information gathered in ExecutionPlan to generate data observations, 173
SQL, 47
    applications providing queries executed by databases, 186
    captured in audit logs, information from, 142
    code generation and, 133
    dbt, SQL-first transformation workflow, 177

About the Author

Andy Petrella has been in the data industry for almost 20 years, starting his career as a software engineer and data miner in the GIS space. He has evangelized big data for more than a decade, especially Apache Spark for which he created the Spark-Notebook that has recorded more than 3,000 stars on GitHub.

During his time evangelizing Spark and helping hundreds of companies in the US and in EU work on their data pipelines and models, he has witnessed the lack of visibility and control of data jobs after they are deployed in production.

Since 2015, he has been talking to tech and data-savvy people to build a sustainable solution for this problem. That is: "how to make data observable" in a way that can be adopted smoothly by any data practitioner.

Today, he is regularly invited to companies to educate their data teams, while running Kensu, which has more than 50 years of total development time dedicated to building the set tools to help data engineers and their peers to build trust in what they deliver.

He is in ongoing talks with advocates such as Gartner to create a definition of *data observability* that refers to all its important facets. Finally, he has written books, blogs, slides, training materials, etc. since 2013, including many materials with O'Reilly.

Colophon

The animal on the cover of *Fundamentals of Data Observability* is an ornate hawk eagle (*Spizaetus ornatus*). Native to Central America and parts of South America, the ornate hawk eagle has a reddish-orange neck, a white throat, orange eyes, and a black-and-white chest. In addition, it has a crest (which indicates excitement depending on whether it is raised or lowered) and feathered tarsi (the tarsus is the part of the leg between the "knee" and the "ankle"). In general, the bird lives in forests and feeds on a variety of prey, from medium-to-large birds to small-to-medium mammals (and sometimes even reptiles).

Ornate hawk eagles have an extended commitment to their young from incubation to independence. Each clutch is only one egg. While the egg incubates for 44 to 48 days, the female sits on the nest while the male provides food for both the female and himself. Even when the egg has hatched, the male continues to provide food, dropping it close to the nest so the female can directly feed the young hawk eagle. Once the fledgling has started flying, the male takes over primary care of the offspring. The entire process, from laying the egg to letting the young ornate hawk eagle go, is a little less than two years, on average. Because of the time involved in raising their young, ornate hawk eagles tend to breed every other year.

The current conservation status (IUCN) of the ornate hawk eagle is "Near Threatened." Many of the animals on O'Reilly covers are endangered; all of them are important to the world.

The cover illustration is by Karen Montgomery, based on an antique line engraving from *Histoire Naturelle*. The cover fonts are Gilroy Semibold and Guardian Sans. The text font is Adobe Minion Pro; the heading font is Adobe Myriad Condensed; and the code font is Dalton Maag's Ubuntu Mono.

O'REILLY®

Learn from experts.
Become one yourself.

Books | Live online courses
Instant answers | Virtual events
Videos | Interactive learning

Get started at oreilly.com.

Printed in the USA
CPSIA information can be obtained
at www.ICGtesting.com
JSHW061723170823
46725JS00003B/20

9 781098 133290